Electronic Music
PIONEERS

by Ben Kettlewell

ProMusic
press

236 Georgia Street, Suite 100
Vallejo, CA 94590

Library of Congress Catalog Card Number: 2001088667

Production Staff: Mike Lawson, Publisher; Patrick Runkle, Editor;
Stephen Ramirez, Art Director

ProMusic Press is an imprint of artistpro.com, LLC
236 Georgia Street, Suite 100
Vallejo, CA 94590
707-554-1935

Also from ProMusic Press
Music Copyright for the New Millennium
The Mellotron Book

Also from EMBooks
The Independent Working Musician
Making the Ultimate Demo, 2nd Ed.
Remix: The Electronic Music Explosion
Making Music with Your Computer, 2nd Ed.
Anatomy of a Home Studio
The EM Guide to the Roland VS-880

Also from MixBooks
The AudioPro Home Recording Course, Volumes I, II, and III
I Hate the Man Who Runs This Bar!
How to Make Money Scoring Soundtracks and Jingles
The Art of Mixing: A Visual Guide to Recording, Engineering, and Production
The Mixing Engineer's Handbook
The Mastering Engineer's Handbook
Music Publishing: The Real Road to Music Business Success, Rev. and Exp. 5th Ed.
How to Run a Recording Session
The Professional Musician's Internet Guide
The Songwriters Guide to Collaboration, Rev. and Exp. 2nd Ed.
Critical Listening and Auditory Perception
Modular Digital Multitracks: The Power User's Guide, Rev. Ed.
The Dictionary of Music Business Terms
Professional Microphone Techniques
Sound for Picture, 2nd Ed.
Music Producers, 2nd Ed.
Live Sound Reinforcement
Professional Sound Reinforcement Techniques
Creative Music Production: Joe Meek's Bold Techniques

Printed in Auburn Hills, MI
ISBN 1-931140-17-0

About the Author

Composer, musician, and writer Ben Kettlewell has been involved with almost every aspect of music for over three decades. He began playing guitar at age 14 and began playing professionally at the age of 19, touring with singer/songwriter Tim Hardin. This venture led to performances with music legends, such as Patrick Sky and Spider John Koerner. He has played lead guitarist in several well-known rock/blues and jazz ensembles since the early '70s, and now records and tours with Celtic singer/writer Mairéid Sullivan.

Ben has been involved in public radio and Community Theater since 1980. From 1982 until 1991, he hosted a weekly series on NPR affiliate WOMR-FM, called *Imaginary Voyage*, one of the first electronic music radio series aired in the United States. In 1986, he was awarded a grant from the Massachusetts Council on the Arts and Humanities to produce a radio series for National Public Radio. This series focused on the evolution of electronic music, featuring interviews with leading figures in electronic music. It was broadcast on public radio in 39 cities in the United States and Canada.

He has written and performed commissioned scores for several film and theater productions. His recordings have been released on Electronic Dreams in the UK, and in the U.S. on Generations Unlimited, CMC Distribution, Poison Plant Records, and Tarheel Productions. He is featured on several compilation albums of electronic music. In addition to these recordings, Ben has produced soundtracks for numerous Cablevision productions and multimedia projects.

He has been a music journalist for over twenty years, contributing to such publications as *Airwaves, Electronic Musician, Music of the Spheres, Heartsong Review, Sound on Sound, Dulcimer Times, Dreams Word Magazine*, and *"i/e" Magazine*. His features have included interviews with Tod Machover, Robert Moog, Steve Roach, Bernd Kistenmacher, Klaus Schulze and many others.

Ben is the editor of Alternate Music Press, an online music archive at **www.alternatemusicpress.com**.

Acknowledgements

This work is dedicated to the memory of my Grandfather, Wayland L. White, whom I grew up with, until my twelfth year, on our farm in North Carolina and whose noble spirit has guided me all through my life.

Heartfelt thanks go to:

All my Scottish and Cherokee ancestors who started me on the path.

The memory of Arnie Manos and to Tom Conklin at WOMR-FM in Provincetown, Massachusetts, for their commitment to excellence, for sharing their love of music with me, for believing I had something to say, and for helping me obtain the grant to produce the radio series upon which this book is based.

To my old friend, Tony Kahn, a great musician, newspaper editor and journalist, for all the good press that kept my inspiration going full-tilt over the years.

To everyone I've interviewed for this book for their creative spark, friendship, enthusiasm and mindfulness of details. To all the people who contributed photographs for the book, who include Roger Luther, Jeff Winner, Faith Frenz-Heckman, Bob Moog, Suzanne Ciani, Michael Stearns, Steve Roach, Neil Nappe, Bill Rhodes, Christopher Franke, Klaus D. Mueller, Joel Chadabe, Joe Paradiso, Don Buchla, and Wendy Carlos.

And, most of all, to Mairéid Sullivan, the treasure of my life, for her abundant love and support, and for inspiring me to write this book, and for her tireless help in editing the book.

Preface

Music has the means to offer a major contribution to the shifting paradigm of our new era and global communication technology is the leading facilitator. High technology has been necessary to the growth and expansion of intelligence. That's because communication multiplies the effect of cultural movements. Biological evolution alone could not have given us the capacity for communication that we have available to us today.

A visionary worldview is the mechanism that makes dreams real. The scientific concept of a new "paradigm" has come into everyday use to help define a new worldview that expands understanding of human potential.

This new sensibility is reflected in the way we live, our circle of friends and the work we choose to do. Contemporary trends in music have always been a direct reflection of this growth. Musicians are sounding out the harmonics of a full life through the use of adventurous new technologies available to them.

New music technology makes it possible, as never before, to capture a sense of "the music of the spheres": Music is a kind of truth our bodies know, expressing rhythms and reflections of what we feel.

Imperfect as they are, the new concepts of music have helped to free up the restrictive forms of older musical styles. Artists can experiment within a broader frame of reference to convey new feelings and messages to meet the needs of people who have learned to blend old and new.

The arts have the power to touch the heart, cut through claustrophobic dogmas, abstract ideologies and social stratas of age and class. Scientists are studying the effects of music on tachyonic and quantum consciousness as well as on the electromagnetic fields of our body's subtle levels, while more and more artists are taking control of their creativity so that they may serve more effectively. New music technology offers that opportunity.

Mairéid Sullivan
www.maireid.com

Foreword

Electronic sound has a broad past and an even more diverse present, having infiltrated nearly every genre of music over the last decades. Most literature on the topic, however, is somewhat partisan. As can happen all too often in artistic spheres, tastes can win out over history, and various writings can have a particular slant, covering certain bodies of work and quickly skipping or ignoring others. When Ben Kettlewell sent me a draft copy of his text for *Electronic Music Pioneers*, however, I was delighted to see that this one was an exception to this rule, covering most of the bases.

It's rare to see a complete survey of the early instruments together with an introduction to what was happening in academic research and composition that also discusses the Berlin musicians of the 1970s and the impact of the synthesizer on more popular genres. Due to its reliance on cutting-edge engineering, electronic music also has another axis that further complicates things: artists vs. technologists. I was likewise happy to see that Ben addresses this one as well, covering both aspects; e.g., that of the designers of these often intricate and complicated machines and the now-legendary musicians who eagerly learned how to use these confusing and temperamental devices to push the boundaries of music.

Thinking back to the time when I first met Ben over a decade ago, this is hardly surprising. It was a beautiful summer evening, and I was walking down Commercial Street in Provincetown, Mass. with my wife during a weekend on Cape Cod. We noticed his gallery, Elements, the front dominated by interesting and appealing pieces of glass, sculpture, and jewelry, not entirely out of place in the whimsical atmosphere there. We couldn't resist wandering in. In the rear of the gallery, there were CD's and tapes for sale. Expecting the usual new-age collection, I sauntered over. Needless to say, I was completely wrong; Ben had amassed an amazing genre-crossing collection of avant-garde and electronic music. Although there are now a multitude of independent and electronic music retailers on the internet, back in the early '90s, this music was nearly impossible to find, usually carried by a small set of mail-order retailers who relied namely on word-of-mouth for advertisement (hence the word "obscure" was always attached to such music).

Being an avid collector, I bought a bunch of discs, which launched a great conversation with Ben that was continued on my many subsequent visits. Although we'd never previously met, the electronic music scene was quite small in Boston then, and we knew several people in common; from my end as a synthesizer builder and from Ben's as a musician and radio presenter. It was a time of change for both of us though; within a couple of years, I was to join the MIT Media Lab to collaborate with Tod Machover on hyperinstruments and later start my own research group focusing on new interfaces for computer-human interaction and electronic music, while Ben left Provincetown to pursue new musical opportunities on the West Coast. Good music shops never lasted too long in those days, especially in the general Boston area...

As I read through the draft of *Electronic Music Pioneers*, I remembered what it was like to grow up in and around Boston across the cusp of the '60s and '70s as a technically inclined kid with a passion for new sounds. Much as today's youth is encountering the revolution of media convergence and social computing brought by cheap PC's and widespread internet penetration, our generation saw the rise of consumer electronics, as transistors and integrated circuits redefined radio, television, hi-fi, and musical instruments. As long as I can remember, I'd had an interest in electronic audio, perhaps because my dad had an ancient Revere open-reel, monaural, tube-driven tape recorder, which offered endless fascination in my toddler days (it was great sport to play with the transport when he wasn't looking and snarl the reels). When I was old enough to get my own library card, these interests expanded upon checking out those wonderfully strange electronic music LP's on the Folkways label, which somehow had infiltrated their collection. I promptly took possession of my dad's old Revere, and had a great time exploring the sonic possibilities when it was operated outside of its normal bounds. It survived (barely) and is still somewhere in the corner of the attic.

Perhaps the fatal blow was given by my Uncle Jake, the subversive relative who first turned my on to rock music by giving me his old 45's (over vehement protests by my parents). I guess this kind of thing repeats with each generation; every kid needs an Uncle Jake in the family. In 1968, Jake gave me a copy of *Switched-on Bach* (he was always pretty hip). Life was never the same again. The sounds were fascinating, but after the Folkways records, that wasn't too unusual. The image of the Moog modular on the cover is what did it. All those knobs and phone jacks sprouting from an ominous black cabinet out of a telephone operator's nightmare, with the musical keyboard totally out of place below. And that person standing beside it in 18'th century garb; could that be Wendy Carlos dressed up like Bach? In those days of Paul Revere and the Raiders, that wouldn't be entirely out of the norm. The liner notes were fascinating, but after having read them a dozen times (and squinted at the blurry labels on the modules in attempts to decipher them), I had little idea of what this device actually was. But one thing was for sure... I had to have one someday.

Synthesizer records would become more common over the next few years. But while most were of little consequence (e.g., everything you'd never want to hear anyway, but played on the Moog), some were groundbreaking. And the amazing thing is that, because they were so novel, they were often widely available. The best examples that I remember were Morton Subotnick's Nonesuch releases. Nonesuch was a budget classical label. I used to see them in common department stores. I'd browse through the stacks while my parents were shopping, and Mort's records would jump right out, with their colorful 60's Peter-Max-ish covers and those muddy photos of Mort in front of the Buchla modulars, like a madcap pilot held prisoner in a macabre cockpit. And at around two dollars a pop, I could even afford them on my allowance!

My high school and early college years were the golden era of progressive rock. My friends and I flocked to some awesome, ground-breaking concerts then; it was indeed a privilege to see Pink Floyd pre-*Dark Side* with speakers scattered all over the theater, King Crimson with their temperamental mellotrons, ELP with that massive Moog modular, and eventually Tangerine Dream with a stage full of blinking lights and sound-producing silicon. Fusion jazz was just beginning then; it didn't even have a name yet, and was far from settling down into a middle-of-the-road boor. In Boston, the Jazz Workshop, a small, intimate club in a basement beneath Copley Square, was the only place to see these groundbreaking fusion bands perform. While most groups sported a tiny ARP Oddessy or Minimoog, the most memorable event was seeing Herbie Hancock's Crossings-era band with Pat Gleeson playing a full-up E-Mu modular. This is the period that essentially clinched it for me; I needed one of these things.

Buying a synthesizer was out of the question. Minimoogs cost well over a thousand dollars, and modular systems ran at least ten times that amount. Aside from the poor economics dictated by the limited market for modulars, the sheer amount of labor involved in wiring up all of the panels and circuitry was formidable. I had no choice but to build one. I was hardly alone in that aspiration. Dave Rossum, co-founder of E-Mu and their main synthesizer architect over most of their products, recently told me that music synthesizers had supplanted ham radios in those days as lightning rods to absorb the lives of technically-inclined tinkerers. I have a feeling that he was on the mark; many of us got our electronics chops that way.

There wasn't much literature on the innards of synthesizers back then. Manufacturers tended to protect their secrets, as the competition was fierce. Don Simonton's low-budget PAIA kits were the exception, however, as he published the circuitry across several issues of Radio and Electronics. Likewise, Don Lancaster (author of the famous TTL and CMOS cookbooks) published some great articles in the popular electronic press about very interesting ways to use common IC's in musical contexts, and Walt Jung's Op-Amp Cookbook was a bible full of synthesizer-relevant circuitry. Barry Klein's tome, *Electronic Music Circuits*, was a gold mine of information, but wasn't to be released for several years, and the various "Electronotes" issues were fantastic, but nearly impossible to get ahold of back then.

I started my first modular in a room in my parent's basement when I was a freshman in college, back in 1974. The room was painted totally black. It had served as a canonical psychedelic dungeon and hangout in my high-school days (a few of the flashing lights and 6' x 8' color organs still worked), and functioned part-time as a darkroom (setting the ambient odor), as I was also an avid photographer. I built the wooden synth cabinet in the center of the room. It measured 3' x 3', and had four rows waiting for modules. As I had only a vague idea of what to put in there, I wrote to every synthesizer manufacture I knew of for brochures to try and figure out what went into these things. I also called every university around to see if I could visit their electronic music studio (we had nothing of the sort at Tufts then). Phoning MIT led me to my present colleague at the Media Lab, Barry Vercoe, who informed me that "MIT only does digital synthesis." I hit the gold mine though when phoning Harvard, where I got connected to Serge Tcherepnin's brother Ivan, who ran their electronic music program and invited me over to see their facility. This was another life-changing experience. Ivan took me right past the rows of hulking, dark Buchlas in their attic studio, and over to a small Serge that he had in the center of the room. He went through his brother's masterpiece module-by-module in the hour that ensued, and I soaked the experience up like a sponge. The Serge's revolutionary concepts, such as the interchangeability of control and audio signals, cast long shadows onto my evolving plans.

My original modules started out with ideas from the Simonton and Lancaster articles. The oscillators weren't very stable and the filters were somewhat dull, but I was able to amuse my friends and annoy my family by crosspatching them to make chaotic soundscapes that I'd let go on for hours at significant volume. I had little money at the time, and had to really scrounge for parts. The potentiometers (i.e., knobs) came from old TV monitors that were being thrown away at a Rt. 128 company that made computer terminals, where I worked during high school. I had a part-time job during college writing software at Draper Laboratories, an MIT spin-off famous for designing guidance systems for missiles and spacecraft. I befriended the technicians and engineers there, who gave me old panels full of pin jacks (the patch cord standard that I adopted from the PAIA designs), provided me with resistors and capacitors, and let me sneak into their printed-circuit facility to make my boards. It was a great gig, indeed. I bought my semiconductors at Eli Heffron's, a surplus electronics store in Cambridge full of the electronic effluent cast out of the Rt. 128 and Cambridge establishments (it was rumored that some of the junk on Eli's floor could compromise America's best military secrets if it fell into the wrong hands). The guys there got to know me pretty well; it wasn't too unusual to be building a synthesizer then, but I was their most fanatic such customer, and they gave me good discounts.

As my quest for components grew more and more esoteric, I wandered one day into a little-known surplus electronics store in a warehouse in downtown Salem. Although I didn't expect to find such an enterprise there, it turned out that these guys had just started a side-business producing the Aries synthesizer kits, comprising modules of much higher quality than the PAIA units. I had a great, high-bandwidth conversation with one of the managers, who thought for some reason that I had enough money to buy his products. In the half-hour that we chatted, I came away with some important gems, e.g., go with exponential oscillators rather than the linear scheme sported by the PAIA system, and check out Dennis Colin's article in the *Journal of the Audio Engineering Society* to find out how to build a great voltage-controlled filter. He also pulled out a schematic in the course of our conversation, but I noticed that the critical, temperature-compensated exponentiator circuitry covered by a black hunk of thermal epoxy on the circuit board was also blacked out on the schematic. Such was the state of this competitive field back then; when I asked about the hidden circuitry, our chat came to a quick close. Regardless, the stability and controllability of my home-made system benefited greatly from this exchange.

I gradually filled the wooden cabinet up with 37 modules after many dedicated evenings and weekends and countless solder burns and minor injuries from totally improper machining practices. Although I had ideas left for many other modules, I ran out of both space in the cabinet and hours to build more. From 1977 to 1982 my synthesizer-building activities took a hiatus, as there was little time free during my graduate physics studies for such leisure. The main exception was a dual-oscillator module that I built to play around with computer-controlled synthesis during a break in my Ph.D. research. This clandestinely fit into an instrument crate that we used for our experiment at the CERN physics laboratory in Geneva, surprising many of my colleagues as it spontaneously erupted into cacophony once an hour (my thesis advisor, in his heavy German accent, termed it "old crow").

Things changed at the end of 1982. I was a postdoc at the Swiss Federal Institute of Technology in Zurich at the time; I'd been there for about a year, and due to a relentless schedule of toil, I was significantly ahead in my work. Zurich, at the time, was a fascinating place, full of stimulation and conflict. The music scene was fantastic; there was an active branch of Recommended Records (later to become RecRec) in town, and I saw countless wonderful concerts from alternative musicians who would never make it to the USA. These ranged from the avant-garde "Rock in Opposition" bands like Sweden's Von Zamla and Belgium's Univers Zero through electronic artists like Klaus Schulze. Likewise, the youth of the city were erupting in protest against the establishment "opera crowd," and it wasn't uncommon to inhale a bit of tear gas together with the clear Alpine air. But it was a city very difficult to participate in, especially as a foreign, workaholic physicist. Thus it was a dangerous mix: I had access to a fantastic electronics lab, time on my hands, lots of musical stimulation, and countless ideas churning on new synthesizer modules to build.

It started with a fairly simple scheme; I purchased one of those cheap Casio "VL-Tone" toy keyboards that had just come onto the market. This was probably the first "throw-away" digital keyboard. After spending a night probing the circuitry, I found several interesting "hidden" points where strange and delightfully ugly intermediate sounds were produced. This led to my first "Frankenstein" construction, where I replaced the toy keyboard of the Casio with a full-sized organ manual, and brought all of the internal patch points that I'd discovered out to a pin jack panel, so I could process them further with my modular gear. Others in this tradition followed (over the next years, the modular system assimilated a Casio CS-101, a Casio SK-1, a Minimoog, a Moog Satellite, and the Radio Shack/Moog MG-1).

I then started making more modules. Many integrated circuits had been recently released that had great musical potential (for instance, a phoneme synthesizer for computer-generated speech that I'd heard babbling away in a gas system designed by some of my German physics colleagues). In the package of a module, which would take me at most a few evenings to fabricate, I'd be able to embed such chips and immediately start experimenting and making sounds with them. Granted, at the time, one could consider building a computer-based system (the DX7 had just been released, and essentially all analog synthesizers at the time were being controlled by microprocessors), but this was a complicated endeavor doomed to fast obsolescence and wouldn't make a sound until everything was completed. On the other hand, I could turn my modules out quickly, and immediately start using them to explore sonic ideas. And these ideas kept coming. During this period of my life, the passion of building synthesizers turned into an obsession. By the time I left Zurich at the end of 1983, I'd constructed an armada of about 80 modules, most of which were unusual devices not found in common modulars. I packed them up into boxes labeled "domestic equipment," and somehow they slipped through U.S. customs and arrived here unscathed and uninspected. After settling back in the Boston area, I found a bookshelf maker in Cambridge who I contracted to build the enclosures, then essentially finished the system. Together with the modules that I'd built previously (which I'd since refurbished), the world's largest homemade synthesizer now dominated my living room.

Although I've designed and built many electronic music devices and interfaces since, some of which have attracted a bit of notoriety, my modular system is happily completed, and the demons that drove me to build the thing have found other fertile fields in which to plant their suggestions (although I still have wild dreams about the appropriate MIDI interface). As I type now in my basement many years later, the modular surrounds me, with its myriad of knobs, switches, buttons, LED's and patch jacks; a sleeping giant waiting to be coaxed into life with a flip of the power switches. It's a very special, fragile, and intimate interface indeed. With all of those degrees of tangible freedom to create and sculpt sound, one rapidly creates unique timbres, easily nudged about with a tweak on any of dozens of possible controls immediately at your fingertips. And every sound you make with it is a unique event; once those patches get pulled, it never comes back the same way twice. And it makes such dirty, gritty, grungy sounds indeed...the beauty of analog!

My main use for it now is to make gigantic sound installations with huge patches that I continue building over several hours, until I run out of patch cords. The process is perhaps closer to sculpture than music, where one starts with a small "seed" patch, and continues augmenting it until it becomes a monster (perhaps a close analogy to the process of building the synthesizer itself). These are mainly autonomous, babbling and droning on for hours and days, never repeating, until it's turned off (see **http:www.media.mit.edu/~joep/synth.html** for representative audio clips). I periodically am tempted to make a MIDI interface for it, but perhaps this beast is best left to roam out on it's own, not lashed down by a demanding stream of MIDI commands.

I often wonder what drove me to make such a titan, and particular answers are elusive. I guess it comes down to being a technical kid growing up in the golden era of the great modulars and witnessing the dawn and synergy of progressive, psychedelic, electronic, and avant-garde music. I've tried to give somewhat of a feeling for what it was like in this text, and Ben expands on it greatly in the chapters that follow. Things were probably quite different for kids growing up in the '90s though; these were difficult days for home-built electronic music, since cutting-edge synthesizer technology was then embodied in specialized integrated circuits that were essentially impossible to work with without corporate resources.

It's a changed world now. Standard personal computers have enough processing power to begin allowing the functions of real-time music synthesizers to be assimilated into software programs and plug-ins. This will only improve as computers follow Moore's Law, packing exponentially more processing power into a desktop footprint. The synthesizer as an external piece of dedicated hardware is an endangered species; it will quickly become a set of rules and algorithms followed by a computer program. This process, started by Max Matthews at Bell Laboratories four decades ago, is blending diverse populations such as academic composers and techno musicians; both are now using the same sets of tools. By running algorithms based on physically derived models, software synthesis is shedding its static, pristine clarity and acquiring the expressiveness of acoustic instruments or the grunge of the early analog synths. Together with the music distribution process likewise being thrown into disarray with the widespread trading of MP3 files over the Internet, mediated through search programs like Napster and Gnutella, we are living in revolutionary times, where the paradigms behind composing, playing, producing, distributing, and interacting with music are all being redefined and wonderfully democratized. Now, it's not academics at large institutions, engineers at musical instrument companies, big-name musicians, or record company execs who will build and define it, but instead talented folks in front of their personal computers-perhaps kids growing up in the post-convergence age, with open ears, lots of ideas, a dose of dedication and commitment, and time to follow their dreams. Although they may suffer from RSI (at least until we stop typing at our computers), this generation can avoid the burns from the soldering iron and cuts from the machine shop. And in whatever form it takes, I can't wait to download the music.

Joe Paradiso
Principal Research Scientist and Technology Director, MIT Media Lab **www.media.mit.edu/~joep/**

Introduction

Since you've already picked up this book, and have turned to this page, you must have some degree of interest in technology. In 1989, in Melbourne, Australia, at an international conference on computer science and technology, an esteemed American computer scientist was asked the question, "How long do you think it will be before we'll have technology that communicates information directly to our brain?" He quickly replied, "We already have it. It's called a book."

Electronic Music Pioneers is based on a radio series originally produced in 1987 by writer and musician Ben Kettlewell at NPR affiliate WOMR-FM in Provincetown, Massachusetts, and funded by a grant from the Massachusetts Council on the Arts and Humanities. The title of the series was *Electronic Pioneers-The Roots of a Musical Revolution*. The programs were aired over a two-year period on 39 public radio stations across the United States.

This book expands a great deal on that radio series, as we explore the development of instruments that create and shape sounds electronically. *Electronic Music Pioneers* focuses on the human side of this history by including interviews with the inventors of these electronic instruments, and the musicians conceiving the music produced with them. It demonstrates their creative interconnection with the technology.

It has been said by many that to play an instrument from another culture properly, the musician must first understand the tradition of that instrument and then go beyond it to find his/her own voice. This way of thinking has much in common with the philosophy of electronic music. The entire aesthetic concept of music is perpetually being redefined, and our expectations from music are greater than ever before.

Electronic Music Pioneers gives comprehensive insight into the historical context of the explorers of electronic music to show how the music and the instruments evolved to open up new, exciting horizons of music creation, inspiring generations to come. As these new forms of music were beginning to emerge and take shape, the technological medium for their creation was also advancing at a rapid pace. In the early days, the center of attention was on the impressive nature of the sounds the instruments produced, rather than on the music that musicians and composers created with them.

In the nineteenth and twentieth centuries, new advancements in technology allowed a much more diverse musical palette for the musician or composer to choose from. Combined use of traditional instruments and this new breed of musical instruments expressed some of the many possibilities that now exist for interaction between various musical cultures. Technology gave birth to new generations of electronic instruments that were distinct in their sound as well as their way of interfacing with the musician.

The goal of the artists and the music discussed in this book is not only to respect the ancient heritages of traditional forms of music, but also to bring something new to the illustrious musical legacies that flourish around the world. As a result of these new forms of exploration, by the mid-1970s music created with synthesizers and other electronic instruments quickly became the most influential development in the modern musical panorama.

This book includes interviews with artists and inventors, a selective photographic gallery of inventors, instruments and musicians, and short features on many inventors and musicians who, as pioneers in the electronic medium, created their own distinct musical signature. Together they give the reader a clear picture of the development and incorporation of these instruments in every form of music.

It would take many volumes to cover every instrument, every genre, every musician involved in the many facets of electronic music. As in the analogy of many layers of an onion, every time we think we're really getting a grasp on the history and evolution of music technology, we discover another "layer of reality," and realize we're just scratching the surface.

As you read the interviews, you will see that the majority of them have been conducted in two stages: the first in 1986, and then again in 2000/2001. What was new and exciting in the late 1980s may seem amusingly archaic compared with the quantum leap made in technology since the time of the first round of interviews. Keeping that perspective is vitally important because these interviews are focused on the historic relevance, as well as the current state of the art in music technology. The insights and predictions of the people being interviewed have all manifested into reality since these artists and inventors were first interviewed. I'm sure you will find their observations visionary, educational, and entertaining.

Contents

PART ONE: ANALOG

PART TWO: DIGITAL

Part One
Analog

Redefining Genres: The Musical Evolution towards New Artistic Concepts

Robert Moog's invention of commercially available synthesizers changed the world of music radically, redefining previously existing genres and at the same time creating new ones. After news of his incredible modular systems reached the public, orders poured in from innovative musicians who felt compelled to explore new musical horizons.

Moog with his creations.

Photo courtesy Roger Luther, MoogArchives.com

Moog recalls in our interview *(chapter 3)*: "My first synthesizer customer was the choreographer Alwin Nikolais. He composed all his music on tape, and wanted additional sonic resources. Then, Eric Siday, who was doing very well as a composer of radio and TV commercial music, ordered a modular system. After that we (R.A.

Moog Co., Trumansburg, NY) sold instruments to Vladimir Ussachevsky of the Columbia Princeton Electronic Music Center, Lejaren Hiller of the University of Illinois, George Rochberg of the University of Pennsylvania, and Gustav Ciamaga of the University of Toronto." After extensive dialog with each of the composers, Moog intuitively knew the requirements of each one, and then proceeded to construct personalized modular components for them.

Eric Siday is credited with creating the first stages of the now widely accepted medium of the television soundtrack. Siday was a pioneer in recording musical scores for television and radio advertisements during the 1960s with Bob Moog's first generation of modular synthesizers. Siday, however, was no newcomer to new forms of music. In the mid-'30s Siday was enchanted by the prepared piano compositions of John Cage and the dissonant timbres of Musique Concrete. Beginning with this experimental background, Siday utilized variations of these techniques in creating music for radio and television commercials. By incorporating multiple recording techniques, Siday realized that his experiments had evolved into an ingenious new way of creating music.

Eric Siday and the 2nd Moog synthesizer, 1964.

Nearly all of Bob Moog's first customers were either experimental composers, working in Universities, or producers of music for radio and television commercials. These instruments were way beyond most working musicians' budgets. For example, the prices in Moog's 1968 catalog ranged from $125 for an envelope generator to $395 for an oscillator and $1,225 for a sequencer. The R. A. Moog order form included an illustration where the customer could specify the arrangement of modules within the cabinet, with a sidebar, reminding the customer that the modules could easily be re-arranged.

In September 1968, composer Wendy Carlos released the first successful commercially released all-synthesizer album, *Switched-on Bach*. It was a hallmark for the synthesizer as well as collaborative musicianship. Carlos performed the music of J.S. Bach on a large customized Moog modular synthesizer. Carlos spent months refining the timbres and "patches" for each track, creating an exciting new translation of baroque masterpieces. The record was done in collaboration with Rachel Elkind, who served as Carlos' producer for many years. *Switched-on Bach* brought Wendy Carlos a great deal of acclaim, including three Grammy Awards. The album implanted the synthesizer deeply into public awareness, and was followed by Carlos' 1969 release, *The Well-Tempered Synthesizer*. Carlos was the first composer to use Harald Bode's invention, the Vocoder, in a feature film, for the soundtrack for Stanley Kubrick's classic *A Clockwork Orange*. She was introduced to the wonderful sound capabilities of the Vocoder at the 1964-65 World's Fair in the Bell Labs pavilion, and, no doubt, was immediately impressed with the instrument's possibilities.

Wendy Carlos

In 1972, Carlos recorded *Sonic Seasonings*. It was, in some ways, the beginning of a new genre, a hybrid of the impressionistic music of Satie, and Debussy, and the minimalism of Steve Reich, combined with environmental sounds like thunder, rain and wind. It was a precursor of American new age music in many ways, especially combining classical music with nature sounds, which became very popular with new age artists in the 1980s.

Carlos worked towards obtaining a degree in both music and physics at Brown University, and later received an M.A. in music composition at Columbia University. It was during the days at Columbia, the first electronic music center in the United States, where she studied with electronic music pioneers Otto Luening and Vladimir Ussachevsky. Carlos graduated from Columbia and was working as a recording engineer in Manhattan when she met Robert Moog at the 1964 AES convention in NYC. Along with Eric Siday, Alwin Nikolais, and Vladimir Ussachevsky, Carlos became one of Moog's earliest clients. Bob Moog personally delivered her first synthesizer to her brownstone apartment in Manhattan, where Moog spent the weekend helping her set it up.

During the late 1960s, Wendy Carlos played a major role in promoting interest in synthesizers, as the musicians recording and performing with these instruments gradually shifted from academia to more mainstream musical genres. Because of the rapidly growing demand for the instruments, it took almost a year and a half, from early 1969 to mid-1970, for Moog and his crew in Trumansburg to catch up on filling orders for his instruments.

During this period, composer David Borden, who lived nearby in Ithaca, NY, began experimenting with Moog's instruments. Bob Moog and his associates at the Trumansburg factory collaborated quite a bit with David Borden and his ensemble, Mother Mallard. Borden's group was one of the very first all-synthesizer performance groups in the world. The contributions of Borden's ensemble in the late 1960s and 1970s were seminal in developing the skills of live synthesizer performance.

In England, Keith Emerson first heard Wendy Carlos' *Switched-on Bach* in 1969, and, consequently, purchased one of the earliest commercially available modular Moog systems. The modular Moog synthesizers of that era were large unwieldy beasts, hard to maintain and control in a studio and even harder to tame on the road. Emerson became the first performer to actually tour live with the instrument, proving that the synthesizer was an instrument capable of breaking down musical barriers and exploring new territory in a live concert setting.

Keith Emerson with Moog Modular System, 1974.

In 1967, Emerson joined drummer Brian Davison, bassist/vocalist Lee Jackson, and guitarist David O'List, in the band (called the Nice) to accompany American soul-singer and former Ike and Tina Turner backing vocalist Patricia Ann Cole (P.P. Arnold). They soon gained their own solo position in local clubs in London, and began performing a distinctive fusion of jazz, blues, classical music, and rock. Emerson quickly emerged as the leader of the band, both musically and as a performer, and set a precedent in rock music with the main focus of the group on the keyboards, predominantly the Hammond Organ. The Rolling Stones' manager, Andrew Oldham, after catching a live gig, was very impressed and signed the band immediately.

The Nice performed at the Royal Albert Hall in London, made regular appearances on British television, and went on to tour throughout Europe and the United States. After releasing five LPs within a three-year period, Emerson was feeling restrained by the other members. The band dissolved in 1970.

It was then that Emerson teamed up with bassist/vocalist Greg Lake and drummer Carl Palmer to form the legendary group Emerson, Lake & Palmer (ELP) in 1970. Their live performance debut at the Isle of Wight Festival brought the trio instant fame. The performance began with a re-working of Mussorgsky's classic *Pictures at an Exhibition* ending with a huge volley of cannon fire, which drove the audience into a frenzy. The band's first single, "Lucky Man," ended with arguably the first lead synthesizer solo to ever appear on a recording.

The electronic sound of ELP took the pop music world by storm, and the band became a rock institution, releasing six platinum albums between 1970 and 1977, including a live recording of Mussorgsky's *Pictures at an Exhibition*. The group headlined the immense 1974 festival, California Jam, playing to a capacity audience of over 500,000. ELP disbanded in 1979, and Emerson began a solo career in 1980. During the '80s, Emerson turned to motion picture soundtrack composition, composing and producing several film scores including the Stallone action vehicle *Nighthawks*, the Dario Argento film *Inferno*, and a full length Japanese animated film called *Harmagedon*.

From the mid-1970s, Keith Emerson won the Overall Best Keyboardist award in the annual *Keyboard* magazine Readers' Poll many times, and now holds a seat of honor on their advisory board. The Smithsonian Institute in Washington, D.C. recently honored Emerson for his pioneering work in electronic music.

ELP were not alone in the new world of synth-based rock. Pink Floyd's double LP, *Ummagumma,* an album whose mystical-sounding title turned out to be a Cambridgeshire euphemism for sex, was released in 1969. One of the albums was live, the second LP in the set featured solo compositions from each member of the group. This second LP was a result of keyboard player Rick Wright's dissatisfaction with being in a rock band. Rick wanted the opportunity to compose "real music," so each member of the band was given half an album side to work on solo projects. Four years and four albums later, in 1973, the band released *The Dark Side of the Moon*, which sold over 25 million copies and remained on the Billboard charts for 14 years.

Another English group to make a successful crossover into synth-based rock was Yes. By April 1971, with the band's third LP, *The Yes Album,* they had defined their new sound, with compositions that resembled tone poems, rather than the standard pop format compositions. Tony Kaye's Moog synthesizer and organ, Steve Howe's guitar solos, Chris Squire's bass, and Jon Anderson's falsetto vocals all contributed to induce a series of imaginative sonic landscapes. Yes began work on their next album, *Close to the Edge*, but were interrupted when keyboard player Tony Kaye left the group in August of 1971 to join ex-Yes guitarist Peter Banks in the group Flash. Former Strawbs keyboard player Rick Wakeman played his first shows with Yes in the fall of 1971, replacing Kaye. Wakeman was a far more dramatic musician than Kaye.

Wakeman used an arsenal of a dozen instruments, including a Mellotron, various synthesizers, a Hammond organ, at least two pianos, and an electric harpsichord. This group, comprised of Anderson, Squire, Howe, Wakeman, and Bruford, while short lived, is generally considered to be the best of all the Yes personnel configurations. The sounds of groups like ELP and Yes spread their influences around the world.

English composer Brian Eno, born in 1948, was one of the pioneers of a new genre known as ambient music.

Perhaps best known as a musician and producer, Eno is also an artist, professor and theorist. Brian Eno's work as a composer, performer, and producer has greatly impacted all facets of both the experimental and rock genres of music. He is well known for his success as a record producer with rock legends like U2, David Bowie and James, as well as for his work for films, including music for *Trainspotting*, *Velvet Goldmine*, and *Heat*. He has also created music for many television programs and commercials, including the memorable Windows 95 startup sound.

Brian Eno first achieved fame as a synthesist, and for his manipulation of tape effects for the British glitter band Roxy Music between 1971 and 1973. Eno used the Sequential Circuits Prophet Five synthesizer, not as a standard keyboard instrument, but as a tool for creating and manipulating new sounds, creating imaginative pads and atmospheres. His passionate involvement with experimental music has resulted in a prolific personal career of numerous achievements. Eno launched the Obscure Records label in 1975, which focused on promoting avant garde and experimental music. Many of the leading composers in these genres were involved, including Gavin Bryars, Christopher Hobbs, John Adams, David Toop, Jan Steele,

John Cage, Michael Nyman, Simon Jeffes, John White, Harold Budd, and Tom Philips. The compositions were tranquil and quiet, characterized by Eno's *Discreet Music*, released in 1975, in which the score for the music was an actual diagram of the tape delay system utilized in the recording.

Eno conceived the idea for ambient music while convalescing after an accident. Confined to bed and under medication, he was listening to an album of 18th century harp music playing almost inaudibly on his stereo with only one channel functioning. Since he didn't have the energy to get up and turn the machine off, or change the record, it played repeatedly for hours. He realized that he was listening to the music as part of the ambience of the environment. He had an epiphany while comparing the tranquil sounds he was hearing to the color of light and the ambience of rain in the environment, sometimes falling below the brink of perception.

Eno created a series of albums that incorporated ambient atmospheres to produce a backdrop for music to exist within, giving birth to the ambient genre. The best example of this type of composition is exemplified in Eno's 1978 release, *Ambient 1–Music for Airports*, which has become a classic of the genre. The complete score for *Music for Airports* was recently re-recorded in 1998 by the New York-based acoustic chamber ensemble Bang on a Can (Opal Productions, in affiliation with Warner Bros.).

Besides recording music, Brian Eno has been very active in creating film and multimedia, creating over a hundred installations around the world. These are specially designed spaces that include sound, sculpture and lighting effects, combined to generate evolving ambient atmospheres. In 1998, Brian Eno began exploring algorithmic music and creating interactive software that offered the person using the software the ability to construct his or her own combinations of musical events. This concept was first realized by New York composer/software author Laurie Spiegel in 1974 with her VAMPIRE system (Video And Music Playing Interactive Real-time Experiment).

In Greece, Vangelis was born Evanghelos Odyssey Papathanassiou on March 29th, 1943 in the eastern port city of Volos, Greece. His musical genius first became evident to his parents when he spontaneously began composing music on the piano at age four. The young Vangelis refused to take music lessons but continued to play the piano and presented his first public performance of his compositions at the age of six.

Vangelis had enjoyed tremendous success in music during his student days in Greece. In the late 1960s, he formed Aphrodite's Child with singer Demis Roussos and drummer Lucas Sideras. This innovative trio created the groundwork for a metamorphosis from the symphonic rock styles of Yes and ELP into the integration of an entirely new musical genre. They went to Paris and recorded the song "Rain and Tears," which was inspired by Pachelbel's "Canon in D," and released it as a single. It became a huge success, and took on special meaning because of its association with the 1968 student riots in Paris.

During their stay in Paris, the political atmosphere had changed radically in Greece and they were unable to return to their homeland. Aphrodite's Child continued to record successful albums. After the controversial double album *666*, which Vangelis seemed to dominate, the group split up in 1970/71 and both Demis Roussos and Vangelis went on to greater success with their own separate solo careers.

Vangelis remained in Paris for a few months, recording soundtracks for Frederic Roseau, a French film director. These included the classic *L'Apocalypse Des Animaux* and *La Fete Sauvage*. He recorded his first solo album, *Fais que ton rêve soit plus long que la nuit*, in France in 1972. The following year, he recorded his first internationally successful album, *Earth*.

In 1974, Vangelis moved to London. There were widespread rumors that he would be keyboard player Rick Wakeman's replacement in the group Yes. After rehearsing with Yes for several weeks, Vangelis walked out, explaining that his musical theory and directions and the group's were in opposition. It was during his encounter with Yes that he and singer Jon Anderson became friends and musical collaborators, a relationship that would produce four albums and a memorable friendship that would endure for many years to come.

Soon after the experiment with Yes, Vangelis signed a recording contract with RCA Records and constructed his own 24-track studio, which he named Nemo Studios. The first album Vangelis produced in this studio for the RCA label was *Heaven and Hell*, a collection of exceptional and powerful music, which immediately catapulted him to the vanguard of popular music in Europe and the United States. After this, Vangelis made a series of very successful and innovative RCA albums in the '70s, followed by a string of memorable albums for Polydor in the '80s.

The music of Vangelis is too diverse to be described in any music category. He eloquently explains his musical concepts in the liner notes to his 1981 greatest hits collection: "I have always felt that you should not borrow knowledge from others, because personal experience and development are of utmost significance."

Vangelis has received a multitude of awards, among them an Oscar in 1982 for the soundtrack for the film *Chariots of Fire*. Ten years later, in 1992, he was awarded the Chevalier Order of Arts and Letters, one of France's most prestigious honors. His most celebrated studio was the "Epsilon Laboratory" in Paris, constructed primarily out of glass perched on top of a skyscraper.

Vangelis has always lived a secluded lifestyle, focusing on creating original sounds for his recordings and composing music. During his career he has lived in Greece, Paris, London, Athens, with most of his recordings since 1993 having been created in Athens. He has also recently become involved in many Greek cultural events, including a large open-air concert in the Temple of Zeus for his *Mythodea* album and several large productions for the opening and closing ceremonies of sporting events in Athens.

In 1960s Germany, a new generation of young West Germans was growing up in the aftermath of the "cold war," amidst the tensions between East and West Germany. There was an impetus to recapture a German cultural identity after the destruction of World War II, which gave rise to a new era of music and films. Karlheinz Stockhausen, an eclectic composer of the Darmstadt school, who was active between the 1950s and the 1990s, became a profound influence on early German rock. Many German music students were interested in performance art, and utilized this medium to express their feelings.

In 1967, two German musicians, Florian Schneider and Ralf Hütter, met and the Kunstacademie in Remschied, near Düsseldorf, They were both classically trained musicians. While they continued their studies at the Düsseldorf Conservatory, they formed Organisation in 1968. Their early music was comprised of a collage of sound, audio feedback and strong driving rhythms. The band took part in various performances at art galleries and universities. They changed their name to Kraftwerk (German for "power plant") in 1970, performing eclectic music based on synthesizers, drum machines, and sequencers.

The group released three albums in Germany between 1970 and 1972. During the summer of 1974, Kraftwerk released their first international album, *Autobahn*, which brought them immediate global recognition. During the recording of *Autobahn*, Florian Schneider and Ralf Hütter sang through a Vocoder designed to their specifications. In 1970 they had constructed their own studio in the center of Düsseldorf in a large rented loft next to the railway station, where it is located today. They named the studio Klingklang, filling it with homemade oscillators and altered electronic organs that were augmented by metallic rods and 'found objects.' Tape splices and loops were incorporated to enhance the recordings. Kraftwerk's studio, over the next two years, evolved into a sophisticated laboratory, with various prototypes and customized modules of new models of synthesizers and devices, developed by various companies, to augment their sound exploration. The rest is history, as there are few electronic musicians today, especially those working in pop, who don't count these pioneering German artists among their influences.

In France, during the early seventies, composer Jean-Michel Jarre, son of Oscar-winning film composer Maurice Jarre (*Lawrence of Arabia*), also began to work with electronic music. Jarre merged classical music, live opera, and experimental music to create a new fusion of these elements.

In 1964, at the age of 16, Jean-Michel organized his first band, Mystere IV. Later, Jean-Michel attended the Paris Conservatoire and studied with the renowned Jeannine Rueff. This classical background was to prove very useful to Jarre's future projects.

In 1968, Jean-Michel left the Paris Conservatoire and met the man most responsible for altering his perception of music and technology, Pierre Schaeffer of the Group de Recherches Musicales (Music Research Group), originator of Musique Concrete. This was his first introduction to the techniques of electroacoustic music. The following year, Jean-Michel recorded his first electroacoustic music composition, *La Cage*.

In 1972 Jean-Michel met Francis Dreyfus, owner of Dreyfus Disques, an internationally distributed recording label, and went on to compose and record a group of original compositions for his first album, *Deserted Palace*. Two years later, Jean-Michel met Michel Geiss, who created custom instruments for him. Two of the most notable inventions by Geiss were the Matri-Sequencer and the Digi-Sequencer. 1976 was the year that really launched Jean-Michel's career, with the French release of the now legendary album *Oxygene*. Shortly after its release, Jean-Michel received the "Grand Prix Du Disques" award for *Oxygene* from the Charles Cross Academy. During that same year, he also met actress Charlotte Rampling, his future wife.

The following year, Polydor licensed *Oxygene* and all future recordings for worldwide release. *People* magazine declared Jean-Michel the Personality of the Year. His success during the mid-1970s with *Oxygene* and *Equinoxe* was greatly enhanced with the release of his 1980 best seller, *Magnetic Fields*. Two weeks after the album was released, it hit the top ten in every European Country.

On October 15th, 1981, sixty musicians and sound technicians departed from Paris for Peking transporting fifteen tons of stage equipment. Jarre performed five concerts in China, which became known as "The Concerts in China," preserved in a double album set on Polydor. He was the first western musician to be invited to perform a concert in China.

Jarre produced a compilation of all his earlier recordings in late 1983. He also received rave reviews and achieved great financial rewards with the release of his much-anticipated 1984 release, *Zoolook*. This album marked the point where we can hear how Jarre established the creative foundation that provided the impetus for several avant-garde sub-genres of pop music to germinate and flourish during the 1980s and 1990s.

Perhaps the greatest of Jean-Michel's achievements was his understanding and investigation of the enormous music potential of the digital sampler, which had just been developed. On *Zoolook*, Jarre ingenuously incorporated the use of digitally sampled human voices and animal sounds, collaborating with world-renowned performance artist Laurie Anderson.

In 1986, NASA commissioned Jarre to compose music for the celebration of the 30th Anniversary of the National Aeronautics Space Agency. Out of that collaboration the highly acclaimed album *Rendezvous* was conceived. It will go down in history as one of the highlights of modern electronic music history. The concert, which took place in Houston (NASA's Manned Spacecraft Center), engulfed the entire city with musicians, instruments, and loudspeakers positioned on top of skyscrapers throughout the city. The musicians involved were successful in assembling a solitary system of musical output from these various locales thanks to the miracle of telecommunications technology, which had also entered a new phase of development at this time, with wireless remote digital systems and MIDI. The concert took place on April 5th 1986, at 8:15pm. This was one of the most spectacular concerts in the history of music.

By 1990, Jean-Michel Jarre had achieved enormous success as a composer, which made his father extremely proud. In retrospect, we can see that Jean Michel's interest in music technology definitely had an influence on his father's later compositions. In 1986, Maurice Jarre began to incorporate synthesizers into his own scores, which were previously performed exclusively by orchestra and acoustic instruments. Both generations had made a major impact on instrumental music of the twentieth century.

In Japan, composer Isao Tomita, inspired by the success of Wendy Carlos in the United States, began to create his own synthesizer recordings of baroque and classical music.

Born in 1932, in Tokyo, Tomita was already an established composer of conventional classical music when Wendy Carlos' *Switched on Bach* captivated his imagination. He admired Carlos' academic attention to detail and virtuoso musicianship. Tomita purchased his first modular Moog synthesizer, a System III, along with a sequencer, in 1971. The first results of Tomita's fourteen months of experimentation in this new medium was the best-selling 1974 album, *Snowflakes Are Dancing*, a collection of Tomita's synthesized, multi-layered interpretations of some of Claude Debussy's most engaging works. The album was so successful that it won a Grammy in 1974 and was voted that year's classical record of the year by the National Association of Recording Merchandisers.

Subsequent Tomita interpretations of classical works included the 1975 interpretation of Igor Stravinsky's *Firebird*, and the highly acclaimed 1976 of Gustav Holst's *Planets*. Holst's heirs sued Tomita for abusing their father's great composition. As a result, *The Planets* was removed from the market for a few years by court order from Gustav Holst's relatives. RCA withdrew some 30,000 records from circulation. While the album remained off the market for two years, it became one of his most popular recordings.

Tomita's concerts have been major events. In 1984 Tomita presented a concert in Linz, Austria, which he called Mind of the Universe, and drew a crowd of 80,000 people. In 1986, Tomita presented a performance art event, Back to the Earth, in New York, in celebration of the centennial of the Statue of Liberty. In 1988, Sound Cloud, another multimedia concert, was presented in Sydney to commemorate the Australian Bicentenary.

Celebrating over 40 years in music, Tomita still remains very active. He is currently the Honorary President of the Japan Synthesizer Programmers Association.

In Russia, Eduard Artemiev is a composer best known for his prolific movie soundtracks for legendary Russian directors Andrei Tarkovski, and Nikita Mikhalkov. In 1960, he met electronic engineer Eugene Murzin and immediately became attracted to the possibilities of electronic music. Murzin and his colleagues had developed the ANS- Synthesizer two years earlier. The soundtracks Artemiev scored for Tarkovski's films *Solaris*, *The Mirror* and *Stalker* gained international recognition in 1989. Also that same year, Artemiev composed *Three Glimpses on the Revolution* for the Bicentennial of the French Revolution, a work commissioned by the organizers of the Electronic Music Festival in Bourges, France. As a creator of over one 120 soundtracks, Artemiev established himself as a leader of Russian electronic music.

In the United States, jazz was also beginning to be influenced by this new technology. The result came to be known as jazz fusion, in which jazz musicians endeavored to expand the boundaries of jazz by incorporating elements from the energy and attitude of rock with the harmonic complexity and improvisational freedom of jazz. Jazz fusion musicians incorporated odd meters, superimposed rhythmic structures and other unorthodox rhythmic constructions in their new modes of musical articulation. The electric guitar, guitar synth, and electric bass, driven through various effects devices and synthesizers, replaced traditional jazz instruments such as the piano, saxophone, and upright bass.

Many people believe that the genre was born with the 1969 release by Miles Davis, *Bitches Brew*. This historic album was originally released as a 90-minute double LP, and was re-released in 1998 with lots of previously unheard music from the sessions in a four-CD box set. Some of the giants of this fledgling genre played in those sessions, including pianists Herbie Hancock, Chick Corea, and Joe Zawinul; bassist Dave Holland; soprano saxophonist Wayne Shorter; bass clarinetist Benny Maupin; drummers Jack DeJohnette, Billy Cobham, and Lenny White; and percussionist Airto Moreira. It was the beginning of a new era in jazz.

One of the most important elements of jazz fusion was the synthesizer, which was usually keyboard-based. Players like Pat Metheny, John McLaughlin, Alan Holdsworth, and Steve Morse also pioneered the use of guitar synthesizers in the genre during the 1970s.

Two of the most influential figures in jazz fusion are Josef Zawinul, the founder of Weather Report (later the Zawinul Syndicate), and Jan Hammer, who worked with many innovative giants of jazz during the sixties and seventies, and also established his own successful solo career.

Josef Zawinul was born in Austria on July 7, 1932. Zawinul has amassed an immense catalog of work, which spans over four decades. He immigrated to the United States in 1959. Since then, Zawinul has proved himself a true trendsetter, defining the path for future generation of musicians. Always one step ahead of his peers, Zawinul shares the pedigree of his European heritage with the wealth of musical experience gathered from American Jazz. He is one of the few jazz artists who remain immune to trends, instead following his heart and artistic instincts as he pushes the musical frontier forward. Zawinul developed his musical ideas while gigging with Maynard Ferguson, Cannonball Adderley, and the revolutionary Miles Davis

Group during the late sixties, before creating Weather Report with brass virtuoso Wayne Shorter in the summer of 1971.

Zawinul was the first musician to play on two separate keyboards simultaneously. He would sit between two independent ARP 2600 synthesizers, and use his left hand for bass lines and chords, and his right hand for leads and harmonies. The 2600 he used for bass and rhythm parts was reversed, with the upper registers on the left, and the lower registers on the right, closest to where he was sitting. This style of layering timbres became a significant tool for musical expression, later used by Keith Emerson, Jan Hammer, and many others.

With Weather Report, Josef Zawinul and Wayne Shorter formed the core of a band which attracted the foremost jazz drummers, percussionists and bass players of the 1970s and 1980s until its demise in 1986, following the tragic death of visionary bassist Jaco Pastorious. Fusion seems like a modest description of the music Weather Report produced, drawing its inspiration from musical styles and techniques from around the planet. Zawinul and his ensemble are currently recording and touring as the Zawinul Syndicate. This band continues to expand on the best ideas of Weather Report.

Another virtuoso player who was a key figure in this genre was Jan Hammer. Born in Prague, Czechoslovakia in 1948, Jan Hammer's musical career is as firmly rooted in the fundamentals of classical, jazz and rock as it is dedicated to the future of electronics, synthesized sound, interactive media, television, film and animation. His studio is lined with Grammy awards and gold and platinum plaques from around the world. His recording career spans includes award winning solo albums as well as collaborations with musicians such as the Mahavishnu Orchestra, Jeff Beck, Al Di Meola, Mick Jagger, Carlos Santana, Stanley Clarke, and Elvin Jones.

Hammer's mother was a well-known Czech singer and his father was a doctor who worked his way through school playing vibes and standup bass. With their musical background, his parents provided an encouraging musical environment. He began playing piano at age four, and began formal classical instruction two years later. He was performing and recording throughout Eastern Europe with his own jazz trio at the age of 14. He entered Prague Academy of Muse Ans where he became engrossed in classes in harmony, counterpoint, music history, and classical composition. This education came to an abrupt halt with the Russian invasion of Czechoslovakia in 1968. Jan immigrated to the United States, and shortly after received a scholarship to attend the Berklee School of Music in Boston.

Jan Hammer and talk show host Charlie Rose

After graduating from Berklee, Jan spent a year as keyboardist/conductor with Sarah Vaughan. In 1970 he moved to a loft in lower Manhattan, and played keyboards on albums by Elvin Jones and flautist, Jeremy Steig. In 1971, he became a member of the original Mahavishnu Orchestra. This was the most successful jazz-rock fusion group to both record and tour in live performance, selling over two million records worldwide, and performing 530 live shows before their December 31, 1973 farewell concert.

The following year, in 1974, Jan recorded an album with Mahavishnu violinist Jerry Goodman. They recorded the album *Like Children* at the band Chicago's Caribou Ranch Studio in Colorado and Trident Studios in London, which was released on the Nemperor Records label.

Then, in 1975 Jan's solo career was launched with the landmark recording *The First Seven Days*, produced and recorded at Red Gate Studio in his upstate New York farmhouse. Over the next decade, Jan produced and performed on nearly twenty albums with his Jan Hammer Group, and toured and recorded with musicians such as Jeff Beck, Al Di Meola, and Neal Schon of Journey, among others.

During the 1980s, Jan scored numerous motion pictures and TV documentaries in the United States. In the fall of 1984, Hammer's most formidable musical challenge was presented to him, when director Jan Eliasberg and the producers of *Miami Vice* commissioned him to write music for their new show. The soundtrack album remained #1 on the Billboard chart for 12 weeks, hitting quadruple-platinum by selling over four million copies in the United States alone, with worldwide sales in excess of eight million albums. This was the first TV show theme to be #1 since Henry Mancini's "Theme from *Peter Gunn*" in 1959.

In the complex world we live in, music is often regarded as entertainment. A lot of people think of it as a business. But music can be a way of life, a language that speaks of worlds your voice could never describe. During the late 1970s, many musicians began a personal quest for inner peace and harmony. As the counter-cultural interests in spirituality and alternate lifestyles expanded, new genres of music evolved in response. They were simple and unadorned, directed from the heart, embodying a deep spiritual significance that came from a personal sanctuary, and could become a center for reflection for the listener. In many senses, this music possesses a Buddhist attitude, the convincingness of which is not drawn from any melody, or segment of the music, but from the entire process, from the gradual, slow journey the listener undertakes to the inner realms of consciousness. This is the period in time when ambient music, or 'space music' began to develop. Small independent labels, like Klaus Schulze's Innovative Communications, Peter Baumann's (Tangerine Dream) label Private Music, Ekhart Rahn's Celestial Harmonies, and Brian Eno's Obscure Records emerged.

Soon, larger companies wanted to exploit this new genre of music, and needed a marketing term to describe it. 'New age music' became a generic term for anything not immediately identifiable as jazz, folk, classical, etc. The term was unappreciated by most musicians who were composing and playing various forms of electronic music at the time, but the stigmatic label stuck despite years of protest.

During the 1970s and 1980s, there was a cornucopia of new electronic music composers creating incredible music. Although the ideas for this new music began with innovative artists like Klaus Schulze, Cluster (Dieter Moebius, Hans Joachim Rodelius and Conny

Plank) and Tangerine Dream, in the late 1960s, and early 1970s, one of the first artists to break through and reach a worldwide audience was Mike Oldfield and his album *Tubular Bells*. Millions of moviegoers recognized and embraced his theme song when it was used in *The Exorcist*. Oldfield's instrumental became was an astonishing smash hit upon its initial release in Britain, and later in the U.S. after *The Exorcist*. Later the same year, Brian Eno released *No Pussyfooting* with Robert Fripp, one of their first ventures into this new musical hybrid of influences. The album contained two long atmospheric compositions. Some of the most noteworthy artists of the new genre of ambient music were Eberhard Schoener, Robert Fripp, Peter Michael Hamel, Michael Nyman, Harold Budd, Michael Stearns, Steve Hillage, Michael William Gilbert, Kerry Leimer, Steve Roach, Stomu Yamashta, Robert Schroeder, Deuter, Thierry Fervant, Masanori Takashi (Kitaro), and the Spanish synth trio Neuronium, led by Michel Huygen.

CHAPTER 2

A Timetable of Musical Technology

Before the innovators who re-invented music throughout the sixties and seventies could make their mark, technological innovators had been working on the concept of creating sound with electronics for more than a century. This chapter gives a thorough overview of the earliest inventors and inventions that led to the development of the first commercially available synthesizer in 1964. It presents a chronicle of the significant musical and scientific events that led to a revolution in many aspects of music during the twentieth century.

French physicist Charles-Augustin de Coulomb (1736-1806) introduced the concept of electrical charge to the world in 1785 when he published the results of his experiments on the quantitative description of force. The work of English scientist Joseph Priestly, whose research introduced the laws of electrical repulsion, inspired Coulomb's research. Technically, Coulomb demonstrated that the force between two electrical charges is proportional to the product of the charges and inversely proportional to the square of the distance between them. To put it more simply, two like electric charges, either positive or negative, will repel each other; two unlike charges, one positive and one negative, attract each other along a straight line joining their centers. This phenomenon became known as the Coulomb's force, or Coulomb's interaction, and a unit of electric charge was named a Coulomb in his honor. One of the main forces in atomic reactions in known as the Coulombic force.

In 1831 Michael Faraday discovered electric induction when he found that by changing a magnetic field he could induce an electric current in a nearby circuit, thus converting mechanical energy to electrical energy. Within two years the first hand-turned generator, using magnets around coils, was demonstrated in Paris. This was followed by an English model, which used rotating coils revolving in the magnetic field of a fixed magnet. By 1850 electric generators were widely manufactured using permanent magnets, until, in 1866, "self-excited generators" were created by using electromagnets powered by the generator itself.

Understanding the laws of electrical force became the new science of the nineteenth century and had reverberations across all studies, from science to the arts.

Europeans contributed the most consistent major force to the development of early music technology through the application of the laws of electricity to electronic technology, which could synthesize sounds by breaking tone down to its component parts and putting it back together by electronic synthesis.

Experiments with electromechanical elements such as solenoids and motors were conducted throughout the nineteenth century, along side experiments with more accessible "automatic" instruments and new modes of creating tones and microtones of sound in music.

By the 1920s, basic electronic music technology such as amplifiers, filter circuits, and loudspeakers had been invented. Basic circuits for sine wave, square, and sawtooth wave generators had been invented to isolate and define sound. A sine wave was defined as signals made up of pure tones, without overtones. Square waves consisted of component tones in the natural harmonic series of notes. The square shape of each fluctuation of the component tone indicates that voltage or current immediately increases to its maximum or peak value and polarity, and remains there throughout that fluctuation. Then the voltage waveform instantly changes its polarity, or the current waveform reverses its direction. Sawtooth waves were defined as fundamental tones and related overtones produced when a voltage or current increases from zero to its positive peak value at a linear rate, and rapidly changes to its negative peak value. The waveform then decreases back to zero at a linear rate.

This inter-disciplinary technological and conceptual exploration has made every aspect of the creation, recording, reproduction and marketing of music accessible from the home studio. Any individual who is interested in new spheres of musical creativity can contribute to this ongoing wide-open exploration of creative expression.

ELISHA GRAY

Elisha Gray, an American electrician and engineer, was born in 1835 in the town of Barnesville, Ohio. After graduating high school, he studied physical science at Oberlin College, and later taught in the Physics department from 1873 to 1900. The first electronic instrument was Elisha Gray's Musical Telegraph, which evolved out of his experiments with telephone technology. In February 1876, Elisha Gray arrived at the U.S. Patent Office to file a caveat announcing his intention to patent his invention "for transmitting vocal sounds telegraphically." Alexander Graham Bell arrived at the patent office an hour or two before Elisha Gray, to actually patent his invention designed to achieve the same end. After years of litigation, Bell was named the inventor of the telephone, even though Gray's apparatus as described in his caveat was proved to work, while Bell's apparatus would not have worked as described in his patent. History will remember Bell as the inventor of the telephone, while Elisha Gray will be remembered for his invention of the first electronic musical instrument.

In the early 1870s, before the invention of the telephone, information was telegraphed all around the world. The fundamental operating principal of the telegraph relied on the use of electricity to create a magnetic field around the telegraph wire. The magnetic field was generated by sending an electric current through the wire, thus creating a magnetic field around the telegraph wire, which was carried along the wire as an electric pulse. The fact that a telegraph line could transmit only one message at a time created limitations in the development of telegraph technology.

The first intention of many telegraphic experimenters was to invent a new method of transmitting multiple messages on a single telegraph line. Elisha Gray's keen interest in telegraphic technology led him to develop several advancements such as a telegraphic switch and the Annunciator, which he patented in 1867. Elisha Gray was working on this research when his nephew showed him a strange experiment for generating sound. Using an electric oscillator to vary voltage, he put his hand in water to conduct electricity through the water into his hand. Thus, he used his body as an amplifier, and generated sound.

Gray developed his nephew's experiment with varying voltage using an electric oscillator in what he referred to as his "electric bathroom." Electric oscillations were transformed into acoustic vibrations through the oscillation of the electrified hand. Gray reproduced the experiment and developed the principle of self-vibrating electromagnetic devices.

Gray refined this invention by using the body of a violin and a metal plate instead of immersing his hand in water. He claimed that the new instrument was like a hybrid of the sound of a violin and the tones produced in his "electric bathroom."

Elisha Gray used the principles of electromagnetic technology to create single note oscillators with a pitch range of two octaves. Gray invented the technology for generating and transmitting sounds with electricity and went further with his experiments to transmit many combined signals, notes, and tonal chords on a single telegraph line.

His Musical Telegraph, also referred to as the Harmonic Telegraph, generated sounds through a series of small steel reeds. The sounds were transmitted by electromagnets over a standard telephone lines. In order to make the oscillator more audible, Gray used a vibrating diaphragm to generate a magnetic field, thereby creating the first loudspeaker. For his second generation Musical Telegraph, Gray used an electromagnet to activate a small, thin metallic strip, which, when oscillated by electric current, emitted a sound from the loudspeaker. Gray had now created the primary elements of an electronic musical instrument: the oscillators and transducers, and the loudspeaker that transforms an electric signal into an audio signal. In 1874, Gray demonstrated his magnificent instrument on a concert tour. The early experiments of Elisha Gray evolved into today's synthesizers, samplers, and studio electronics.

Among his later inventions were appliances for multiplex telegraphy and the Teleautograph, a machine devised for the electric transmission of handwriting. Besides his scientific addresses and monographs, Gray wrote two books, *Telegraphy and Telephony* (1878) and *Electricity and Magnetism* (1900). Gray's experiments won him the highest accolade, the Legion of Honour, at the Paris Exposition of 1878. Elisha Gray died in Newtonville, Massachusetts on January 21, 1901.

EMILE BERLINER AND THOMAS EDISON

Emile Berliner was born in Germany in 1851, and began his career as a printer, but later became a clerk in a fabric store. It was here that his talent as an inventor first began to surface. In 1869, he invented a new type of loom for weaving cloth.

Berliner immigrated to the United States in 1870, at the age of 19, and studied Physics part time at the Cooper Institute, which became the Cooper Union for the Advancement of Science and Art, in New York. He took a zealous interest in electricity and sound.

In the summer of 1876, after seeing Alexander Graham Bell's new invention, the telephone, at a Centennial Celebration exhibit in Philadelphia, he observed that Bell's invention had a reliable receiver but had an inferior transmitter mechanism. (This is the famous convention where a forum on the future predicted that there would be a telephone in every city of the world by the year 1976.)

Emile Berliner immediately went to work to solve the problems posed by the limitations of Bell's transmitter mechanism. His first transmission of sound was over the telephone he had installed between his apartment and his landlady's apartment. Berliner patented his discovery on June 4th, 1877, and immediately sold it to the newly formed Bell Telephone Company in Boston. Berliner's invention of his primitive microphone allowed Bell's invention to be used over any distance, making it possible for the Bell company to mass produce the telephone.

In 1877, Thomas Edison and Emile Berliner simultaneously invented the first prototypes of the phonograph, designed for playing pre-recorded sounds. Berliner's invention recorded sound by tracing grooves in a spiral on a flat disc. Edison's invention recorded sound by creating an indention on a sheet of tinfoil wrapped around a rotating cylinder, with a vibrating stylus. The Bell Company bought Edison's invention, preferring the cylinder method of recording to the disc. The problem with Edison's technology is that each wax cylinder had to be recorded separately. No mass reproduction of the sounds was possible. These "talking machines" were originally sold as novelties in toy stores and bicycle shops.

Berliner was quick to understand the potential for "automatic music" as a means of disseminating culture as well as a form of entertainment. He continued to develop his recording technology until he invented the means to play a recording over and over on his gramophone. He invented shellac gramophone disks, which were fabricated with a zinc base, coated with beeswax, and etched with chromic acid. These were the predecessors of shellac LP records. Berliner received his American patent for his invention of the gramophone and a disc that could be played on it on September 29, 1887.

In 1898, after a decade of further experimentation and refinement of the technology, Berliner returned to Europe and launched Berliner Gramophone Records with his brother Joseph. For the Gramaphone Co. Ltd., in London, Berliner adopted a picture of a dog listening to a recording, "His Master's Voice," as his trademark.

Berliner founded Deutsche Grammophon Gesellschaft (DGG) in his hometown of Hanover, Germany, in the same year. His factory in Hanover became the first manufacturing center in the world, producing several million records a year within 10 years. Berliner was also responsible for producing the first disc recordings available in the United States. Emile Berliner's disc revolutionized the relationship between artists and their public, because for the first time, music lovers could experience music in the privacy of their homes. Two legendary opera singers, Australia's Dame Nelly Melba and Italy's Enrico Caruso, were among the first artists recorded on records at the turn of the twentieth century. It was 1910 before the first orchestral recordings were made, and in 1913 Beethoven's Fifth Symphony became the first symphonic recording, on double-sided records capable of playing five minutes of music per side.

After World War I, the Gramophone Co. and its German subsidiary, Deutsche Grammophon Gesellschaft, parted ways. In 1924, the London-based Gramophone Co, and its famous trademark, "His Master's Voice," was bought by the Canadian Victor Talking Machine Company, which merged with RCA in 1929 to become RCA Victor. Following a severe heart attack, Emile Berliner died on August 3, 1929.

In 1941, Deutsche Grammophon was bought by the giant German electronic company Siemens & Halske. In 1962, Siemens joined forces with Philips to create the DGG/PPI Group, which in turn led to PolyGram. In 1998, PolyGram was acquired by Seagrams Company Ltd., of Canada, to form the Universal Music Group.

Deutsche Grammophon Gesellschaft is now part of Universal Classics, and still has its headquarters in Hanover, where it continues to record the world's leading artists and is committed to continuing the development of new recording technologies.

Until the early 1980s, when CD technology was developed, almost a century later, the masters for LPs were still made with Emile Berliner's technology.

ALEXANDER GRAHAM BELL

Alexander Graham Bell, 1862-1939, was an impassioned explorer of communication technology, most renowned for his invention of the telephone. Bell was driven by a powerful desire to test new ideas over many years of concentrated research. In 1876, at the age of 29, he completed his designs for the telephone. The telegraph was about to be replaced with a completely new communication technology. "Talking with electricity" was a far more radical development than any efforts to expand the capability of the existing telegraphic dot-and-dash system of communication.

Bell won the French Volta Prize from the French Academy of Science in 1881. He used the $10,000 award to launch an electro-acoustic research facility, the Volta Laboratory in Washington, D.C. His cousin, Chichester Bell, and Charles S. Tainter worked with him on the development of a method of recording sound optically. This invention, the Photophone, transmitted speech sounds by light rays, using a selenium crystal and a mirror, which vibrated in response to sound. This technology is based on principles that eventually led to laser and fiber optic communication systems. Bell was one of the co-founders of the National Geographic Society, and he also founded the journal *Science* in 1883. By the 1890s, Bell's experiments and inventions were focused mainly on the fields of aeronautics and marine propulsion.

CLEMENT ADER

French engineer and inventor Clement Ader (1841-1925) introduced the first public broadcast of entertainment with his Theatrephone, or "musical telephone." His invention was celebrated at the International Electricity Exposition in Paris, in 1881. Ader demonstrated his technology by transmission of musical performances through telephone lines, which were laid through the sewers from the Paris Opera to the Exhibition Hall at the Palais de l'Industrie.

Ader invented ultra-sensitive microphones, which he placed on either side of the stage to create the first stereophonic transmission signals. The sound was enhanced by earphones, or receivers, which the listeners wore over both ears as they gathered in special "Telephonic Salons" in the early stages of the service. In 1890, Compagne du Theatrophone was launched in Paris to broadcast concerts from various theatres, as well as news and lectures, to home subscribers and to coin-operated telephones installed in hotels and cafes around Paris. Transmissions were also sent over longer distances, to Brussels and London, and even Budapest, until the service was discontinued in 1932.

MELVIN SEVERY

During the late 1880s and early 1890s, Melvin Severy, with the assistance of George B. Sinclair, spent nine years designing and building the Choralcello. The Choralcello Manufacturing Company, in Boston, was formed in 1909, to mass-produce and market the instrument. The Choralcello was an enormous organ designed for use in very large homes, for social recitals and concerts of high society. It was a high-tech player piano, incorporating a player piano paper roll mechanism to play pre-recorded music. Because of its prohibitive high cost and limited market, only a few were sold.

The Choralcello used an electromagnetic tone wheel sound generator with electro-magnetic piano strings, and two keyboards. It used a set of Hammond organ-style stops to operate timbre and tone variations. To create varying tones, it used resonators made of cardboard, hardwood, softwood, glass, and steel.

THEO WANGEMANN

On December 2, 1889, Theo Wangemann, an engineer working with Thomas Edison, made a recording with composer Johannes Brahms, which caused nearly a century-long controversy. Brahms recorded a segment of Strauss' "Libelle," and a few selected segments of Brahms' own 1872 arrangement of the first "Hungarian Dance" for solo piano.

The Brahms cylinder recording is a rare primary source of material for Brahms' research, and a rare document, due to the uniqueness of the technology. However, for nearly a century the amount of noise that masked the music has been the source of great frustration for musicologists and audio technicians alike. In addition to the enormous amount of noise in the recording, it was difficult to trace documentation regarding the history of the Brahms cylinder.

In 1998, the mystery was solved by composer Jonathan Berger from Stanford University, mathematicians Ronald R. Coifman from Yale, and Maxim J. Goldberg from York College of Pennsylvania, when they devised a de-noising technique that brought the century-old cylinder back to life. Their idea was that digital analysis and sampling commonly used to sharpen visual images could be applied to sound, to distinguish music from noise. To prove this theory, they set out to achieve the impossible. They found a vinyl copy of the original Brahms cylinder and were able to completely re-create the clarity of the original Brahms cylinder, thus resurrecting an important part of music history.

JULIAN CARRILLO

Composer, violinist, and music theorist Julian Carrillo was born in 1875, in San Lui Potosi, Mexico. Carillo's thesis, "The Thirteenth Sound Revolution," was his proposal for the incorporation of micro-intervals into the musical system. The number 13 was not suggesting a scale consisting of thirteen sounds, but rather symbolized the break with the traditional 12-tone scale that has traditionally been the basis of the Western musical system.

As a young music student at the National Conservatory of Music in Mexico, Carrillo studied the physics, acoustics and mathematical basis of the laws governing the generation of fundamental intervals in music. He noticed 16 clearly differentiated sounds between the pitches of G and A, emitted by the violin's fourth string, while he played his violin. This became the springboard for his celebrated contribution to new music.

In 1899, the President of Mexico, General Porfrio Diaz, heard Carrillo play his violin and was so impressed that he granted Carrillo a special music scholarship to study in Europe, where he was admitted to Leipzig's Royal Conservatory. He later entered Gante's Royal Conservatory of Music in Belgium to focus on his study of the violin, where he won awards for excellence.

In 1900, Carrillo presented his ideas on the nature of microtones before a convention presided over by Camille Saint-Saens, at the International Congress of Music in Paris, which published his paper.

In 1904, Carrillo returned to Mexico to great acclaim for his outstanding achievements in Europe. In 1906, he became a professor at the National Conservatory in Mexico City. He returned to Europe frequently over the coming years, presenting his papers at several music congresses throughout Europe.

Following the fall of the Huerta government, Carrillo fled to the United States, where he organized the celebrated American Symphony Orchestra. He returned to Mexico in 1918, and took up the post of Principal at the National Conservatory from 1920-1921. He conducted the National Symphony Orchestra from 1918-1924, introducing the works of the great European and Mexican composers. His orchestra became so popular that it sustained itself financially, without grants.

Julian Carillo's theories of microtones, and the 96-tone scale, led to the construction of new instruments, which reproduced tone divisions as small as a sixteenth tone. He demonstrated his instruments in New York City in 1926. The instruments included an Octavina for producing eighth tones and an Arpa Citera for sixteenth tones. There are several existing recordings of Carillo's music, primarily his string quartets.

EDWIN S. VOTEY

In 1896, Edwin Votey of Detroit, Michigan completed his construction of the first Pianola. The first instrument was comprised of a large wooden cabinet placed on the floor in front of a piano, where the piano bench normally stood. Protruding from the back of the cabinet, was a row of flat wooden rods, which were manually aligned with the keyboard of the piano to play the keys in much the same manner as a human pianist.

The Pianola was operated by pumping a pedal with the feet, which created the suction power to control the pitch via a perforated paper music roll. Pianola music rolls were marked in pencil, with reference to the original sheet music, and perforated by a technician. The "tracker bar" was a pneumatic reading device with a row of equally spaced holes; one for each note, over which the piano-roll passed. The greater the suction, the louder a particular note or chord would sound. There are no changes of tempi, rubato, or phrasing on normal Pianola rolls, therefore, the Pianola player had to develop techniques for control of the dynamics by rapid and subtle use of their feet.

Votey's design combined a number of existing mechanisms to make his creation the first truly musical automatic player piano in the world. Aeolian Company acquired the rights to launch an improved version of the Pianola to the American market in 1897, and, two years later, to the European market.

WILLIAM DU BOIS DUDDELL

British physicist and electrical engineer William Du Bois Duddell (1869 –1942) was educated at Cannes and served his engineering apprenticeship at Colchester, England. In 1893, he attended the City and Guilds Institute, where he remained for a number of years because of their state-of-the-art experimental research facilities. Later he opened his own studio on Victoria Street in London. Duddell showed a great talent for designing and building various electric apparatus. His first invention was the Duddell Galvanometer, or Oscillograph.

During the late 1800s, carbon-arc electric street lamps dimly lit the streets of Western Europe, many years before Edison invented the light bulb in America. Electric light was created by the continuous flow of electric sparks between two carbon nodes of the lamps. But these electric sparks emitted an annoying constant humming noise, which became intolerable. William Duddell was asked to find a solution to this problem.

As a result of his experiments with varying voltages supplied to the arc lamps, using a resonant circuit consisting of an inductor and a capacitor, he discovered that subtle changes in voltage modulation created variations in the audio frequencies they produced. He experimented with a method of altering the arc's rate of pulsation, creating distinct musical notes by connecting a musical keyboard to the arc lamps. Thus, in 1899, Duddell demonstrated one of the earliest instruments to generate musical tones by purely electric means. His "singing arc" created the first electrically generated sounds that were not dependent on transmission through a telephone system. The results of his experiments on the resistance of the electric arc were published in the *Proceedings of the Royal Society* in 1901.

William Duddell toured all over England demonstrating his invention, which he never patented. He received the esteemed Friend of the Royal Society Award from Queen Victoria and held office in several learned societies. William Duddell died on November 4, 1917.

VALDIMIR POULSEN

In 1900, Danish engineer Valdimir Poulsen (1869-1942) demonstrated the principle of magnetic recording with his invention of an electro-magnetic phonograph, which he patented in 1898. The telegraphone was a magnetic sound recorder, which registered sound by the alternating magnetization of a steel wire. Thus, magnet tape was first designed for sound recording. In 1903, he founded the American Telegraphone Company, with American investors, who were basically unsuccessful in their efforts to manufacture and market Poulsen's version of the technology. In the following years researchers in Europe and the United States developed magnetic recording techniques using a variety of recording devices.

Poulsen went on to contribute a major development to radio technology when he created the first device for generating continuous long-wave radio broadcasting. This was an adaptation of William Duddell's "singing arc," transformed by Poulsen to generate continuous audio waves by creating an arc between a copper cathode and a carbon anode in a hydrocarbon gas atmosphere and a transverse magnetic field. It was patented in England in 1903 and became known as the Poulsen Arc. By 1920, further development of Poulsen's device made long-wave radio broadcasting a reality.

THADDEUS CAHILL

Thaddeus Cahill was born in 1867 in rural Iowa. At an early age he became interested in the physics of musical sounds. When he was 14, he constructed his own telephone receiver, because the Bell Company had refused to sell him a telephone to use in his own experiments.

Cahill patented the first truly significant electronic musical instrument in 1897. When the blueprints became reality, almost nine years later, it was introduced to the public in 1906 as the Telharmonium.

The Telharmonium, also known as the Dynamophone, was a machine that produced music by using an alternating current (AC) to run an electric generator. This was commonly known as a Dynamo at the time. This was the first 'additive synthesis' device. An article in the April, 1906 issue of *McClure's* magazine stated, "…democracy in music…the musician uses keys and stops to build up voices of flute or clarinet, as the artist uses his brushes for mixing color to obtain a certain hue…it may revolutionize our musical art."

Cahill described the instrument as a large system capable of electrically generating, controlling, and modeling sounds, which could be reproduced through a loudspeaker system. The instrument in many ways was a direct forerunner of the modern synthesizer. Cahill, in his patent application, actually used the term "synthesizing" to describe the instrument's operation.

A complex system of alternators called "rheotomes" (gears with a precise number of serrated teeth) was accountable for creating the sound of the Telharmonium. These rheotomes rotated against a series of wire brushes, and, depending on the rheotome's diameter, the teeth would strike the brush a precise number of times each second. This contact created an electrical oscillation of a sine wave. Various rheotomes, or gears, controlled by a standard piano-style keyboard, were grouped together on a rotating axle with one axle corresponding to one note of the chromatic scale.

Like the piano, the Telharmonium keyboard was touch-sensitive, a feature that was incorporated into modern synthesizers almost a century later, in the early 1980s. The instrument had a console that was used to mix and filter the sounds, and to emulate the tonal qualities of various orchestral instruments. It produced a range of seven octaves, with 36 notes per octave.

In 1900 Cahill built the first display model of the Telharmonium. Two years later, Cahill sought financial support from fellow Washington D.C. resident George Westinghouse by transmitting Telharmonium music over a telephone line to Westinghouse's home. This was the first experiment in Cahill's larger scheme to connect his instruments to homes, hotels, restaurants, and other businesses. Cahill envisioned this would be accomplished as a subscription-based service. Cahill's invention was the first system to utilize telephone lines to transmit information other than conversation. It predated computer data transmission by 70 years. This was the first enterprise designed to transmit live musical performance over telephone lines.

In 1902, Cahill moved his laboratory from Washington to Holyoke, Massachusetts. In the spring of 1906, Cahill displayed his second model to the public. On March 16,1906, composer Edwin Hall Pierce presented a series of Telharmonium concerts that were transmitted a little over a mile by standard telephone cable. This extended from Cahill's assembly plant to the Hotel Hamilton's ballroom, using a telephone receiver covered with a large paper horn to amplify the transmission signal.

This Telharmonium was a colossal instrument utilizing 145 rheotomes, and incorporating nearly 2,000 switches to produce its unique sound. Historical reports vary on its size, claiming the instrument was between 30 and 60 feet in length. We do know it was enormous, weighing over 200 tons. The entire system was transported on 30 railroad flatbed cars from Holyoke, Massachusetts to New York City. Cahill spent over $200,000 in building, dismantling and moving it. This was one of the largest and most expensive musical devices ever constructed. Author Thomas Holmes, in his book *Electronic and Experimental Music* presented a detail of expenditure for the three instruments which Cahill constructed: "It is estimated that the total expenses for all three Telharmoniums from 1902-1914 amounted to some $1,899,733... In average 1991 dollars, the Telharmonic capital investment was worth $28,367,800."

The New York Electric Music Company proposed to introduce live Telharmonium performances to a group of subscribers over telephone lines from the "Telharmonic Hall," a building located at 39th Street and Broadway in New York City, where the instrument resided for over 20 years. Although Cahill found an adequate number of people to subscribe, complaints about interference with other telephone service became more frequent, and this, combined with the fact that the success of the technology fell short of Cahill's expectations, led to the project being abandoned in 1916.

LEE DE FOREST

American inventor Lee De Forest was born in Council Bluffs, Indiana on August 26, 1873. He was educated at the Shieffield Scientific School at Yale, receiving his B.S. in 1896 and his Ph.D. in 1899. Lee De Forest is remembered as the "Father of Radio," which is also the title of his autobiography. While working for the Federal Telegraph Company, Lee De Forest was asked to develop an amplifier for the recording of high-speed radiotelegraph messages through a receiver known as the Tikker. He was the first person to use the alternating current generator and transmitter, which were later universally employed in wireless transmission apparatus.

In 1904 he was awarded a gold medal for his work in wireless telegraphy at the St. Louis Exposition. In 1906, De Forest invented the Triode, or Audion tube, the first vacuum tube, or valve. De Forest inserted a third electrode between the cathode and anode to make his Audion tube. Connecting an antenna to the tube's grid, he picked up radio signals. His tube revolutionized the field of electronics and became a key component in nearly all radio, radar, television, and computer systems until the transistor was introduced in the early 1960s. In the spring of 1910, the first radio broadcast occurred in New York City. (The first independent radio station was constructed in New York City ten years later.) He also designed and installed the first high-power radio stations for the U.S. Navy.

Lee De Forest created the first vacuum tube instrument, a major breakthrough in technology in 1915. The Audion Piano, as he called it, was a rudimentary keyboard, incorporating what De Forest referred to as a beat-frequency heterodyning oscillator system. Like Leon Theremin's later instrument, the Audion used body capacitance to control pitch and timbre. It was, like most electronic instruments of the era, a monophonic instrument. Like many inventors of his time, De Forest searched for a method of creating greater polyphony. He designed an updated model of the instrument that incorporated separate valves for each key to allow full polyphony, but the instrument never materialized.

His invention of the Triode amplifier liberated electronic instruments from dependence on telephone systems as signal amplifiers. He received a gold medal from the Panama Pacific Exposition in San Francisco in 1915. In 1921, he was the recipient of the Elliott Cresson medal of the Franklin Institute for his invention of the Audion.

After 1921 he devoted himself to the development of the phonofilm, a talking motion picture, which involved the synchronization of sound and motion by the use of a photographic representation of sound waves. De Forest also received a medal from the Institute of Radio Engineers and a prize from the Institute of France in 1923. Lee De Forest owned over 300 patents for his inventions by the end of his career.

FERRUCCIO BUSONI

Italian composer, pianist, conductor and author, Ferruccio Busoni (1866-1924) believed that the current twelve-tone musical system was severely limited. Bosoni's devotion to the progress of modern music led him to invent several new scales. He shocked his public, in 1907, with his statement that instrumental music was dead. His treatise on aesthetics, *Sketch of a New Music*, discussed his visions for the future of music. He studied at the Graz in Vienna, and was a member of the Academia Filarmonica of Bologna. In 1868 he was appointed Professor at Helsinfors, and in 1899, was appointed Professor at the Moscow Conservatorie. His international concerts brought him worldwide fame as a virtuoso musician. Although he composed an enormous amount of music, including concertos, orchestral works and the operas *Turandot* and *Doktor Faust*, Bosoni's most important contributions were in fostering modern music, in teaching, and in transcribing, arranging, and annotating much of the keyboard music of J.S. Bach, in particular, the *Well-Tempered Clavichord*. His critical writing was collected in English translation in *The Essence of Music* (1965).

LUIGI RUSSOLO AND FILIPPO MARINETTI

In 1912, Italian painter Luigi Russolo joined the Italian Futurist Movement, created initially as a literary movement in 1909 by poet Filippo Marinetti, with his manifesto "Le Futurisme." Marinetti's mission was "to present the musical soul of the masses, of the great factories, of the railways, of the transatlantic liners, of the battleships, of the automobiles and airplanes. To add to the great central themes of the musical poem, the domain of the machines and the victorious kingdom of Electricity." This resonated with many radical artists, including Luigi Russolo, at the beginning of the twentieth century.

Russolo gave a tremendous impetus to realizing the Futurist Movements' ideas on music and art, by engaging in some of the most radical musical experiments of the early twentieth century.

In 1913, Russolo wrote "l'arte di rumori," proposing that "the Art of Noise" could release the artist from the limitations of conformity that "pure sounds" had placed on music. In "The Art of Noises," he describes the historical evolution from pure silence to sound, leading to noise to sound, culminating in a final cacophonous musical noise. He wanted to take us back to the roots of sound. His point of view is best illustrated by a quote from "The Art of Noises": "Ancient life was all silence. In the nineteenth century, with the invention of the machine, noise was born. Today, noise triumphs and reigns supreme over the sensibilities of men."

Russolo passionately argued that the limited range of current musical instruments could no longer appease modern man's thirst for music. Noise Intoners, 'Intonorumori,' or Noise Machines, were families of acoustic sound generators designed by Russolo, and another painter in the movement, Ugo Piatti. They refined their instruments to create the range of sounds he tried to describe in "The Art of Noise": The collectively built orchestras of "cracklers, roarers, bubblers, thunderers, busters, etc.," performing their own improvised microtonal explorations or compositions created especially for them by Russolo. They presented their first concert in 1914 in Milan.

Later versions of the Noise Machines, developed by Russolo in Paris, included "Rumorarmonio" or "Noise Harmonium" or the "Russolo-Phone" which combined several noise machines with a fundamental keyboard. Unfortunately, plans for mass production of the "Russolo-Phone" never materialized. Russolo became disillusioned and returned full time to the study of philosophy and his first love, painting.

The instruments and music created by Russollo, although not electronic, led to the incorporation of noise and environmental sound in modern music. They were a primary source of inspiration for many composers, including Ravel, Stravinsky, Edgard Varèse, Pierre Schaefer, and John Cage.

VLADIMIR BARANOFF-ROSSINÉ

Russian futurist and painter Vladimir Baranoff-Rossiné (1888-1944) studied at Odessa, and at the Imperial Academie des beaux-arts of Saint Petersbourg.

Rossiné constructed his hybrid instrument, the Piano-Optophonique, while living in Paris from 1910. He gave his first presentation in Paris in 1912, and toured to Oslo and Stockholm in 1916. He returned to Russia after the 1917 revolution to assist with the revolutionary movement's artistic activities. He gave two piano-optophonique concerts, assisted by his wife, Pauline Boukour, in Moscow, in 1924, at the Theatre Bolchoi, before returning to Paris with his wife and children in 1925. Over the following years, he continued to exhibit his work through this unique presentation throughout Europe.

The Piano Optophonique was an audio/video synthesizer; an electronic optical instrument that generated sounds while directing a light beam through a series of Rossiné's hand-painted, revolving glass disks. These revolving kaleidoscopic patterns were projected by use of mirrors and lenses to refract and project the rays and patterns of light around the room. The lenses and disks were selected by manipulating controls on the keyboard. Each key produced continuous varying musical tones to accompany the projections. This was a direct predecessor of the color, or light organs, used in the late 1960s. The following is an extract from an original text by Baranoff Rossiné, written in 1916.

The Mechanism of the Piano Optophonique

"Imagine that every key of an organ's keyboard immobilizes in a specific position, or moves a determined element, more or less rapidly, in a group of transparent filters which a beam of white light pierces, and this will give you an idea of the instrument Baranoff-Rossiné invented. … There are various kinds of luminous filters: simply coloured ones optical elements such as prisms, lenses or mirrors; filters containing graphic elements and, finally, filters with coloured shapes and defined outlines. If on the top of this, you can modify the projector's position, the screen frame, the symmetry or asymmetry of the compositions and their movements and intensity; then, you will be able to reconstitute this optical piano that will play an infinite number of musical compositions. The key word here is 'interpret,' because, for the time being, the aim is not to find a unique rendering of an existing musical composition for which the author did not foresee a version expressed by light. In music, as in any other artistic interpretation, one has to take into account elements such as the talent and sensitivity of the musician, in order to fully understand the author's mind-frame. The day when a composer will compose music using notes that remain to be determined in terms of music and light, the interpreter's liberty will be curtailed, and that day, the artistic unity we were talking about will probably be closer to perfection..." (Reprinted with permission © Dimitri Baranoff Rossine)

LEON THEREMIN

Lev Sergeivitch Termen (Anglicized to Leon Theremin), born in St. Petersburg, Russia in 1896, became one of the most influential pioneers in the development of electronic music at the time when electronic engineering was in its infancy. His work in electronic musical instrument development has been referred to as the corner stone of electronic music in the early twentieth century, through his instrument, the aetherphon, a.k.a. thereminvox, later known as the theremin. The theremin was the first electronic instrument with a repetoire of concert music written specifically for it by major composers.

(NOTE: According to Bob Moog, theremin is written in lower case only.)

Leon Theremin

Professor Theremin invented his first prototype thereminvox in the winter of 1917, while he was a student at the University of Petrograd. The original theremin was housed in a wooden cabinet approximately eighteen inches wide and a foot deep. It stood about three and a half feet high from the ground. The top of the cabinet was slanted to form a music stand. On the upper right hand corner of the cabinet was a vertical antenna rod, for controlling the pitch of sound. Control switches and tuning knobs were located at the front of the cabinet. When properly tuned the pitch ranged from lower than two octaves below middle C, to over two and a-half octaves above. Protruding from the left-hand side of the cabinet was a tubular loop antenna, which controlled the volume, from complete in-audibility to full volume. Inside were large electric coils, which created a magnetic field around the external metal antennas. The antennas responded to anything that would carry an electrical capacitance, being able to collect an electrical charge, like a human hand or a metal rod. It was necessary for the player to stand motionless, exerting firm discipline over body and head motions as well as hand motions, while creating variation in the phrasing and modulation of sounds by precise movement of the hands over the two antennas.

In 1927, Theremin arrived in the United States after lengthy and successful performance tours of Europe. The Wurlitzer Company sponsored his tour of the United States. The tour included sold-out concerts at Carnegie Hall and the Metropolitan Opera House, with rave reviews and headlines such as "Soviet Edison Makes Music from Air," "Famous Russian Scientist and Inventor, Professor Leon Theremin," and "10,000 See Radio Shows Marvels." He was embraced by members of the leading families in American society, such as the Fords, the Kreislers, as well as celebrated composers, Rachmaninoff and Toscanini, who flocked to meet him at his "by invitation only" first appearance in New York.

A US patent was granted to Theremin for his invention of the thereminvox in 1928. RCA Victor, inspired by the instruments commercial potential, aggressively marketed the theremin in North America during the late twenties and most of the 1930s.

Theremin set up a studio on West 54th street, and found a large following and numerous patrons among New York's elite society. Theremin's success allowed him to subsidize his continuing experiments by building an enormous studio, which he equipped with a variety of newly invented technologies, for building and showcasing his inventions.

Theremin hosted many elegant parties in his famous studio, where guests were astounded by his new technology. Theremin's studio must have seemed totally alien to his friends, students and fashionable visitors, many of whom would never have experienced such technology before. His collection of inventions included the prototype for the color television, which he used to communicate between floors of this studio. His visitors could see his electronic inventions at various stages of construction: Several offspring of his theremin, the "rhythmicon," the world's first drum machine, the "keyboard theremin," a theremin with a fingerboard controller attached, the "Electronic Cello," and the "Terpistone," a raised dance floor that was actually an instrument in itself, and included devices for creating customized light shows.

In 1930, Leon Theremin, who was originally a cellist, invented the Theremin-Cello. As a result, one of the first infinite sustain instruments was born. It could sustain a note for as long as the finger was pressed against the fingerboard. There were no strings on this instrument. Instead, the Theremin-Cello had a flexible, black plastic film fingerboard. The film was constructed as a substitute for the cello's strings. Volume was controlled with a small lever, while pitch was defined by the placement of the hand on the fingerboard, much like a conventional cello, only without the strings.

The Theremin-Cello body had two rotary knobs used for tone control. Composer conductor Leopold Stowkowski commissioned Theremin to design and build a bass Theremin-Cello. The project was soon abandoned, due to the unbearable cacophonous subharmonic frequencies created by the instrument.

Theremin's Rhythmicon, also invented in 1930, was the first electronic rhythm generator, or "drum machine." The project was commissioned by the avant-garde American composer Henry Cowell, who wanted a machine that could transform harmonic data into rhythmic data. The 17-key polyphonic keyboard Theremin constructed produced a single note that was repeated in periodic rhythm as long as the key was depressed. Rotating disks, which interrupted light beams that triggered photoelectric cells generated the rhythmic structure, and an extra beat in the middle of each bar was generated by pressing the 17th key. The Rhythmicon became popular with film music composers, and found its way into many popular films between 1953 and the late 1960s. Some of the most memorable were *Battle Beneath the Earth, The Rains of Ranchipur* and *Dr Strangelove*. It has also been used by many of the great pop bands of the late sixties and early seventies. The classic *Rubicon* album by Tangerine Dream featured the Rhythmicon as a part of the percussion.

Leon Theremin adapted his theremin technology to create the Terpistone, an instrument used primarily by dancers and theatre companies. The control antenna was fabricated in the form of a large metal sheet that was normally disguised beneath the surface of a dance floor. The performer's movements on the floor, above the metal sheet, shaped variations in pitch in response to the movements of the performers' bodies. This instrument was often used for various forms of live theatre presentations and light shows throughout the thirties.

There are conflicting reports regarding Theremin's return to Russia in 1938. Some believe Joseph Stalin ordered Theremin be transported back to Russia, where he was accused of disseminating anti-Soviet propaganda while in the U.S. On the other hand, some say that Stalin sent members of the Russian Intelligence organization, the NKVD (which later became the KGB) to kidnap Theremin from his home in the presence of his wife, the famous African American

Ballet dancer Iavana Williams. Some believed that Theremin was in fact a Soviet spy, whose mission was to gather information on U.S. military technology and political strategies. During that period, rumors of his execution were broadly circulated in Europe and North America, particularly in the technology and music communities.

As we know, Theremin was not executed. It is believed he was employed by the Russians in further research, and as a result of his outspokenness, he soon landed on the official "disapproval list." He was incarcerated for seven years in a prison called Magadan, an infamous labor camp in Siberia.

In return for his compliance with the government, Theremin was released, but he was not allowed to leave Russia. He began teaching music theory at the Moscow Conservatory of Music. Shortly after, he was discharged without notice for continuing his research in electronic music. Stalin's Soviet ideology held the view that modern music was detrimental to society.

Theremin went on to develop new ideas in electronic research, apart from music. Some say the Soviet authorities forced Theremin to work on cold war spy technology, such as a hidden microphone apparatus—known as the buran or "bug"—for eavesdropping, espionage and surveillance. It is also believed he supervised the installation of wiretapping devices in both the American Embassy and Stalin's private apartment. He also invented an alarm system that could be triggered by movement in an electromagnetic field, using the motion-sensitive technology of the theremin.

In 1947, Theremin was awarded Russia's highest honor, the First-Class Stalin Prize.

The theremin was featured on several movie soundtracks between 1940 and 1960, as well as on several sci-fi television series, such as *Lost in Space* and *The Twilight Zone*. It has also played an important role in pop music culture, including the spacey introductions on the Beach Boys' hits "Good Vibrations" and "Surfin' USA." Led Zeppelin's lead guitarist, Jimmy Page, can be seen playing a theremin in the film *The Song Remains the Same.*

Until just before his death in 1993, when he made one final lecture tour to America, Leon Theremin was unaware of the fact that his inventions were a great success in the United States. The

1994 movie *Theremin: An Electronic Odyssey* documented his life and work.

CLARA ROCKMORE

Clara Reisenberg Rockmore is generally believed to be the greatest thereminist ever. Born in Russia in 1911, the youngest of three musically gifted sisters, Clara was a true child prodigy, with perfect pitch and a gifted sense of music. At the age of two, she could pick out a melody on the piano or sing any melody she heard. Her career as a violinist began when her uncle gave her a quarter-size violin for her fourth birthday. At the age of five she was admitted as an exceptional student to the Imperial Conservatory of Music in St. Petersburg (now Leningrad). She was the youngest student to receive this honor. She became one of Professor Leopold Auer's most promising pupils. At the age of nine in 1920, she received permission from the Russian government to leave her native land in order to perform in concerts around the world. Clara and her sister, Nadia Reisenberg, a well-known concert pianist in her own right, embarked on an extensive tour of Europe. Finally, their recital circuit led them to New York City, where Clara met Leon Theremin for the first time in 1928, after one of his performances at the Plaza Hotel. She was deeply impressed with "this very interesting, fascinating man and hearing this ethereal and heavenly sound coming from the air." Theremin courted Clara for some time. As a surprise for Clara's eighteenth birthday, Theremin made her a cake, which lit up and revolved when anyone came close to it.

Clara Rockmore

Clara Rockmore spent several years collaborating with Leon Theremin, while he made further refinements to the theremin's sensitivity as an instrument capable of performing a wide range of musical styles.

In 1934, Clara Rockmore gave one of the first theremin concerts in the United States. Clara then embarked on a celebrated performance career in the U.S. and Canada. Her appearances as a soloist with several orchestras, including the New York Philharmonic, the Philadelphia Orchestra, and the Toronto Symphony, set the definitive standard for theremin performance technique.

Clara Rockmore appeared in the 1994 movie, *Theremin: An Electronic Odyssey*. Following the release of this highly acclaimed film the theremin developed an "overnight" mass following. As a consequence of her appearance in the film, Clara Rockmore became equally popular as a concert artist once again. She, almost single-handedly, throughout her long music career, established wide spread respect for the theremin. Shortly before her death in 1998, she starred in her own autobiographical video documentary, "Clara Rockmore, the Greatest Theremin Virtuoso." The film was released in 1999.

DARIUS MILHAUD

French composer Darius Milhaud (1892-1974) trained at the Paris Conservatoire as a violinist and composer. Throughout his career, he was prolific in a wide range of compositional styles and genres, from classical music to the folk music of North and South America, Europe and the Middle East. He was particularly inspired by the capacity of music to articulate his mystical love of nature. His music incorporated polytonality, jazz, and Brazilian elements. He is considered a forerunner of rap and hip-hop DJ's because of his experiments with electronic audio equipment.

During WWI he traveled to Brazil for two years, as secretary to the French diplomat and poet Paul Claudel's French delegation. He returned to France when the war was over, in 1918. He collaborated in musical compositions with a diverse group of French composers known as Les SIX. He was celebrated for his operas, ballets, symphonies, chamber music works, and music for film and the theater. He moved to the U.S., because as a Jew it was unsafe for him to stay in Europe during WWII. He taught at Mills College in California. Among the best known of his more than 400 compositions were the ballet *La création du monde* (1923), the opera *Christophe Colomb* (1930), and the orchestral suite, *Suite Provencale* (1937).

"Notes without Music" was the title of first autobiographical work. He later added to it and changed the title to "My Happy Life."

A unique insight into his "happy life" is presented to us in his reply to a letter from someone who quoted Wagner as saying that all art "springs from suffering, unhappiness, and frustration." In response to this, Milhaud replied, "I am glad you decided to me about your problem (with Wagner's view): here is my point of view, if you want it. I had a marvelously happy childhood. My wife is my companion, my collaborator; we are the best of friends, and this gives me great happiness. My son is a painter who works incessantly, and he is sweet and loving to his parents. Thus I can say that I've had a happy life, and if I compose, it's because I am in love with music and I wouldn't know how to do anything else…Your Wagner quote proves to me once again that he was an idiot."

JÖRG MAGER

In 1926, German engineer and musician Jörg Mager first presented his series of electronic instruments, known as the Sphäraphon range of electronic instruments, to the general public at the Donaueschingen Festival.

Mager's first instrument was the Electrophon, an instrument without a keyboard, whose notes were created by turning a metal handle that regulated the wavelength of the sound, creating a glissando effect. The Electrophon was specifically designed to create micro-tonal music. It was later upgraded to include filters for improving the timbre, regulators for controlling the glissando, and foot pedals for volume control. This was known as the KurbelSphäraphon. A modified version of this instrument, the Klaviaturspäharaphon, used two short keyed monophonic keyboards to create a duophonic tone which could be tuned to microtonal tunings.

In 1929, Mager was given the use of a small castle in Darmstadt, where he created his studio, the Studiengesellschaft fur Elektro

Akustische Musik. In 1930, Mager introduced the Partiturophon, a four and five keyboard/voice version of the Klaviaturspharaphon, and, in 1939, the Kaleidophone, so named for its "Kaleidoscopic" tone combinations. These were monophonic instruments, implementing keyboard controllers, each voice with its own keyboard, combining to create many registers. These instruments were used predominantly in theatrical productions. Unfortunately, they were destroyed during World War II.

GEORGE ANTHEIL

Born on 8 July 1900 in Trenton, New Jersey, George Antheil studied with Constantin von Sternberg, Ernest Bloch, and with Clark Smith at the Philadelphia Conservatory. In 1922, he traveled to France to pursue a career as a concert pianist, performing in recital many of his own works such as "Mechanisms," "Airplane Sonata," and "Sonata Sauvage."

His spectacular *Ballet Mécanique* broke all conventions in a production. It was scored for pianos, xylophones, pianola, doorbells, and airplane propellers. The *Ballet Mécanique* was a highly rhythmic and very aggressive composition, blending atonal music and jazz, with sounds of the industrial age. His concerts routinely caused riots all over Europe, which was a sign of genius among his European artistic peers.

He was considered to be a revolutionary genius for his inventive use of unusual sound sources and his radical combinations of instruments and mechanical apparatus. He was thought to be, musically and technically, far ahead of his time. Antheil's early compositions expressed the emotion and energy of jazz of that era, while his later compositions were influenced by neo-romantic and neo-classic styles and included full-scale symphonic, operatic and film scores; e.g. *Symphonie en fa, Piano Concerto* and *Transatlantic*.

Antheil lived in France during the "roaring" '20s, at the center of English-language culture in Europe. He lived in the Latin Quarter of Paris, above Sylvia Beach's legendary Shakespeare & Co. bookstore on the Rue de l'Odéon. (James Joyce's *Ulysses* was published originally by Sylvia Beach.) Antheil moved among the Parisian elite: musicians, painters and writers, including James Joyce, Ezra Pound, Ernest

Hemingway, Gertrude Stein, Salvador Dali, Pablo Picasso, Eric Satie. Antheil left Paris in the late '20s and went to Berlin, where he met Igor Stravinsky who became an important influence on his compositional style. In 1936, as German society began to fall under the influence of the Nazis, he returned to America, settling in Hollywood where he began writing scores for film and television. He wrote over 300 musical works in all genres, including symphonies, operas, chamber works, and film music.

Of all of his compositions, the *Ballet Mecanique* caused the most controversy. Although it was a great success in Paris, it was a sensational failure when it came to New York's Carnegie Hall. Consequently, it was not performed again for over 60 years. Antheil's reputation as a "serious" composer never fully recovered after the riots at Carnegie Hall. In 1953, he revised the composition, creating a much shorter piece than the original versions, which has been performed and recorded several times, using a very different instrumental ensemble, including four pianos, four xylophones, two electric bells, two propellers, timpani, glockenspiel, and various percussion instruments.

Antheil, who died in 1959, was an extremely articulate man, an excellent writer, an inventor, and a student of many disciplines, including endocrinology, criminal justice, and military history. Still in print, his autobiography, *Bad Boy of Music*, reveals the heart and soul of the early twentieth century avant-garde movement in music.

PIERRE TOULON

In the summer of 1927, French engineer Pierre Toulon, with Krugg Bass, created the Cellulophone, an electro-optical tone generator based instrument. This photo-electric sound system used two eight-octave manual keyboards and a foot pedal board, much like Hammond's later organ designs popularly used in many churches and theaters, only this instrument was much larger. The Cellulophone incorporated rotating disks, each octave (twelve-note scale) comprised one disk, that generated sound by masking light, which was transferred to a photoelectric cell. The speed of the rotating disk determined the frequency of the output signal. A vacuum tube oscillator was used to create the output signal.

RENÉ BERTRAND

French electrical engineer René Bertrand invented the Dynaphone, which made its concert debut in 1928. Bertrand worked with French composer Edgard Varèse to design an instrument that could achieve a sound frequency higher than any instrument available at the time. The Dynaphone was a portable table-top instrument, which created sounds through electrical oscillations much like the theremin. Its timbre was compared to that of a saxophone, french horn, cello, or low flute, very similar to other monophonic, vacuum tube oscillator instruments developed around the 1930's.

The pitch was controlled with the right hand by turning a circular wheel, which was mounted on a calibrated disk. A switch was used to select either the upper or lower range of five octaves within a full seven-octave range. The left hand was used to control the volume and timbre of the instrument. Vibrato was created by moving the right hand back and forth slightly touching the dial. It also had a push button sound articulation mechanism.

Bertrand later improved on the instrument design, and created the 'Radio-Electric-Organ'. This was a forerunner of the modern 61-note synth keyboard, with one exception, the note being played could be doubled at the fifth and octave, which we are still incapable of achieving with 21st century technology.

MAURICE MARTENOT

While in charge of a wireless station as a sergeant in the French army shortly after World War1, French cellist and radio telegraphist, Maurice Martenot (1898-1980), developed an interest in the purity of vibrations produced by the new radio tube technology, which led to his investigations in sound and electronics.

Martenot was introduced to Leon Theremin in 1923, when he began experimenting with Theremin's instrument, and listening to his theories on instrument design. Martenot designed his own instrument based on oscillating radio tubes which produced electric pulses at supersonic sound-wave frequencies. Martenot patented in April 1928 and called it the Ondes-Martenot, which in English means Martenot's waves. The Ondes-Martenot was designed so that an orchestral musician would feel comfortable playing it, rather than feeling alienated by the many experimental electronic music instruments of that era. The Ondes-Martenot was designed to perform orchestral music, not to create a new type of music. The tone of the Martenot was like the sound of a glass harmonica.

The Ondes-Martenot could be played in two different ways. The first technique used a keyboard with a seven-octave range. The player's right hand played the keyboard while the left hand controlled dynamics and timbre by manipulating switches that controlled sound filters. The keyboard allowed parallel movement of the keys, which made it possible for the player to create vibrato by vibrating his/her finger on the key. In the second mode of operation a metal ribbon was used to create varying tonal inflections ranging over seven octaves. The player moved a finger ring attached to the metal ribbon, which controlled the frequency, to give a wide glissando. The keyboard was played with the right hand, while the left hand controlled a key that created sound much like the bow of a violinist. With a touch of the finger on the key, the player controlled the timbre, harmonics, attack, intensity and volume. There was also a knee lever that could be used as a substitute for the key, freeing the left hand to join the right on the keyboard.

Martenot presented his new musical instrument to the public in May of 1928 at the Paris Opera. This was the first concert in Paris to include an electronic instrument. Well known classical composers of the period, such as Edgarde Varèse, Maurice Jarre, Olivier Messian, Arthur Honegger, and Pierre Boulez, wrote many works for the Ondes-Martenot. In 1938, Hindu poet, Rabindranath Tagore and his musician friend, Alain Danielou, commissioned Martenot to create a variation of the instrument, which featured microtonal tunings for playing Hindu music to accompany Tagore's readings. Ten years later, in 1948, Martenot became a professor at the Paris Conservatoire, training young students on the Ondes-Martenot.

ARMAND GIVELET AND EDUARD COUPLEAUX

As a radio engineer and physicist, Armand Givelet was very interested in electronic instrument design. In 1928, Givelet demonstrated his silent recording technique in Paris, while working at the radio laboratory at the Eiffel Tower. Givelet found a way to record music for radio broadcast without using microphones. He completely revolutionized radio broadcasting techniques, alleviating hiss and hum from the signal when he connected the electronic instruments directly into the radio transmitter or sound recorder.

Armand Givelet and organist Eduard Coupleaux were working on creating an inexpensive alternative to the pipe organ, expressly designed for use with his silent recording technique. This was decades before the Dolby noise reduction system was introduced. They produced a monophonic vacuum tube oscillator instrument called the "Clavier à Lampes." They continued to work on refinement of their design to create an instrument that could reach a much broader commercial market. This led to the development of their second instrument, the "Orgue des Ondes," later known as the Wave Organ. The Wave Organ incorporated Givelet's silent recording technology, by-passing microphones, by using an output jack connected directly to an amplifier or radio transmitter. The Wave Organ was a large instrument, using over 700 vacuum tubes to produce a six-octave range, and was one of the first polyphonic instruments sold commercially.

Another of their inventions, the Coupleaux-Givelet Organ, known simply as the Givelet, was a polyphonic instrument which used punched paper rolls long before this method was exploited commercially by RCA and Hammond. The Givelet was sold commercially and was popularly used in French churches before Hammond Organs became readily available in the late 1930's.

LAURENS HAMMOND

In 1929, in the United States, a clockmaker named Laurens Hammond built the first Hammond Organ. The original Hammond organ used a mechanical system, tone wheel generators or oscillators, to produce its individual pitches. The Hammond Organ used ninety-one rotary electromagnetic disk generators, driven by a synchronous motor, and operated by gears and tone wheels.

Laurens Hammond began the mass-production of his instruments in the spring of 1935. His Hammond Organ Company produced affordable electronic organs, which became very popular with the general public. Depending on the model, about 100 spinning disks create the individual pitches, creating pure sinusoidal flute tones, to create a wide selection of tonal combinations with the ability to mix the pitches at varying degrees of amplitude. The Hammond organ generated sounds in much the same way as Cahill's Telaharmonium, by using a tone wheel. Pitch was controlled by an AC synchronous motor, operating on a 60 Hz line frequency feeding off the incoming 120 volts. The Hammond maintained stable intonation, never deviating from the correct frequencies, which was an ongoing problem with most other electronic instruments of that era and a plague that haunted keyboard designers until the DX7 in 1983.

In the early stages of Hammond's production, there were three models, all incorporating two sixty-one key manuals; the lower manual, which Hammond called the Great console, and upper manual, which Hammond called the Swell. The instrument had a bass pedal board, which was comprised of twenty-five individual foot pedals. The larger concert models had a thirty-two key pedal board, which produced nearly three octaves.

In 1939, Laurens Hammond and Charles Williams designed the Hammond Novachord. The Novachord was the first commercially produced polyphonic electronic organ. Within the following three years, the Hammond Organ Company produced and sold over a thousand units. The Novachord was the first instrument in which Hammond used tube-based technology. The Novachord's sound was generated by twelve oscillators, powered by 169 vacuum tubes, to produce a six-octave range. The Novachord used a pressure sensitive, seventy-two note keyboard. Because of various technical difficulties, the instrument was discontinued in 1942.

Hammond's portable organ, the B3, was introduced in the 1950s. Its rotating speaker system, built by Don Leslie, revolutionized the electric organ sound, and became known as The Leslie. The B3 became popular with jazz, blues, and rock musicians. It was also popular with groups like the Moody Blues, who featured it on their 1967 hit, "A Whiter Shade of Pale."

Hammond also developed and patented one of the first reverb units based on the helical torsion of a coiled spring. This was imitated in later electronic instruments and accessories, especially guitar amplifiers.

NIKOLAY OBUKHOV, MICHEL BILLAUDOT AND PIERRE DUVALIE

In 1929, in Paris, Russian composer Nikolay Obukhov commissioned Michel Billaudot and Pierre Duvalie to design and build the Sonorous Cross. It was similar in design to the theremin, in that it was based upon experimentation with the beat frequency of heterodyning oscillators. The difference in Obukhov's instrument was mainly in its appearance. The antenna was designed like a large brass crucifix with a central star, and the circuitry and oscillators were constructed inside a metal sphere.

Like the theremin, the Sonorous Cross' oscillator frequency was controlled by the body's capacitance, by gestures of the hands concentrated around the star in the center of the cross. Nikolay Obukhov was a prolific composer. He wrote many two-part compositions using his instrument and the Ondes-Martenot, culminating in his most celebrated work, "Le Livre De Vie." In 1934, Obukhov upgraded the components of the Sonorous Cross and designed two other instruments, the Crystal and the Éther. The Crystal resembled a psaltery, in its use of mallets to strike a row of crystal spheres. His third invention, the Éther, which is on permanent display at the Musée de L'Opéra in Paris, is a large electronic instrument, which uses a large turning paddle wheel to generate ominous humming drones.

PETER LERTES, BRUNO HELBERGER AND SCHNEIDER-OPEL

In 1929, in Leipzig, Germany, electrical engineer Peter Lertes, and pianist Bruno Helberger worked together to develop the monophonic vacuum tube instrument known as the Hellertion. Schneider-Opel, in Frankfurt, joined forces with Lertes and Helberger and helped construct modified versions of the original instrument. The Hellertion was often used in tandem with a piano in concert performance settings.

The Hellertion used a fingerboard and continuous controller instead of a keyboard. The amount of pressure applied controlled the volume of the output signal. Correct pitch was found by following the markings inscribed on the fingerboard strip. When pressing on the fingerboard strip, the resistance opened the circuit, thus creating variation of pitch over a range of five octaves. The original instrument had one fingerboard strip. Later models extended this to four, and eventually, six fingerboard strips were placed side by side, horizontally, at the height of a piano keyboard. The four and six strip models allowed four and six voice polyphony.

Much like modern pre-MIDI keyboard performances on multiple keyboards, the melody lines on the Hellertion were played with one hand, and chordal accompaniment was played on a piano with the other hand. The playing styles of artists such as Keith Emerson or Jan Hammer are a good example of this method.

In 1936, a new version of the Hellertion, called the Heliophon, was constructed by Bruno Hellberger. Unfortunately, it was destroyed during World War II. After the war, Hellberger moved to Austria, where he kept updating the Heliophon until his death in 1951. Within a few months Woflgang Wehrman, an electrical engineer, became interested in his work, contributing further developments to the instrument.

Heterodyning vacuum tube oscillator technology was used in the production of the Heliophon. Instead of using fingerboards, like its predecessor the Hellertion, Hellberger used two fifty-eight note, pressure sensitive keyboards. Three different pitches and tones could be produced simultaneously from each keyboard. A fingerboard was mounted just above each keyboard to provide variations in timbre and glissando. The output volume of was controlled by a foot pedal and a knee lever was incorporated to add vibrato.

ROBERT HITCHCOCK

Robert Hitchcock, an engineer at Westinghouse Electric Manufacturing Company, was asked to design the Westinghouse Organ. Hitchcock and his assistants completed the instrument in 1930, and unveiled it at Pittsburgh's KDKA radio station. It was a semi-polyphonic multi-vacuum tube electronic organ, and one of the first commercially marketed organs in the United States.

FRIEDRICH TRAUTWEIN

German engineer Friedrich Trautwein (1888-1956) invented the Trautonium in 1930. During the early 1930's, the pioneering German electronics company, Telefunken, commercially developed and sold the Trautonium. The first Trautonium was a monophonic instrument, which used an oscillator with a "glimmer" lamp to produce continuous variations of tone, using a fingerboard. The fingerboard had a chromatic scale etched into a metal rail, with a resistance wire drawn out horizontally over the rail. The rail was connected to a neon tube oscillator, which was amplified by a loudspeaker. To play a note, the player pressed the wire onto the rail, completing a circuit. The frequency of the note and the pitch of the oscillator varied, depending on the resistance created by the position of the musician's finger along the wire, and contact with the rail. The tone was controlled by the circuits, which amplified the harmonics of the fundamental note, producing a unique series of sub-harmonics.

The Trautonium became popular with several celebrated composers of the era, including Strauss, Genzmer, Höffer, Varese, Weismann, Hindemith, and Oskar Sala.

In 1936, Trautwein also invented an amplified harpsichord and "Electronic Bells." In 1947, shortly after World War II, Trautwein worked in Paris on aviation research. In 1948, Dr Freidrich Trautwein was commissioned by the Electronic Music studio of North West German Radio Studios, Köln, to design and build the Monochord, which he modeled on the concert Trautonium. Until then the studio had only one synthesis module containing one sine wave generator and an uncomplicated filter system.

In 1950, Trautwein set up a school for recording engineers in Düsseldorf. Friedrich Trautwein produced his last instrument, the Elektronische Monochord, in 1952.

OSKAR SALA

Oskar Sala, who was born in Germany in 1910, became a virtuoso player on the Trautonium. He also designed and built his own variations on the instrument. After World War II, Sala discovered a new circuit, with which he was able to create sub-harmonic mixtures of tone on the Trautonium.

Between 1949 and 1952, Sala designed and constructed the Mixturtrautonium, based on the design principles of the Trautonium. In later models built in the nineteen-sixties, Sala replaced the triode lamps with semi-conductors, which enabled him to enhance the precision of the sub-harmonic frequency range. In 1958, Oskar Sala opened his independent studio, which soon became a workshop for electronic film music, and Sala became occupied more as a composer, than as an inventor. The most famous example of Sala's film music work is Alfred Hitchcock's thriller *The Birds*. Sala has produced over 300 film music soundtracks, and received many awards for his compositions.

FRITZ PFLEUMER AND INGMAR FARBEN

In 1928, Electrical Engineer Fritz Pfleumer developed and patented a system for recording on paper coated with a magnetizable, powdered steel layer. AEG, a large German electrical manufacturer, created and developed plastic audio tape in 1930, after first purchasing the patent rights from Pfleumer. Imgmar Farben, an employee of AEG, continued the research, coating tape with carbonyl iron powder in his effort to refine this recording medium. Under the auspice of AEG, Farben, went on to design a marketable prototype of a tape recorder.

RUTH CRAWFORD SEEGER

With American composers such as Aaron Copland and Henry Cowell, Ruth Crawford Seeger (1901-1953) is a key member of the 1920s American musical avant garde. Included in Seeger's small but impressive body of original music is her String Quartet, composed in 1931. This composition was one of the first works to employ extended serialism, for systematic organization of pitch, rhythm, dynamics, and articulation. Seeger's legacy extends into the American folk music revival as well, in her collaboration on folk song arrangements with poet Carl Sandburg, during in the 1920s, and with the famous folk song collectors, John and Alan Lomax, in the 1930s. Seeger's impact on American folk songs in children's music education is comparable to Bartok and Kodaly. Radicalized by the Great Depression of the 1930s, she spent the following two decades working for cultural change, along with her husband, and her stepson the famous folk singer-activist Pete Seeger.

FREDERICK SAMMIS AND ART LESTI

In 1931, the American engineering team of Frederick Sammis and Art Lesti built the "Radio Organ of a Trillion Tones." This instrument utilized a vacuum tube oscillator to create pitches and timbres along with a series of rotating photo-electric disks, which intermittently changed a light beamed at various frequencies to produce changes in pitch. In 1934, the improved and updated model of the "Radio Organ of a Trillion Tones," renamed the "The Polytone Organ" was introduced. This instrument was comprised of a large three-part keyboard that controlled a multi-timbral organ. This became the first commercially available multi-timbral organ.

During the fall of 1936, Frederick Sammis invented the "Singing Keyboard." It was a direct predecessor of modern sampling devices of the 1980s, such as the Kurzweil, Synclavier, and Fairlight series. The Singing Keyboard played electro-optical recordings of audio waves stored on small strips of 35mm film. These audio waves were triggered and pitched when the player pressed a key. Sammis' Singing Keyboard technology inspired the development of other, similarly triggered and pitched, magnetic tape recording technology of the '60s, among these the Mellotron and Chamberlin.

NICHOLAS LANGER

Nicholas Langer, a Connecticut based American Engineer, built the Emicon in 1932. Like many of the tube-based instruments before, the Emicon was a monophonic instrument that relied on a vacuum tube oscillator. It was controlled with a standard keyboard. A separate self-contained portable amplifier was made available a few months later. According to marketing brochures, the Emicon could produce timbres comparable to a violin, trumpet, saxophone, guitar, oboe, mandolin, and bagpipe. It was a piano-like keyboard, similar to most modern 61-note synthesizer keyboards.

A. RIMSKY-KORSAKOV AND ANTON IVANOV

The Emitron, (not to be confused with the Emicon), was designed by Anton Ivanov and A. Rimsky-Korsakov using neon-tube oscillators as a sound source to create glissando effects. Like most other instruments developed in the Soviet Union in the 1930s, their instrument used an electronic fingerboard, although future models of the Emitron were constructed with a standard keyboard.

YEVGENY ALEXANDROVITCH SHOLPO

Russian inventor Yevgeny Alexandrovitch Sholpo constructed his Variophone in 1932. This instrument was based on a new form of sound generation, which Sholpo called optical synthesis. It was considered to be a refined spin-off of Vladimir Baranoff Rossiné's 1916 Piano Optophonique technology.

In a totally unique approach to synthesis, morphing visual art with music, Sholpo drew sound waves directly onto transparent 35mm film. He created his musical compositions by photographing drawings, and then using the optical synthesis generator in his Variophone to create soundtracks based on the photographs of the drawings.

MILTON TAUBMAN

In 1934, Milton Taubman constructed the Electronde, which was a spin-off on theremin technology. It was a portable battery-powered unit, with the addition of a volume pedal. Like the theremin, it used capacitive space control of pitch.

LEON STOKOWSKI AND IVAN EREMEEF

The Gnome was invented by electrical engineer Ivan Eremeef in 1933. It used rotating electro-magnetic tone wheels for tone generation.

In 1934, Ivan Eremeef and Leon Stokowski collaborated in their invention of the Syntronic Organ. The sound engine was based on an electro-optical tone generator. By using film on tone wheels, which were fed into an optical generator, much like a slide projector, the Syntronic Organ was capable of creating an hour-long pattern of continuous variations of tone. Eremeef also built a similar instrument, which he called the Photona, for a radio station in Philadelphia.

LLOYD LOAR

A virtuoso classical mandolinist and well-respected acoustical engineer, Lloyd Loar joined Gibson, a year after Orville Gibson's death in 1919. He is best remembered for his acoustical scroll design shape for Gibson mandolin bodies. In 1924, five years after being a member of Gibson's engineering team, Loar constructed a prototype of an electric bass. When Loar's radical bass guitar design was not accepted by Gibson management he resigned in 1924. In 1934, Lloyd Loar constructed the Vivatone, a modified acoustic/electric guitar, and the forerunner of the electric guitar. Loar's refinements of Orville Gibson's concepts brought about the L-5 guitar and the Master Model F-5 mandolin, the finest mandolin ever built, which featured the first "f" holes ever used on fretted instruments. The L-5 was the first guitar to be used in the orchestral line-up and soon replaced the tenor banjo as a popular rhythm instrument. Although there is photographic evidence that an L-5 existed in late 1922, no surviving instrument is dated earlier than 1924. Lloyd Loar's L-5 also launched Gibson's dominant role in the new field of arch-top guitars.

HARALD BODE

In 1936, German born designer of electronic instruments, Harald Bode, in collaboration with C. Warnke, designed and built his first instrument, the Warbo Formant Orgel, while studying at the Heinrich-Herst Institut für Schwingungsforschung at the Technische Hochschule in Berlin. The Warbo Formant Orgel was a semi-poly-phonic four-voice keyboard instrument.

Harald Bode collaborated with the inventor of the Grosstonorgel, Oskar Vierling, to create the Melodium, a monophonic, touch-sensitive keyboard instrument, which debuted in 1938. The instrument had a vibrato pedal and a knob that could adjust tuning and transposition.

The German Electronics Company, Hohner GmbH, commercially produced Harald Bode's Multimonika in 1940. It was an electronic/acoustic hybrid with two separate keyboards. The upper keyboard was a lead synth, with an electronic monophonic sawtooth wave generator. The lower 41-note keyboard was a wind-blown (Wuviend Reit) reed harmonium.

In 1947, Harald Bode built another monophonic keyboard instrument based on vacuum tube technology, the Melochord. By incorporating switches, Bode extended the instrument's thirty-seven-note range from three to seven octaves. He used a standard twelve-note scale keyboard, and a foot pedal for volume control. Bode also built a two keyboard version, where the second keyboard controlled the timbre of the first keyboard.

The German company, Apparatewerk Bayern, and the American company, Estey Organ Co, commissioned Bode to design several conventional electronic instruments. The most popular were the Polychord, which he designed in 1950, the Cembaphon, built the following year, and the "Bode Organ," also designed in 1951. These three instruments were the forerunners of Bode's Polychord III, Tuttivox, and the concert Clavioline. Harald Bode also designed the Combichord, which was a combination of a Clavioline and a Tuttivox.

Harald Bode emigrated from Germany to the United States in 1954, and soon was commissioned by the Wurlitzer Organ Company to develop a new model of the Wurlitzer Electric Piano. While he privately continued his own research, Bode worked at Bell Aerospace laboratories' micro circuitry department until his retirement in 1974. While working at Bell Labs, Bode developed a modular signal processor comprised of a ring module and a voltage control module. In 1963, Bob Moog hired Bode to help with research and development. Bode's own private company, called Bode Sound, built miscellaneous sound processing modules, such as the Vocoder and an "infinite phaser," during the 1960s and 70s. These became very popular with many pop bands of that generation. The Vocoder became internationally known through the music of artists like Kraftwerk, Peter Framton, Laurie Anderson, and Jean-Michel Jarre.

During the early days of the Electronic Studio at Bonn University, Dr Werner Meyer-Eppler explored the capabilities of Harald Bode's Melochord. Later, the North West German Radio studios in Köln installed a Melocord. The Elektronische Musik Group, a collective of artists working at the studio, including Karlheinz Stockhausen, used the Melochord and Monochord throughout the 1950s.

The Melochord played an historic role in the future development of electronic music. Meyer-Eppler's lectures at Darmstadt New Music School, and his inspiring thesis, "Klangmodelle," were all based on the possibilities of the Melochord. Bode's 1961 thesis, explaining the significance of transistor based technology over valve based synthesis, revolutionized electronic musical instruments. In the early 1960's, Robert Moog, Don Buchla and others adopted and developed Harald Bode's ideas on modular and miniature self-contained transistor based equipment.

ORSON WELLES

Orson Welles, in his 1937 broadcast *War of the Worlds,* was the first director to use studio electronics, as well as the fade and dissolve technique first seen in his film *Citizen Kane.*

KARL WAGNER

As Director of the Heinrich-Hertz-Institut in the 1940s, Karl Wagner was responsible for early development of voice synthesizers, which contributed to the development of the Voder and Vocoders in the United States. He was also credited for designing many of the electronic instruments built in Germany between 1932 and 1940.

EDWIN WELTE

Edwin Welte's Light-Tone Organ, developed in Germany in the early 1930s, was an electronic instrument using electro-optical controlled tone generators. This was actually the third generation of this technology, beginning with Vladimir Baranoff Rossiné's 1916 hybrid instrument, the Optophonic Piano.

By printing eighteen various waveforms onto a glass disk, Welte created three different tones for every octave register of each individual note. Timbre and pitch were controlled by a glass tone wheel, which revolved above a sequence of photoelectric cells, which filtered tiny concentrated shafts of light.

OSKAR VIERLING

In 1936, Oskar Vierling, along with Winston Kock, and his associates at the Heinrich-Hertz-Institut in Berlin, designed the Grosstonorgel. This instrument was a vacuum tube oscillator based organ. In 1937, he designed the Electrochord, a forerunner of the Fender Rhodes, and many other electric keyboards. Vierling, a highly respected member of the Heinrich-Hertz-Institut, was acknowledged for his role in fostering the growing interest in electronic music technology in Germany during that era.

GEORGES JENNY

In 1938, Georges Jenny developed the Ondioline, while undergoing therapy in a tuberculosis sanatorium. After his release from the hospital, he continued to work on the refinement of his instrument in Paris, at his Les Ondes Georges Jenny, which soon became La Musique Electronique. He constructed, developed and built each instrument himself, until his death in 1976. He also designed instrument kits for musicians who wanted to build their own instrument. The Ondioline was a small eight-octave touch sensitive monophonic keyboard instrument, based on vacuum tubes and an oscillator. It had a six-octave range and was tuned by a mechanism, which Jenny called an octave transposer. Complex waveforms could be created with a series of filters. A touch wire was used to change the timbre of the sound waves. The attack of the note was altered by a vertical finger movement, and, by moving the finger horizontally, glissando or pitch modulation was produced. A knee lever was installed for volume control.

The Ondioline became popular in film and theatre music of the 1940s. In Germany, the Ondioline was promoted as the "Pianoline." In The Netherlands it was sold as the Orcheline and, during the Brussels World Fair in 1958, it made a conspicuous presentation on the roof of the Atomium Building in Brussels. Del Shannon's 1958 pop hit, "Runaway," used the Ondioline to create dreamy, organ-like tones in the chorus background.

JOHN CAGE

In 1938, American composer John Cage began his musical experiments incorporating his concept of indeterminacy with his first performance of his composition *Imaginary Landscape No 1*. This performance required several performers to play selected recordings on several record players, changing the frequencies and variable speed settings on each machine as the performance progressed.

In 1952, John Cage composed "4'33"," with the aim of liberating the performer and the composer from the need to make any conscious decisions. The only sounds produced in this composition were those made by the audience.

In 1960, John Cage composed his piece "Cartridge Music." Continuing with his mission to change the expectations and opinions of his audiences on the purpose of performance art, Cartridge Music, was an indeterminate score performed by several people whose task was to apply microphones to various objects.

John Cage's experiments in the use of indeterminacy culminated in *Music of Changes*, a work based on charts from the *I-Ching*, the Chinese book of Changes. Cage continued creating electronic music pieces, such as *Roaratorio*, written in 1979, and a series of *Europeras*, composed between 1987 and 1991. During the following years, Cage remained active as a composer, and a devout advocate of new and electronic music. He died on August 12, 1992.

HOMER W. DUDLEY

Homer W. Dudley, a research physicist at Bell Laboratories, worked on developing new methods of speech analysis and re-synthesis. In 1939, he invented the Parallel Bandpass Vocoder, and in the following year, he introduced the Voder speech synthesizer. Dudley's Vocoder (Voice Operated reCOrdDER) incorporated an electronically generated voice and an analyzer. The purpose of the analyzer was to read the energy level output of sequential sound samples, which were then processed by a series of narrow band filters for identification within the full audio frequency spectrum. The synthesizer then scanned the data from the analyzer, and reversed the process so that a feedback network of analytical filters, energized by a noise generator, could receive the transmitted signals and create sound from the data.

TRISTRAM CARY

Tristram Cary built a sound studio in London where, during the late 1940s, he created compositions using electronic instruments made from World War II surplus electronic parts. He has been a composer of electronic music during many stages in the development of the technology, from the first tape recorders of the 1950s, to analog synthesizers in the 1960s and 1970s, and later, development of computer-based systems. In 1968, Cary co-produced the first concert of live computer music at Queen Elizabeth Hall, in London. As an engineer, Cary was a partner in the creation of one of the first generation of synthesizers in the UK, the EMS VCS-1 or "Putney" as it was nicknamed. In the late 1960s, Cary became well known as a composer when he created the music for several episodes of the popular BBC science-fiction series "Doctor Who." He gained critical acclaim for his film scores, including the classic Alec Guiness comedy *The Lady Killers*; *The Children of Lir* (1959), the first major BBC television program with an entirely electronic score; *Birth Is Life Is Power Is Death Is God* (1967), Ray Bradbury's radio play *Leviathan 99* (1972); *Soft Walls* (1980), a work for Synclavier composed upon his arrival in Australia; and excerpts from *The Impossible Piano (Homage to CN')* (1994), a tribute to Conlon Nancarrow for sequencer and sampled piano.

TOM JENNINGS

The Jennings Electronic Development Corporation was founded in the mid-1940s, in Dartford, Kent, England. Tom Jennings began his illustrious career when he opened a shop selling used musical equipment. But, selling used instruments was not enough to survive on, so Jennings began developing and manufacturing electronic music instruments.

Tom Jennings' J. M. I. Company manufactured the Univox, (Latin for single voice) a portable electronic keyboard instrument, designed in 1946 by Derek Underdown, and Tom Jennings. The Univox was a monophonic organ, using vacuum-tube technology to create a sawtooth wave generator, modulated by a diode waveform shaper circuit. It utilized a valve based tone generation system, with a three-octave F to F miniature wooden keyboard, to create a range of tone selections and vibrato effects designed to simulate the sound of various acoustic instruments as well as the human voice. One key could produce multiple octaves by activating a frequency divider. Univox had its own amplification, a tiny six watt amp driving an eight inch speaker. The Univox was the first mass-produced portable electronic keyboard in the UK.

The Univox became extremely popular on the British and European club circuit. In 1962 Joe Meek used it with his group the Tornadoes on their international hit single "Telstar." (See Artistpro's book *Creative Music Production: Joe Meek's Bold Techniques* for the whole story of Joe Meek's unique career.)

Jenning's company later became known as VOX, an English company at the forefront of progressive ideas and new technology, synonymous with fine craftsmanship, progressive electronics and excellent musical-tone.

ALAN YOUNG

Alan Young, an engineer employed by the Hammond Organ Co., designed a monophonic keyboard called The Solovox, which was manufactured in the U.S. between 1940 and 1948. It was designed to play lead lines, simulating the sound of string, woodwind and organ, to the accompaniment of a piano. It was a predecessor of instruments such as the Mini-Moog, the ARP Axe, and Sequential Circuits' Prophet One.

It had a three-octave keyboard, and was designed to be stored on a sliding tray mounted directly under the piano keyboard. The Hammond Solovox had a knee operated volume control, and several big knobs on the front, used to select woodwind, string, organ or mute. It was very popular during the 1940s.

PERCY GRAINGER

The "Free Music Machine" was patented by the celebrated Australian composer Percy Grainger (1882-1961). Grainger and musician Burnett Cross, who assisted Grainger, and his wife Ella Granger, conducted their experiments in Free Music from 1945 until Grainger's death in 1961. Granger's experiments with random music composition have been compared with the work of John Cage, though his work predates Cage by over thirty years. The Free Music Machine's aim was to "free" music from the limitations of conventional tuning systems and the rhythmic inadequacies of human performers. The Free Music Machine composed "Free Music" using eight oscillators and synchronizing equipment, in conjunction with photosensitive graph paper to convert the projected notation into sound. The first of these machines was based on the piano roll system, and produced the sounds utilizing pneumatics instead of electronics.

The following are Grainger's April 1952 notes describing the Free Music Machine, provided by the Percy Grainger Museum, Melbourne, Australia, and the 1946 edition of the Encyclopedia Britannica:

"Eight oscillators, able to play the gliding tones and irregular (beatless) rhythms of Grainger's FREE MUSIC (first thought of around 1892), are manipulated by paper graphs, towered discs and metal arms. A sheet of light brown wrapping paper 80 inches high (called "main paper"), is rolled continually from the "Feeder" revolving turret into the "Eater" revolving turret, passing through a metal cage on its way (the cage keeps the Main Paper, the graphs and the discs in place).

Each of the eight oscillators has its own special pitch control graph and sound strength control graph. To the front of the main paper are attached 4 pitch-control graphs (mauve and greenish paper) and 4 tone-strength control graphs (pinkish paper), their top edges cut into "hills and dales" in accordance with the intervals & tone strength desired. These graphs operate oscillators 1,2,3,4. To the back of the Main Paper are attached 4 additional pitch control graphs & 4 additional tone strength control graphs, operating oscillators 5,6,7,8 The bottoms of these 16 graphs are sewn onto the main paper at various heights but the top of each graph is left unattached. Into each pouch thus formed (between the main paper and the graph paper) is inserted a towered metal disc, the tower riding the upon the top edge of the graph & following its up and down movements. These movements are passed on to the axle and tone strength control box of each oscillator by means of metal arms, causing whatever changes in pitch and volume are intended. The blue-and-white discs controlling tone strengths are smaller than the variously colored discs controlling pitch."

JOHN HANERT

The Hammond Organ Company commissioned John Hanert to design and build his Hanert Synthesizer, or "Electric Orchestra," in 1945. It was described as an "Apparatus for Automatic Production of Music." It consisted of an enormous bank of vacuum tube oscillators, generators, and wave shaping circuits, and a sixty-foot long table. The "automation" was achieved by moving mechanical scanning heads over the full length of the table, which was covered in 11 by 12-inch paper cards, each card encoded, using a graphite pencil, with characteristics of sound, including volume, timbre, pitch, and duration, stored as the graphite marks. These codes were recognized by direct electrical contact with the scanning head. The cards could be moved around to create musical variation and the speed and direction of the scanner could also be changed at any time to alter the tempo of the music. In theory, this was a forerunner of the modern flatbed scanners, used by the graphics and computer industry.

Instruments capable of reading and performing encoded scores such as the "Electric Orchestra" were developed during the 1940s and '50s. Unlike commercial keyboard-controlled organs and related instruments, the score-reading instruments were large, experimental devices.

HUGH LECAINE

Canadian composer, physicist, and inventor Hugh LeCaine produced many innovative technologies and custom-built one-of-a-kind electronic instruments. He was a pioneer in the development of multi-track tape recording and a leader in the development and expansion of electronic music studios. While LeCaine worked at his Toronto laboratory, supported by the Canadian National Research Council, he developed prototypes for a touch sensitive organ, a variable speed recorder, a multi-track recorder, among numerous other electronic instruments. While his inventions were never developed for mass-markets, he made a great contribution to the world of electronic music. Among his inventions were the Electronic Sackbut and the Sonde, one-of-a-kind instruments, custom built for the University of Toronto during the 1940s.

Le Caine demonstrated his inventions with his own compositions and arrangements of well-known tunes, for example, he demonstrated his Electronic Sackbut in 1948 by playing the opening clarinet solo from Gershwin's "Rhapsody in Blue".

In 1952, LeCaine presented his minimal composition, "Dripsody." The single sound source for this Musique Concrete piece was a drip of water.

RAYMOND SCOTT

Raymond Scott constructed his electronic music laboratory in his home on Long Island, NY, where he designed his innovative electronic devices and electronic instruments before incorporating Manhattan Research Inc., in 1946.

Robert Moog had this to say about Scott in his 1997 article, "Memories of Raymond Scott," for the Raymond Scott Archive, (**RaymondScott.com**). *"Raymond Scott was a very creative guy, but an absolute madman! When I first worked for him in the early 1950s, he had a very large laboratory completely filled with rack upon rack of relays, motors, steppers and electronic circuits. I'd never seen anything like it. It was a huge, electromechanical 'sequencer'."* (Scott referred to it as his "Wall of Sound.")

Raymond Scott at work in his lab in 1938.

Moog continued: *"Raymond Scott was definitely in the forefront of developing electronic music technology—and in the forefront of using it commercially as a musician. He was the first—he foresaw the use of sequencers, and the use of electronic oscillators, to make sounds. They were the watershed uses of electronic circuitry. Raymond got a lot of his electronic music into radio and television, but he also went much further out and did pieces of music with the equipment he built. They don't sound as weird anymore, they sound similar to what people are doing today. He didn't always work in the standard ways, but that didn't matter because he had so much imagination, and so much intuition, that he could get something to work. And do exactly what he wanted it to do. Raymond Scott was one of those rare people who was influenced by the future. Not by the past, not by the present, but by the future. He did things that later turned out to be directly for the future. I think Raymond was tuned into the celestial, cosmic network (the one that is out there in time as well as space) to a greater extent than the rest of us."*

Raymond Scott was an accomplished professional pianist and band leader and a major American composer, who trained at the Juilliard School of Music. He began his career as a musician in 1931. Beginning in 1934, Scott wrote and recorded several novel instrumental pieces of music with his band, "The Raymond Scott Quintette," which included his son John Williams, the famous film score composer (*Jaws*, *Star Wars*, etc.) on drums. These recordings became pop hits on radio, selling millions of copies of the records, which led to a 20th Century Fox deal for films scores in Hollywood.

His recordings combined his own unique style with elements of jazz, swing, pop and avant-garde music. Scott was a huge, international pop star for decades, only a notch below the fame of Glen Miller, Tommy Dorsey, etc. A few years later, in 1942, Scott sold the publishing rights to some of his hit compositions to Warner Brothers. Many of these recordings were then used on the scores for WB cartoons from the 1940s on, the most famous of which were Loony Tunes and Merry Melodies, with Bugs Bunny, Daffy Duck, Ren & Stimpy, Duckman and, later, the Simpsons, etc. As a result, Scott's music is among the most recognized of the 20th century, being instantly recognizable from the cartoons that generations of Americans grew so familiar with.

Scott recorded all of his band sessions, with his Raymond Scott Quintet, on lacquer discs, and then edited random blocks of music into complex, almost unplayable compositions. By developing a unique cut and paste technique, he achieved an end similar to that of later algorithmic-based software technology.

In 1946, Scott patented the "Orchestra Machine," his first electronic music instrument. During 1948, Scott built an instrument called the Karloff named after the horror movie star. Scott designed the machine to create sound effects for advertisements and films.

From 1950 to 1957, Scott financed his experiments with electronic music technology through his "day job" as orchestra conductor for the NBC's chart-countdown show, *Lucky Strike's Your Hit Parade*.

In the early-1950s, Raymond Scott began developing a keyboard instrument known as the Clavivox, or keyboard theremin. His original intention was to create a keyboard version of the theremin for his daughter, but by 1956 the Clavivox was far more than a simple keyboard theremin. The sub-assembly circuit was designed and built by Robert Moog, when Moog was a twenty-year old engineering student at Columbia, still living at home and building theremins part time with his father.

As an analog synthesizer, the Clavivox easily predates the Moog synthesizer by a decade. By attaching a keyboard to Moog's theremin, Scott created his Clavivox. The Clavivox simulated the continuous gliding tone of the theremin, each note gliding from one to the next without a break, over a three-octave keyboard. In addition to the "gliding" and expressive playing, the Clavivox could also create staccato attacks, allow on/off vibrato toggling, and many other effects not possible on the theremin. It was completed and patented in 1956.

Robert Moog said, "This was not a theremin anymore. Raymond quickly realized there were more elegant ways of controlling an electronic circuit. ...A lot of the sound-producing circuitry of the Clavivox resembles very closely the first analog synthesizer my company made in the mid-1960s. ... Some of the sounds are not the same, but they are close."

We know that Scott built more electronic instruments in the early to mid-1950s, because Bob Moog has talked about seeing his huge electro-mechanical sequencer from his first visit to Scott's studio in 1955. Scott's first sequencer/synthesizer hybrid was the "Raymond Scott Electro-mechanical Sequencer." It was a very large instrument, thirty feet in length, and over six-feet high, which he had programmed to produce all sorts of rhythmic patterns. Hundreds of telephone-relay switches were used in the sequencer portion of the instrument, along with a modified Hammond organ, an Ondes-Martenot and two Clavivoxes, using a bank of sixteen oscillators to generate the sound.

Scott's most celebrated instrument design was the Electronium, (not to be confused with René Seybold's Electronium or the Electronium-Pi sold by Hohner). According to the leading authority on Scott's life and work, The Raymond Scott Archive. Scott described his instrument as an *"instantaneous composition-performance machine. The Electronium is not a synthesizer—there is no keyboard ... and it cannot be used for the performance of existing music. The instrument is designed solely for the simultaneous and instantaneous composition-performance of musical works."* Robert Moog also constructed modules for two incarnations of the Raymond Scott Electronium.

Scott began his work with Berry Gordy, the owner of Motown Records, in June of 1970 after Gordy saw an announcement about the Raymond Scott Electronium in Variety magazine. In 1972, Scott was officially hired as Motown's director of electronic music research and development. After he retired from Motown in 1977 following a heart attack. Scott went on to use MIDI technology to further his compositional skills. Raymond Scott died in 1994 at the age of 85.

Decades before minimalist musicians such as Phillip Glass and Steve Reich, Raymond Scott used minimalist repetition and sequencing techniques in his compositions. His three-volume set of synthesized lullabies, *Soothing Sounds for Baby,* was originally released by Epic Records in 1963, and reissued on CD in 1997. In response to a popular rediscovery of the musical genius of his original novelty jazz recordings, Columbia Records also released a CD featuring his music, titled *Reckless Nights and Turkish Twilights*, in 1992. Sony released a remastered, expanded version of this CD in 1999. *Manhattan Research Inc*, released on the Dutch label Basta, was nominated by no less than 16 music magazines among the Top Ten Best CDs of 2000. This double CD package comes with a 144-page hardcover book and features previously unreleased recordings and photographs from the 1950s and '60s, including several collaborations with pre-Muppet-era Jim Henson.

Moog demonstrated the Raymond Scott Clavivox as part of a 1997 Raymond Scott Tribute Show and is an active Advisory Board Member of the Raymond Scott Archives.

LEO FENDER

California inventor Leo Fender became fascinated by radio electronics at age thirteen. He mastered the art of electronics, not by formal electronics training, but by repairing radios for his student friends while studying accounting at Fullerton Junior College. While still a student, in 1932, Leo befriended an orchestra leader who contracted him to build a PA system. This experience led him to build and install several public address systems during the 1930s. Between 1934 and 1938, he held various positions as an accountant, before he opened his radio repair shop, Fender Radio Service. World War II marked a major turning point in popular music styles. With the decline of big band era, Leo began developing methods of amplification for hollow body instruments. The first electric Hawaiian lap steel guitar was built by Leo Fender and Doc Kaufman in the fall of 1945, under the name K&F Instruments. Kaufman left the company in 1946, and Leo Fender changed the name to The Fender Electric Instrument Company.

In 1948, he developed the legendary Telecaster (originally named the Broadcaster). The Tele, as it became known, was the first solid-body electric Spanish-style guitar to be manufactured commercially. Because of this, Fender has often been referred to as the Henry Ford of the electric guitar.

Leo Fender continued to create new instruments, such as the first successful alternative to the acoustic or stand-up bass, the Fender Precision Bass.

In 1954, the Stratocaster become the standard of the industry (played by many notable artists, such as Buddy Holly, Jimi Hendrix, Jeff Beck). These were followed by instruments including the Jazz Bass, which featured two pickups, to produce a wider variety of sounds, a slim, fast-action neck and an ergonomic body design for more comfortable playing.

Fender guitars, such as the Telecaster and Stratocaster, have become American classics and the most popular electric guitars in the world, preferred by countless famous musicians.

Leo Fender's first amps, in 1945, consisted of basic circuits that had been around for years. In 1957, Leo Fender introduced tone controls, his foremost contribution to the field of amplifier design. When Fender started producing amps with treble, bass, middle and presence controls, complete control of the instruments' sound became, for the first time, an integral part of the amplifier.

Because of poor health, Leo Fender sold his company to CBS in 1965. He signed a contract promising not to become involved in making guitars or amplifiers, or to lend his name in any product in competition with CBS for ten years. When the contract expired, in 1976, he started the Music Man Company, which soon became the Ernie Ball Musicman. He then went into partnership with George Fullerton, his long-time friend and co-designer of the stratacaster. Being bound to CBS not to use his name, they named their company "George & Leo," or G&L for short, and went on to design guitars reminiscent of their earlier designs of the 1950s.

Under CBS, Fender remained a giant in the music industry until the usual corporate cost cutting on components led to a downturn in the quality of Fender products. Today, pre-CBS Fender amps and guitars are highly prized by collectors, and professional musicians.

When asked why he never retired, Leo Fender is reputed to have said, "I owe it to musicians to make better instruments." Leo Fender worked up until the day before he died, on Thursday March 21, 1991, at the age of 82.

JOHN BARDEEN, WALTER BRATTAIN AND WILLIAM SHOCKLEY

The first transistor was revealed to the public by Bell Laboratories in 1948. The transistor was discovered almost by accident, when, in 1947, Bell Lab researchers, John Bardeen, a theoroetical physicist and Walter Brattain, an experimental physicist, were working together on seeking a solid-state semiconductor equivalent to the vacuum tube. When Brattain and Bardeen failed to come up with a working model semiconductor, they began their own experiments with new elements, following an insight of Baradeen's regarding the behaviour of electrons on crystals. This new insight led to the development of the first point-contact transistor, made from strips of gold foil pushed into contact with a slab of germanium.

Unfortunately for them, their research supervisor William Shockley believed that the person who had the original idea was the sole inventor and should be the only name on the patent. Shockley believed that the original ideas had been his own, even though their transistor bore no resemblance to the one Shockley had envisioned.

In January 1947, Shockley announced, to Bardeen's and Brattain's disapproval, that he fully intended to be the only person on the transistor's patent.

While the Bell Lab legal department began formulating their patent application, they found that, in the 1930s, Julius Lilienfeld had filed a patent for a device almost identical to Shockley's original idea. Since the transistor built by Bardeen and Brattain was different from Shockley's original idea, the Bell lawyers decided to file Bardeen and Brattain original work.

Eventually, the Bell Lab attorneys filed four patents on the initial solid-state amplifier. The first two were on the initial work that Bardeen, Brattain, and a colleague named Gibney, had done based on Shockley's field effect transistor, a third for the new Bardeen and Brattain device, and a fourth for Shockley's improved version, which he called a junction transistor. These were all filed by mid-1948, just before Bell Labs announced the inventions to the press.

The first two proposals were rejected in November 1948, because the U.S. Patent Office found them to be too similar to the Lilienfeld patents of twenty years before. But the second two, for Bardeen and

Brattain's point contact transistor and Shockley's junction transistor, were accepted.

Bardeen and Brattain were vindicated. Shockley was extremely distressed, and remained bitter for years, as he tried in vain to overturn the decision of the patent office. In the end, he failed to prove that his own designs would have worked.

Shockley, Brattain and Bardeen met again in 1956, for the first time since the controversy over their research, in Stockholm, Sweden, when they received the Nobel Prize for their contribution to physics.

Not fully comprehending the importance of their discovery, Bell Labs held a transistor symposium in September 1951, where they offered to license their transistor technology to anyone who wanted it for a fee of $25,000.

The first commercial junction transistors had a maximum collector-emitter voltage of 6 volts, and a maximum collector current of a few milliamps. In 1953, Raytheon released the first mass-produced transistor, the CK722. This made solid-state electronics affordable to the amateur constructor. Improved transistor designs, extending frequency response, lowering noise levels, and increasing power dissipation, developed rapidly. The earliest transistors were made from germanium, a metallic semiconductor. By 1955, the first silicon transistors were commercially available.

In 1962, Bell Labs began mass production of transistors for the blossoming solid-state market, while also manufacturing professional grade amplifiers.

MILTON BABBITT

American composer Milton Babbitt, born in Philadelphia in 1916, is famed for his pioneering musical achievements in the dodecaphonic system. Milton Babbit was a leading proponent of total serialization, which, in lay-terms, was the use of predetermined series of pitches, rhythms, durations, tone colors, and other musical elements, as the basis for musical composition. As one of the twentieth centuries most celebrated American composers, with an extraordinary flexibility of musical style, and a gifted instinct for jazz, he has fostered increased integration of 'serialist' language into many musical styles of the late twentieth century. Babbitt serialized all aspects of pitch, rhythm, dynamics, and articulation by applying 12-tone principles to all the elements of composition: dynamics, timbre, and rhythm, as well as melody and harmony in his compositions, most notably, his 1947 composition, *Three Compositions for Piano*.

In 1959 Babbitt was a part of the team of composers who launched the Columbia-Princeton Electronic Music Center. In 1982 he was awarded a Pulitzer Special Citation for his life's work, which includes *Concerti for Violin, Small Orchestra, and Synthesized Tape* (1976).

MAURICE CONSTANT MARTIN

In 1947, at Versailles, France, Maurice Constant Martin constructed a monophonic keyboard called the Clavioline. This instrument was a battery powered, portable keyboard, and was comprised of two separate modules. The first was a five-octave keyboard, which contained, on the front panel, eighteen switches for controlling various parameters, i.e., timbre, octave range and attack, and two controls for vibrato speed, and intensity. A knee lever controlled the volume. The second module was a separate amp and speaker unit. The avant-garde jazz musician, Sun Ra, one of the first well-known musicians to incorporate electronic instruments into their live performances, performed and recorded with a Clavioline during the 1950's and 60's. The Clavioline was licensed to Selmer and Gibson during the fifties and sixties for worldwide distribution.

HAROLD RHODES

Harold Rhodes built the first prototype of the Rhodes Piano in 1944. It produced its unique tone through a series of metal tines amplified by electrostatic pickups. Rhodes' efforts to build a portable piano that could be used to entertain the soldiers during World War II became his "lap model," or the Army Air Corps Piano Model. In the mid-1940s, the Rhodes Piano Corporation was founded and the Pre-Piano, was built in 1946. In the late 1950s, Leo Fender bought the company, and it became known as the Fender Rhodes. Soon, the first full-size model, the 73-note MkII Suitcase Piano, consisting of two parts, a keyboard and a cabinet with amp/speakers, was introduced. The two MkIII parts could easily be fitted into the special "suitcase," for easy transportation. Two more models were launched during the sixties, a Celeste, and a "Domestic" 88 Student Piano, designed for schools. Not long after, more modified designs were introduced. The Rhodes Mk60 stood on four metal legs, halving the weight, making it perfect for touring musicians. The piano could also be connected to any external amp. The new model was named The Stage Piano Mark I. During the early '70s, many famous artists, such as Herbie Hancock, Stevie Wonder, Chick Corea, and Joe Zawinul, played Rhodes electric pianos.

When CBS bought out Fender, in 1965, they changed the name Fender Rhodes to Rhodes and continued to modify various aspects of its design. CBS also took over Alan R. Pearlman's bankrupt synthesizer company, ARP, and released a new model, the Rhodes Chroma, based on the ARP Chroma. The Chroma Polaris, also know as the Fender Polaris, succeeded this model. In 1983, new models were equipped with the new technology, MIDI. In 1987, Rhodes was sold to the Japanese electronics company, Roland, who released a few new models under the Rhodes name. Unlike the earlier Rhodes models, the new Roland models were digital instruments with built-in, ROM based patches, which created a sound inferior to the unique Rhodes sound. No new models were released during the 1990s. After much negotiation, Harold Rhodes won the rights to use his name on his future inventions.

PIERRE SCHAEFFER

Pierre Schaeffer, born in Nancy, France in 1910, was an electro-acoustic engineer working at Radio-Diffusion-Television Francaise (RTF) in Paris, when he produced several short studies on his concept of free sound, which became known as Musique Concrete. Musique Concrete is a concept based on the use of sounds that are not produced by traditional acoustic music instruments, but rather, sounds from environmental sources; the sound of the voice, the sound of thunderstorms, of waterfalls, steam-engines, steel foundries, etc., recorded on turntable discs, before the invention of tape recorders, and manipulated to create soundscapes.

In October 1948, Schaeffer's early studies were broadcast on French radio in a "Concert of Noises." Schaeffer, and engineer Jacques Poullin, inspired by the reception they received, continued to develop Musique Concrete as a musical concept.

While Musique Concrete had its supporters, Schaeffer found himself surrounded by opponents of his experiments, both from traditional acoustic musicians as well as electronic music composers, whose arguments rested on the source of sound material, as well as on the purpose of music itself.

For Musique Concrete, the character of music is understood as a human activity of listening experience, shaped by and elevating the unique aesthetic of the listener. Electronic Music is based on the idea, the system, and precise control of a machine in a scientific environment.

Schaeffer believed that the French had been liberated politically from German occupation, but that the 12-tone music of the Vienna school, inspired by scientific ideas and mathematical equations, was still an occupying force, to be 'driven back' over the borders.

While Pierre Schaeffer saw himself principally as an electro-acoustic engineer and not as a composer, in 1949-50, with Pierre Schaeffer and Pierre Henry, with the help of Jacques Poullin, he composed "Symphonie pour un homme seul" (Symphony for a Man Alone). The work premiered in Paris on March 18, 1950.

JOSEPH SCHILLINGER

Joseph Schillinger was born in Kharkov, Russia on September 1, 1895. He studied composition and conducting at the St. Petersburg Imperial Conservatory of Music, graduating in 1918. He held several high academic positions; Head of the Music Department, Board of Education, Ukraine; Dean and Professor at the State Academy of Music; Consultant to the State Opera of Ukraine; Conductor and Lecturer at the Institute of Technology; Lecturer of the State Symphony Orchestra of Ukraine, and many other posts. He received an invitation from the American Society for Cultural Relations with Russia to come to the United States, in 1928, to present a series of lectures on the contemporary music of Russia. He became a US citizen in 1936.

Schillinger was a leading intellectual of his time. He left a large body of work, including orchestral and electronic music compositions, as well as his theoretical and scientific papers, which introduced a new interpretation on the workings of music. Schillinger is most renowned for his series of papers on music theory, *The Mathematical Basis of the Arts*, which he presented at several universities in the US, throughout the 1930s. Many of his students, including George Gershwin and Glenn Miller, produced musical compositions using patterns passed on to them by Joseph Schillinger.

PIERRE BOULEZ

Boulez was born on March 2, 1925, in Montbrison, France, and during his long prolific career, he has garnered a reputation as one of the most distinguished composers and conductors of the twentieth century. "Structures for Two Pianos," written in 1952, was one of Pierre Boulez' initial efforts to utilize a small quantity of musical data, which he called cells, for use in pitch, duration, dynamics, or attack points in a highly serialized musical structure. Boulez studied with Messiaen at the Paris Conservatoire between 1944 and 1946 and, privately, under the tutelage of Andree Vaurabourg and Rene Leibowitz. At this time he came to know Karlheinz Stockhausen. It was through this association that he became a leader of the European avant-garde movement. Boulez's compositional style has been referred to as "tonal serialism" which produced works of "feverish conducting." Beginning in the mid 1970's, he concentrated on his work as Director of the Institut de Recherche et Coordination Acoustique/Musique, a prestigious world renowned computer studio located in Paris. His honors include the1995 German Record Critics Award for his contribution to 20th century music. Also that same year, Gramophone magazine dubbed him "Artist of the Year." In 1996, Boulez was presented with the Berlin Arts Prize, and also the Royal Swedish Academy of Music's Polar Music Prize (also awarded to Bob Moog in 2001).

HARRY OLSEN AND HEBERT BELAR

In 1952, Harry Olsen and Hebert Belar, both electronic engineers employed at RCA's Princeton Laboratories, invented the RCA synthesizer, also known as the Olson-Belar Synthesizer. Belar and Olsen wanted to produce an instrument that generated music based on a system of random probability. Their efforts were inspired by the controversial 1948 publication, *A Mathematical Theory of Music* by Joseph Schillinger, who proposed that new forms of commercial music could be created by combining random variations of existing popular music.

The RCA synthesizer was capable of producing four musical tones simultaneously. Encoded in binary form on a perforated paper roll, made with a special typewriter-like keyboard, were pitches, tone colors, vibrato intensities, envelope shapes, and portamento for each of the four tones. The perforations specified the sounds' properties for every 1/30 second, which enabled the composer to produce musical changes faster and more precisely than traditional musicians could play.

Two RCA synthesizers were built; the second, the MK II, was installed at the Columbia-Princeton Electronic Music Center in New York City in 1959.

Twelve vacuum tube oscillators provided the sound source in the Mark I, while the larger Mark II incorporated twenty-four. Mixdown of the tracks from the instrument was monitored on a pair of speakers, while they were copied onto an internal lacquer disk cutter. This process created six concentric grooves, with a total running time of three minutes per groove. The grooves were then combined, and recorded onto a separate lacquer disk. By a means of recycling and bouncing the existing tracks back and forth, the disk was capable of creating up to 216 tracks.

Dr. Harry F. Olson was posthumously awarded the Distinguished Engineering Alumni Award (1996) and the UI Alumni Association's Distinguished Achievement Award (1982). He died April 1, 1982, in Princeton, N.J., only days before the announcement of his Achievement Award reached him.

KARLHEINZ STOCKHAUSEN

German composer Karlheinz Stockhausen was born in 1928. Between 1947 and 1951, he studied piano and music education at the National Conservatory of Music, and philology, philosophy, and musicology at Cologne University. He attended Olivier Messiaen's courses in rhythmics and aesthetics in Paris. While in France, he began his experiments with the Musique Concrète group at the French radio station in Paris. In 1952, Stockhausen worked with Herbert Eimert to create what they called Elektronische Musik, when Eimert launched the Cologne Station of Nordwest Deutscher Rundfunk, later re-named Westdeutscher Rundfunk. The following year, while continuing to pursue research and to compose at the Studio for Electronic Music, he studied phonetics, information and communication theory with Professor Meyer-Eppler at Bonn University.

Stockhausen continued to explore the building blocks of sound to create increasingly complex synthesized sounds from simple pure frequencies, or sine waves, which led him to develop what he called 'flood sounds'. To capture the overtone sound that would normally be, as he said, "going out the chimney," he experimented with placing four microphones in a circle around a rotating loudspeaker with a horn, so that sound could be picked up by each of the four micro-phones as the sound went around the circle. This is a predecessor to the Dolby surround system.

The Cologne Radio Series *Music of Our Time*, in its initial broad-cast of October 19, 1954, used only electronically generated sounds by pioneering electronic music composers, such as Stockhausen, Eimert, and Pousseur.

ROBERT BEYER, WERNER MEYER-EPPLER, AND HERBERT EIMERT

The Cologne studio came into being through the collaboration of several individuals contributing their different skills, technologies and backgrounds.

Dr. Werner Meyer-Eppler, a mathematician, physicist, and director of Phonetics at Bonn University, was one of the leading chroniclers of electronic music technology. In 1948, Homer Dudley, who had just invented his Vocoder (Voice Operated reCOrDER), designed for analyzing and synthesizing speech, brought his new invention to show to Meyer-Eppler, who was impressed. He made reference to it in his account on the history of electronic instruments (Elektrische Klangerzeugung). Dudley was invited to play a recording of Vocoder sounds at a lecture on electronic sound production at North-West German Music Academy. In the audience was Robert Beyer from West German Radio.

Beyer, an inventor and author, was also interested in the use of electronics in music production. He and Meyer-Eppler joined forces and gave a lecture on "The Sound World of Electronic Music" at Darmstadt. Beyer concentrated on design and manufacturing of electronic equipment, and Meyer-Eppler concentrated on research in speech synthesis. Composer, Herbert Eimert, a devotee of 12-tone music, soon joined them. In 1950, Harald Bode brought along his Melochord. They used it to produce music by layering tracks of tones. In 1951 they presented their results at Darmstadt in a lecture entitled "The Possibilities of Electronic Sound Production." Beyer gave a paper on "Music and Technology," and Eimert discussed "Music on the Borderline."

During 1951, a radio station in Cologne broadcast an evening program called "The Sound World of Electronic Music." The show featured a forum between Eimert, Beyer and Meyer-Eppler. The director of the station, Fritz Enkel, was impressed and agreed to establish a studio in Cologne to research electronic music. The studio took two years to become fully operational. Eimert became the artistic director.

During the interim, while the studio was being constructed, Meyer-Eppler gave his lecture on "The Methods of Electronic Tone Generation" to a large gathering of technologists in Bonn. In 1952, in Darmstadt, composer Bruno Maderna presented Musica sue due Dimensioni, which featured flute, percussion, and taped tones projected through a loud speaker. In the audience were future electronic music composers Stockhausen, Klebe, Koenig, Hambraeus, Goeyvaerts and others.

In 1952, while teaching at Darmstadt Summer School in Germany, Robert Beyer, Werner Meyer-Eppler and Herbert Eimert experimented with electronically generated sounds together. Beyer and Eimert composed the first all-electronic works while the Cologne Studio was still in construction: Klang im unbegrenzten

Raum (1951-1952), Klangstudie 1 (1952), and Klangstudie II (1952-1953). Their compositions were premiered in Paris at the highly acclaimed Institut de Recherche et Coordination Acoustique/Musique. As soon as the studio became functional, other composers including Stockhausen began to compose there. In 1953 Stockhausen was appointed assistant director under Eimert. From 1963 to 1978, he was the sole director.

LOUIS AND BEBE BARON

Composers Louis and Bebe Baron built their first private studio in New York City in the mid-1950s. Here they created electronic sound scores for soundtracks in sci-fi films, such as *Atlantis* and *Forbidden Planet*.

OSMOND KENDALL

Osmond Kendall developed the Composer-Tron, an analog synthesis and composition instrument, in 1952 for the Canadian branch of the Marconi Wireless Company. Kendall's aim was to create a composition tool in combination with a synthesis device that permitted the composer to create and control every nuance of the music in real time.

The Composer-Tron control system was capable of reading patterns and shapes, which were hand-drawn on its surface with a grease pencil. The drawing defined the timbre of the note, and, by making marks on a strip of film, rhythmical sequences were created.

LEJAREN HILLER AND LEONARD ISAACSON

In 1955, at the University of Illinois, the first piece of computer-generated music, the *Illiac String Quartet*, was programmed by Lejaren Hiller and Leonard Isaacson, using a Univac computer. The name was derived from a combination of the computer's name and the name of the University. In 1958, the Studio for Experimental

Music was launched at the University of Illinois, under the direction of Lejaren Hiller.

OTTO LUENING AND VLADAMIR USSACHEVSKY

In 1954, composers Otto Luening and Vladimir Ussachevsky collaborated to launch the Columbia-Princeton Studio from their own respective homes.

In 1959, the Columbia-Princeton Electronic Music Center received a five-year grant of $175,000 from the Rockefeller Foundation. This was the first American inter-academic laboratory where electronic musicians and inventors could collaborate and experiment with electronic music technology free of charge and without pressure from commercial concerns. Many renowned composers gave debut performances of their works at the center. The Committee of Direction members, were Professors Luening and Ussachevsky of Columbia University and Professors Babbitt and Sessions of Princeton University, with Professor Ussachevsky acting as Chairman of the Committee.

In 1959, the RCA Mark II Synthesizer was purchased by the Columbia-Princeton Electronic Music Center. The first electronic music concerts at the Columbia-Princeton Studio were presented soon after, in 1960. Predictably, many of the conservative faculty members who attended the concerts reacted with great hostility and animosity towards the new music.

In efforts to explore the synthesizer's full potential, the Mark II opened up many collaborations between composers and designers alike, particularly between Milton Babbitt and Vladimir Ussachevsky. Unfortunately, like many early technologies, the limitations of its interface meant that the Mark II synthesizer would not become a commercially produced instrument, as Babbitt described:

"The machine was extremely difficult to operate. First of all, it had a paper drive, and getting the paper through the machine and punching the holes was difficult. We were punching in binary. The machine was totally zero, nothing predetermined, and any number we punched could refer to any dimension in the machine. There were an immense number of analog oscillators, but the analog sound equipment was constantly causing problems. I couldn't think of anything that you couldn't get, but other composers gave up – it was a matter of patience."

MAX MATHEWS

Dr. Max Mathews of Bell Laboratories was known as the "Father of Computer Music." In 1957, Dr. Mathews directed research into developing analysis and synthesis of sound using computers. His team conducted behavioral and acoustic research. His collaborative research community developed the first software-based computer synthesis programs. His work in speech synthesis led him to realize that it should be easier for a computer to make music than the human voice. *(See Chapter 10 for more information on his significant contribution to computer music.)*

MAURICIO KAGEL

Mauricio Kagel, born in Buenos Aires in 1931, studied music and the history of literature (under J. L. Borges) at the University of Buenos Aires. Kagel immigrated to Cologne, Germany in 1957. During 1958/59, Mauricio Kagel wrote *Transicion II*, the first composition to incorporate a live tape recording as part of a performance. His work was first performed in Cologne. It was written for quartet; one musician performed in the traditional manner on the piano, another played on the strings and wooden portions of the piano, while two other performers used tape recorders simultaneously recording and playing back snippets of the performance.

EUGENI MURZIN

In 1958, after many years of research, Russian engineer Eugeni Murzin, and a team of colleagues constructed the ANS Synthesizer. The instrument was named after famous Russian composer, Alexander Nikolayevich Scriabin. A photo-optic generator, designed by Murzin, operated the instrument. Sound was achieved by a rotating glass disk, which contained 144 optic phonograms of pure tones. It could create a visible image from a sound wave, as well as reversing the process and creating sound from an image. The frequency of the notes increased from the center of the disk to the last "track" near the edge. These "tracks" corresponded directly to the 144 optic tones. The synthesizer, with five rotating disks, all turning at different speeds could produce over 700 tones. To select a specific tone, a separate disk was used. The disk was coated with a non-drying black film, and the "score" was produced by removing a portion of the film in a certain area, allowing the light from the photo-optic generator to pass through. Because the black film remained in a semi-liquid state, mistakes could be easily corrected, and edits to the musical score were simple to negotiate. The only ANS synthesizer in existence is stored at the Moscow State University in Russia.

DAPHNE ORAM

In 1959, Daphne Oram, an electronic music composer at the BBC Radiophonic Workshop, in England, developed a programming technique known as Oramics. By drawing onto a set of ten sprocket-synchronized strips of 35mm film, this monophonic system produced sound via strips of film covering photo-electric cells, and generated an electrical charge to control the sound frequency, timbre, amplitude and duration of the sound. Polyphonic textures were built up via multi-track tape recording. This method offered unparalleled flexibility and control over the nuances of sound, rivaled only by the most advanced analog voltage controlled synthesizers of the era. The instrument was used in many films and theatre scores during the 1960s.

HELMUT KLEIN AND W. SCHAAF

The Siemens Synthesizer, or "Siemens Studio for Electronic Music," was originally designed by Helmut Klein and W. Schaaf, at Siemens & Halske, in Munich, Germany. The studio used an enormous modular composition and synthesis system, similar to the RCA synthesizer, for generating musical sequences, which were then synthesized and recorded.

The Siemens synthesizer produced a range of seven octaves. Photo-electrically generated sounds allowed the scanning of photographic slides using Siemens' specially designed Bildabtaster technology. This technology enabled artists, such as German artist Günter Maas, to explore the possibilities of scanning his paintings for translation into music

Klein and Schaaf continued to work on refining the Siemens Synthesizer for use by the Munich Studio Für Elektronische Musik in Munich. Many well-known European experimental composers used this system during the 1950s and 1960s. Further development of the Siemens Synthesizer came to an end when the studio was dissolved in 1969.

RUDOLPH WURLITZER

Rudolph Wurlitzer was born in Schilbach, Saxony (Germany) in 1829, into a family who had a reputation for making and selling fine musical instruments since the 17th century. In 1853, at age 24, Rudolph Wurlitzer immigrated to America. Three years later in 1856, he founded The Rudolph Wurlitzer Company in Cincinnati, Ohio. Eventually, Wurlitzer began manufacturing his own instruments with the launch of the Wurlitzer piano in 1880. Until then, he imported instruments from his family's Wurlitzer plant in Huhlhorst, Germany. From 1880 on, Wurlitzer developed and manufactured many popular instruments. He introduced the precursor to the jukebox, the first coin-operated electric piano, the Tonophon, in 1896.

During the silent movie era, with the introduction of cinema and theatre organs, the dramatic movie soundtracks of the Mighty Wurlitzer became a popular sensation. Wurlitzer Pipe Organs were in demand for use in theatres and churches, and various models of the Wurlitzer electric piano and player pianos became extremely popular for use in private residences.

Wurlitzer manufactured the first commercial electronic drum machine, the Sideman, between 1959 and 1965. It was designed as an accompanying rhythm section for Wurlitzer organs. It used vacuum tubes to produce ten preset drum sounds, from twelve electronically generated predetermined rhythm patterns, with variable tempos. Its small electronic motor turned a wheel, which had a row of contact points on the outer rim. Each drum rhythm and sound had its own row of points. The speed of the spinning wheel determined the speed of the rhythm. The wheel was controlled by a slider and included a remote control on the organ keyboard, which enabled the keyboard player to switch tempos and drum sounds from a preset selection of ten speeds, ranging from a metronome click through patterns such as tango, foxtrot, or waltz.

TSUTOMU KATOH AND TADASHI OSANAI

Tadashi Osanai, an engineering graduate of Tokyo University and a noted Japanese accordionist, wanted to improve on the capabilities of the Wurlitzer Sideman. He approached Tsutomu Katoh for funding and, in 1962, they launched their company, Keio Electronic Laboratories (Keio being a combination of their names). They rented a small facility alongside the Keio railway line where Osanai and four assistants worked and produced the electro-mechanical drum machine, the Donca-Matic DA-20, or Disc Rotary Electric Auto Rhythm machine, in 1963.

This was the only competitor of the Wurlitzer Sideman rhythm machine in the early 1960s. The DA-20 was a major breakthrough, both in size, quality of sound, and technology. The transition from electromechanical technology to solid-state technology came with the introduction of a new model in 1966, the Donca DE-20. Keio went on to develop keyboard products under the name, Korg Musical Instrument Company (a combination of Keio and organ). In 1975, Korg introduced the world's first hand-held electronic tuner, the WT-10. Korg synthesizers have been some of the most innovative and popular instruments produced in the past 20 years. Mr. Katoh is still dedicated to providing musicians with new and better Korg instruments with which to express their creativity, and as a result of that dedication, Korg has became one of the world's largest and most innovative music electronics manufacturers.

MORTON SUBOTNICK, PAULINE OLIVEROS, AND RAMON SENDER

In 1960, Morton Subotnick, Pauline Oliveros, and Ramon Sender established the San Francisco Tape Music Center, an historic event in "new music" circles, designed to show that important music innovations could be created completely outside the academic and commercial community. The San Francisco Tape Music Center was founded in the attic of the San Francisco Conservatory of Music by a group of like-minded artists who believed that innovative music, as well as ambitious concepts and projects could be created on a shoestring budget. By pooling equipment, in collaborations that depended more on the strength of original ideas than on big budgets, the FSTMC became a significant force in the advancement of electronic music.

The influential SFTMC expanded, and moved on to bigger location when it was officially inaugurated in 1962. The artistic climate in San Francisco continued to grow with vibrantly innovative cultural ideas. Concerts by members of the adventurous collective were based on every available technology. Typically, ingenious technicians creatively linked miscellaneous electronic components, tone generators, and prerecorded material on racks of tape recorders, using loops and delay systems, along with projected images, in combinations of acoustic and electronic instruments, in their innovative collective presentations. The collective undertook regional and national tours during the mid-1960s.

Morton Subotnick, born in 1933, was a major force in the field of electronic music, which included interactive computer music systems. He was one of the most influential members of the SFTMC collective. Subotnick worked closely with Don Buchla to develop the 100 series Modular Electronic Music System, built in 1963.

Subotnick produced a widely performed electronic composition, "Silver Apples of the Moon" (1967), which was the first composition commissioned by Nonesuch Records expressly for the phonograph medium. In 1968 Subotnick premiered his new Buchla piece, "The Wild Bull," at Brandais. For its time, this was a masterpiece of enormous electronic sound. Many of his compositions remain in the repertoire of leading dance companies.

During 1966 and 1967, SFTMC moved to Mills College, becoming part of the Mills Center for Contemporary Music. The facilities were improved, but all of the original people who made up SFTMC departed in 1967.

JACK S. KILBY

In 1958 Jack Kilby created the first integrated circuit at Texas Instruments, revolutionizing the electronics industry and launching a new technological age of computers and electronic instruments. Kilby's first integrated circuit contained a single transistor, while advanced microchips use several million transistors in a single silicon chip by the end of the twentieth century. His efforts proved that resistors and capacitors could exist on the same piece of semi-conductor material. His circuit consisted of a sliver of germanium with five components linked by wires. High-quality, low-cost silicon transistors enabled electronic instrument designers to incorporate synthesizer features in small, convenient instruments, thus revolutionizing the music industry.

JAMES TENNEY

James Tenney, born in Silver City, New Mexico in 1934, was a pianist and composer and one of the first to experiment with computer generated music. He attended the University of Denver, the Juilliard School of Music, Bennington College (BA, 1958) and the University of Illinois (MA, 1961). He has performed with John Cage, Harry Partch, Steve Reich and Phillip Glass. He worked with Max Mathews at the Bell Lab in the early 1960s, developing programs for computer sound-generation and composition. Tenny developed his own music software, PLF 2, which he used to write *Four Stochastic Studies*, *Ergodos* and other computer generated music.

THE BRADLEY BROTHERS AND HARRY CHAMBERLIN

The Bradley brothers, Frank, Norman, and Leslie, bought the Mellotron technology from California inventor Harry Chamberlin in 1963. The story goes that Harry Chamberlin recorded himself playing his organ, and it dawned on him that he could create an instrument that could play pre-recorded music, which could be programmed to play various combined tracks, for instance a piano sound, or a flute sound or a violin sound, etc. In 1948, Chamberlain invented the prototype of his original percussion sampler, known as the Rhythmate 100, leading to several variations of design with he developed and sold at his shop, which opened in Ontario, California in 1960. Chamberlin's inability to keep up with orders, as well as unresolved problems with the tape shuttling system and playback heads, led him to sell the technology to the Bradley Brothers. This came about when, Bill Fransen, a salesman hired by Chamberlin, took a couple of the instruments to England to generate interest in improving and marketing the technology. Fransen contacted Leslie Bradley of Bradmatic Ltd. and asked him if his company could produce 70 matched replay heads. This created a great deal of curiosity, and the Bradley brothers met with Fransen. Bill asked the brothers if they could make a dependable functional instrument with this technology, and thinking the idea was Fransen's, they immediately said yes. The following year, Harry Chamberlain heard what the Bradley brothers were up to, and caught a flight to England. After much heated debate, the Bradley's agreed to pay Chamberlin thirty thousand pounds to acquire rights to the technology. After extensive further development, the Mellotron was manufactured in England, from 1963 until 1987, under the Bradley Brothers new partnership, Streetly Electronics. Harry Chamberlain continued to design his own new instruments, leading up to the development of the Chamberlain M series of the 1970s. During this time the Bradley brothers and Harry Chamberlin exchanged many of the "samples" used in both instruments.

The Mellotron contributed to the unique sound of English pop musicians such as the Beatles, Rolling Stones, the Moody Blues, the Kinks, Pink Floyd, Emerson, Lake, and Palmer, Genesis, King Crimson, the Strawbs, and Yes, who used the Mellotron in their recordings. The Mellotron was the pride and joy of keyboard players in the progressive rock genre. The Mellotron went through many more evolutions, exploring tone and portability. The Novatron was a later model of the Mellotron with basically the same features, but more refined tape mechanisms were incorporated into this model. The Mark II Mellotron used two three-octave keyboards, which made it possible to create a total of 1260 distinct recordings. The Mellotron operated by attaching a sound or "sample," pre-recorded on a strip of magnetic tape, under each key, corresponding to the pitch of each individual key. When the key was pressed, the Mellotron played the sample. When the key was released, the tape head was mechanically returned to the beginning of the tape; thus, the individual attributes of a sustained note were retained. The maximum duration of sample playback time was eight seconds. The instrument used a series of proprietary three track 3/8" recording tapes. The Mellotron was in many ways, the predecessor of the modern digital sampler. In 1987, Streetly Electronics went out of business because of the growing accessibility of synthesizers and financial troubles as a result of their American distributor, but the company has risen again, run by one of the original owner's sons, John Bradley and his partner, Martin Smith.

See Artistpro's *The Mellotron Book* for the complete, fascinating story of this unique instrument.

JOHN EATON AND PAUL KETOFF

Composer John Eaton commissioned engineer and designer Paul Ketoff to design a portable synthesizer in 1963. Ketoff, a Russian expatriate, created a small synthesizer in 1963, which he called the SynKet (after SYNthesizer and KEToff). This machine could fit on a desktop. It had three small closely spaced, tuned touch-sensitive keyboards. John Eaton gave many concerts on his Synket throughout the 1960s and '70s, performing his own compositions written for the instrument.

DON BUCHLA

American inventor, Don Buchla is renowned for having created one of the first generation of analog synthesizers, around the same time that Robert Moog invented his synthesizer. *To learn more about Don Buchla, see chapter 6.*

ROBERT MOOG

In 1964, the fully developed Moog synthesizer was released. The modular idea came from the miniaturization of electronics. Up to this point commercially available synthesizers were non-existent. *See chapter 3 for more.*

SALVATORE MARTIRANO

In the fall of 1969, Salvatore Martirano and a group of composers and engineers at the University of Illinois began designing and building an electronic instrument, The Sal-Mar Construction, which took two and one half years to develop at a cost of $18,000. The instrument was comprised of 39 separate sound-sources, which were divided into four separate "music programs" or ensembles. These ensembles were amplified through 24 speakers, which were divided into specific groups. These speakers could be placed in various parts of a performance hall or studio, so that Martirano could create the effect of four different sets of sounds moving, interacting and colliding around the room.

ALAN R. PEARLMAN

The company, ARP Instruments was formed in 1969 by Alan R. Pearlman with 100,000 dollars of his own money and a further loan of $100,000 from a small group of investors. The company unveiled its first synthesizer, which Pearlman called the ARP 2500 in January 1970.

In late 1970, at almost the same time as the Minimoog was unveiled, the ARP 2600, aka the Tonus, was manufactured. The synth was pre-configured internally, but connections between modules could be over-ridden by the use of patch cords, much like modular synths of that time. Pearlman, quick to notice the attention the Minimoog was getting, set out to design a small performance synth. The result from this engineering brainstorm was the ARP Odyssey, introduced in 1972. 1973 saw the release of the ARP Pro Soloist, later to be renamed the ARP Pro-DGX. It became one of ARP's best sellers. It was a "pre-set" instrument offering a pressure sensitive keyboard, and a variety of orchestral voices, making it quick and easy to use. There are rumors that, in 1973, the people at ARP were developing a String Ensemble synth, which for some reason was abandoned.

The Hal Leonard Publishing Company published a book on ARP and his instruments, written by David Friend, Alan R. Pearlman and Thomas D. Piggot in 1974, *Learning Music With Synthesizers*, a 213-page introduction to the use of synthesizers. Even though the book was intended for ARP Odyssey users, the book also contained a great deal of valuable information on analog synthesizers in general. Pearlman's first instrument, the ARP 2500, will best be remembered as the instrument used by French director Francois Truffaut, to communicate with the aliens in Steven Spielberg's 1977 film, *Close Encounters of the Third Kind*.

TOM OBERHEIM

Tom Oberheim was one of the key pioneers of modern electronic music. Oberheim is the creator of the legendary Oberheim synthesizers, drum machines, and sequencers, including the SEM-1, Two, Four, and Eight Voice Polyphonic Synthesizers, DS-1, OB-1, OB-X, OB-XA, OB-8, DMX, Xpander, Matrix-12, and the Oberheim Performance System. In the late 1970s the Oberheim Company developed the first polyphonic synthesizer, which was a four voice analog instrument. In 1979, Oberheim built the first synthesizers containing a computer interface, the Oberheim OBX and Rhodes Chroma. The interface allowed up to three instruments built by the same manufacturer to be interconnected.

DAVE SMITH

In 1978, the historic synth manufacturing company Sequential Circuits was founded by Dave Smith in his garage. Two of the first products he and partners, John Bowen, and Barbara Fairhurst produced and exhibited at NAMM (National Association of Music Merchants) were the Model 800 digital sequencer and the now legendary Prophet-5. The Prophet-5 was an instant success with keyboard players around the world, and propelled the company to overnight success. Dave Smith was also a key figure in the development of MIDI in 1983, which will be discussed later in the book.

IN SUMMARY:

The styles of music and the instruments that created them diversified a great deal from the mid-1970s. The following chapters will delve more deeply into the expansion of electronic music, and will continue to explore the people, the instruments, and the musical evolution of the past thirty years, and its profound impact upon music and on civilization as we know it.

CHAPTER 3

A Discussion with Dr. Robert Moog

Dr. Robert Moog was born in New York in 1934. His academic degrees include a B.S. in Physics from Queens College (New York City), a B.S. in Electrical Engineering from Columbia University (New York City), a Ph.D. in Engineering Physics from Cornell University (Ithaca, New York), and honorary doctorates from Polytechnic University and Lycoming College.

Bob Moog in the 1960s.

Photo courtesy Roger Luther, MoogArchives.com

When Bob Moog was a 10-year-old boy, he and his father began to build simple electronics hobby projects, such as radios with two tubes and similar devices. At one point they built one or two very simple electronic musical instruments.

Bob started building kits on his own at the age of 12. He built his first theremin from a magazine article when he was 14. When Moog was in high school, he designed and built several theremins. In 1953 Robert Moog wrote his first "how to build a theremin" article, for *Radio and Television News* magazine.

In 1954, while still an undergraduate studying physics at Queens College, Moog founded the R. A. Moog Company. Moog's article,

"A Transistorized Theremin," for the January 1961 issue of the magazine *Electronics World* resulted in hundreds of orders for theremin kits. He sold these kits from his business, which he operated out of his apartment.

Moog designed his first modular electronic music synthesizer components in 1964, and exhibited at the Audio Engineering Society Convention in October of that year. Moog then began manufacturing synthesizers. His first prototype synthesizer was designed in collaboration with composer Herbert A. Deutsch, who wanted Moog to build a device that had techniques to shape sounds through moving pitches and make siren-like sounds that could be produced electronically. Herb Deutsch, at the time, had been working with the theremin to teach ear training.

Bob Moog at work in his Trumansburg factory, 1968.

Photo courtesy Faith Frenz

The R. A. Moog Company became a full-time business in 1964, when Moog invented the components of the first modular Moog synthesizer. The company was located in Trumansburg, a small town 13 miles north of Ithaca, New York. The entire operation—offices, engineering, and production—took place in what was Baldwin's Furniture Store on Main Street. The Trumansburg factory housed a full electronic music recording studio, which brought the resident musical engineers into constant contact with performers and composers. Some of the composers were local regulars at the factory, and included Chris Swanson, David Borden, and Steve Drews. Other composers traveled from various distant places to get hands-on instruction in the operation of their synthesizers.

Many visitors who came to the Trumansburg factory were long-term customers, wishing to keep up with the new technology and simply needing advice on, for example, which collection of modules would best suit their needs. This interaction between the engineers and their 'user group' created a lively exchange of insights, ideas, opinions, and speculations as the Moog team of engineers endeavored to meet requirements for original patches and unique circuit design modifications.

Bob Moog's synthesizer designs represented a significant advance over previous electronic synthesizers, partially because of newly developed semiconductor technology. The new instruments were also less expensive to manufacture, and as a result, Moog's instruments soon became popular all over the world. His synthesizers became referred to simply as Moogs (pronounced with a long *o*). Bob Moog's instruments created the possibility for musicians to fabricate completely new sounds electronically. Many styles of music, such as trance, new age, ambient, techno, house, and hybrids of pop and world music descended from this technology.

The release of Wendy Carlos' album *Switched-on Bach* in 1968 brought Moog's synthesizer to the general public's attention. The album demonstrated that besides creating strange sounds, the synthesizer could be used to make beautiful music.

In 1978, after his bustling early days in the synthesizer business, Bob Moog moved to a picturesque region of the Smoky Mountains in Leicester, North Carolina. He started a new business, Big Briar Productions, in his workshop there. Over the past 25 years, Big Briar has developed a great reputation for building high quality, technically fascinating equipment, like theremins, MIDI interfaces, and analog effects modules. The company recently exhibited a new synthesizer, the Minimoog Voyager, designed by Bob Moog and in production starting in 2001. This was Bob Moog's first new analog keyboard instrument since his Micromoog in 1974. With a special touch-control pad, this new analog synthesizer's state-of-the-art technology is designed for live performance.

Bob Moog and Les Paul

Photo courtesy Roger Luther, MoogArchives.com

From 1984 to 1988, Moog was a full-time consultant and Vice President of New Product Research for Kurzweil Music Systems, and from 1988 until 1992 he also served as a professor in the Music Department of the University of North Carolina at Asheville.

Moog's awards include honorary doctorates from Polytechnic University (New York City) and Lycoming College (Williamsport, Pennsylvania); the Silver Medal of The Audio Engineering Society; the Trustee's Award of the National Academy of Recording Arts and Sciences; the *Billboard* Magazine Trendsetter's Award; and the SEAMUS award from the Society of Electroacoustic Music in the United States. He has written and spoken extensively on subject matter related to music technology, and has contributed major articles to the Encyclopedia Britannica and the Encyclopedia of Applied Physics. Robert Moog was inducted into the Rock-Walk Hall of Fame on January 14, 1988. He is also the recipient of the Polar Music Prize, the Royal Swedish Academy of Music Award, for 2001. The Prize has been awarded since 1992 for exceptional and lifetime achievements, transcending musical genres and breaking down musical boundaries.

The remainder of this chapter contains two interviews with Bob Moog, the first in the summer of 1987, and the second in the summer of 2000. During the 1987 interview, Dr. Moog discusses the building blocks of sound synthesis and takes us back in history, explaining how he developed his first modular synthesizer, and his thoughts on future technologies. The July 2000 interview expands on those revelations as Bob shares his thoughts on the future of music technology.

Robert Moog: The first composer I began working with was Herb Deutsch back in 1964. At that time Herb was working with experimental tape recording. He was making music that consisted primarily of tone color changes rather than conventional pitch and melody. He was interested in developing ways of making new sounds, sounds that had textures and qualities that hadn't been heard before.

The first instruments that we made for him were very experimental. They were made on what electrical engineers call a breadboard. It was a circuit board that I could solder components onto, right out in the open, without any cabinet, fancy power supply or anything. There were two instruments, one called a voltage-controlled oscillator and the other, a voltage-controlled amplifier.

Let me first explain what an oscillator is. An oscillator produces an electronic signal that repeats regularly between 20 and 20,000 times a second, which we hear as a pitched tone. An amplifier simply makes a sound stronger or weaker. A voltage-controlled oscillator produces a pitched tone whose pitch can be changed rapidly by changing the voltage. Imagine my taking two voltage-controlled oscillators, one of which is going fast enough for us to hear as a pitch, and the other going much slower. I used the second oscillator to control the first oscillator. This would enable me to create a sound whose pitch changes rapidly, like a siren, or a trill, or any one of a great variety of new sounds.

This is exactly what Herb Deutsch proceeded to do. He took voltage-controlled oscillator and voltage-controlled amplifiers, and put them together in ways that we just didn't foresee, and came up with the most amazing variety of sounds! He was tickled because these were the sounds he had been looking for, but couldn't obtain with conventional electronic equipment of the early sixties. I was tickled because he was doing something with the circuitry that was familiar to us that had never been done before to our ears.

After Herb and I tried out these two basic modules, which are now very common, we talked about how we would control them, how we would turn the sound on and off. Up until then, Herb would just stick a wire in to make a sound, or turn a switch on. Of course, that's not how musicians work. Herb and I discussed a few possibilities. We talked about whether or not to use a conventional music keyboard, or should we have a whole bunch of buttons to push, or something that you could slide your hand along to change the pitch continuously like a trombone slide or violin bow. We decided to use a standard keyboard because it was readily available, and provided an inexpensive way of turning on and off notes and sounds. The first keyboard we built used an organ keyboard mechanism, along with some circuitry that would open and close the voltage control amplifier every time you pressed a key, which made an envelope on the sound. You could adjust how fast the sound built up by holding the attack, and how fast the sound would decay by manipulating the decay. The envelope generator inside the keyboard opened up the voltage-controlled amplifier every time you pressed a key, and that is how the sound was shaped. By the summer of 1964, these were the components that we had assembled, the voltage-controlled oscillators, the voltage-controlled amplifiers, and the keyboard controller. It was these handmade experimental components that I showed at the Audio Engineering Society Convention in New York City, in the fall of 1964. That was the beginning. During that show in New York, I got my first orders for electronic music modular components. These were modular components, because each of the components did one thing, and one thing only towards generating, shaping, or controlling sound. In order to make a complete musical sound; you had to mix several of the components together. The first circuits were quite basic, actually. The only problem was that the pitch wasn't very accurate in the early prototypes. That didn't bother us at the time, because we were working with composers who didn't care that much about pitch accuracy. My first synthesizer customer was the choreographer Alwin Nikolais. He composed all his music on tape, and wanted additional sonic resources. My second customer was Eric Siday, who was doing very well as a composer of radio and TV commercial music. Only after our synthesizers became commercially important and our customers wanted to produce conventional melodies did we realize that we would have to improve and stabilize our voltage-controlled oscillators.

Vladimir Ussachevsky, who in 1964 was the head of the Columbia—Princeton Electronic Music Center in New York City, gave us an order. He wanted me to design and build an envelope generator that had four parts to the envelope, the initial rise, or attack, the initial fall, or decay, a flat area called sustain, and when you let go of the keyboard or trigger, the fall back to silence, which is called the release. This four part envelope, attack, decay, sustain, release, is now well know to all electronic musicians who play synthesizers. It's called the ADSR envelope. Back then, it was something brand new, an idea Ussachevsky developed for us to design and build.

The last module I want to mention is the voltage-controlled filter, which was ordered by Gustav Ciamaga from the University of Toronto in 1965. This filter is a device that emphasizes or attenuates, (cuts down) various parts of a musical sound, what we call the overtones. In doing so it actually changes the tone color without changing the pitch or the loudness. The voltage controlled filter allowed the tone color changes in the sound to be affected rapidly, and analog synthesizers are distinguished more for their control filter capabilities than any other single function.

Ben Kettlewell: Since you first displayed your prototypes at the Audio Engineering Society Convention in New York in 1964, there have been dozens of breakthroughs in electronic instrument technology, yet modular synthesizers still seem very popular. With the lower prices, and ease of operation of today's keyboards and modules, why do the modular synthesizers still maintain such a prominent position?

RM: Modular synthesizers made by my company back in the sixties were a natural outgrowth and the development of the first modules that I designed. The idea was to put together as many modules as you required, and that the modules were compatible, and able to work with each other. And of course, the more modules you put together, the more complex the sound was, the more rich the timbres, more interesting altogether. Each module has a series of front panel controls and switches that define how it's working, and at what point it's making the sound. For instance an oscillator module would have a knob determining what the pitch was. Another one would select the waveform, etc. Musicians quickly learned what the correspondence was between turning one of these knobs and hearing a change in the sound, and setting up, and manipulating a rich new sound, or sound quality. It was musical texture reduced to simply turning the appropriate knobs.

I think that's why analog modular equipment is still popular. It gives an immediacy, a physical ability to manipulate actual controls and connections whose effect a musician can easily hear, rather than a musician having to conceptualize it ahead of time by determining what sound he or she is going after in a digital instrument.

The following is from a new interview, which took place in July 2000.

BK: Since our last interview, what do you consider to be the most significant changes in music, and music technology since that time?

RM: I don't think that music has changed much within the last 10 or 20 years. Oh sure, there are some new genres, but little about our national or global musical culture has changed. The big change happened 40 years ago, when rock music completely and abruptly redirected our national musical culture. Today we still have rock music, we still have pre-20th-century classical music, and we still have the pre-rock jazz-blues-big band stuff. Musicians are tripping over each other trying to sound like the sixties and seventies. We may be poised for another abrupt change in our popular musical culture, but don't ask me to predict when it will come or what it will be like.

With respect to music technology, the big change here is the total takeover of recorded music production by the personal computer. Any musician who is not yet computer-literate is bound to find himself at the margins of contemporary music making.

BK: What do you think about the evolution of electronic music and its offspring over the past 2-3 decades?

RM: I haven't heard any recent "experimental" electronic music that has broken completely new ground. All the stuff that has been done on the computer has a somewhat different sound, but structurally it seems to me to be evolving from the truly groundbreaking stuff of the '50s and '60s.

In the pop arena, you can really begin to hear the influence of the experimental music of 30-50 years ago. A lot of today's techno and dance music sounds to me like "deja vu all over again."

BK: How do you feel the new technologies are going to alter the way music is created, performed and accessed in the twenty first century?

RM: When I think back over the last 30 or 40 years, I see that nobody was able to predict a whole century's "progress" in the face of rapidly moving technologies. In fact, making accurate predictions even five years ahead is difficult. Eight-channel recorders were just coming into existence during the 1960s. Did anyone back then foresee that, ten years later, there would be 24-track recorders that were synched together? Maybe a few far-seeing people in the tape recorder industry saw it. When Apple came out with its first computer in the late '70s, did anyone foresee that personal computers would be capable of professional-quality sound recording and editing in a mere 20 years? Ten years ago, who foresaw the explosion of web-based music distribution? Do you see what I'm getting at? These days, things are too complicated and moving too fast for anyone to predict anything accurately more than a few years into the future.

That said, I'll try to answer your question for the next five years. I don't think there will be a big change in how music is performed. Musicians still need to play together, and audiences need to listen together. The web is not going to change that, I don't think.

I don't see much change in the way music is created either. Recording music one track at a time is a non-real-time way of approximating a live ensemble performance. That is, the goal of "tracking" is to "sound natural," that is, like you're a group playing together. Furthermore, music recording software is modeled on the multi-track tape recorder, complete with stop, play, record, fast forward, rewind, and pause buttons. So all the latest and greatest technology is now used to produce the illusion of an old-timey musical performance. I don't think that will change very much. Oh sure, the technical details will change. Generalized personal computers are already evolving into configurations that are optimized for musicians. But the way music is created won't change very much within the next five years.

With respect to accessing recorded music, probably the web will become an increasingly bigger part of the picture. ASCAP and BMI can duke it out in Congress. Hey, I remember when the Musician's Union threatened to strike in order to keep the Moog Synthesizer from being used in television commercials. And I've read about the Luddites who, centuries ago, tried to impede progress by destroying mechanical looms. I'm sorry if Tower Records' and Blockbuster's sales plummet. On the other hand, it wasn't that long ago that those megastore chains drove a lot of neighborhood record stores out of business. That's the way it goes these days. Things are moving fast. As the Buddha said, "Everything is changing all the time."

Bob Moog tweaks a VCF, 1968.

An Interview with Klaus Schulze, Father of Ambient Music

In Germany, Klaus Schulze utilized synthesizers and sequencers like Bob Moog's massive modular system to create an entirely new genre of music with his mesmerizing, trance-like soundscapes. Schulze later became known as the father of ambient music, or "picture music" as he called it, which eventually mutated into many new musical forms. The first Tangerine Dream album, *Electronic Meditation,* was released in late 1969, and included Edgar Froese, Conrad Schnitzler, and Klaus Schulze. Schulze left the group in 1970 to form the band Ash Ra Tempel with Manuel Goettsching and Hartmut Enke. During this period, Schulze's work became more trance-like and introspective.

In 1972, Schulze began his solo career with *Irrlicht,* which featured an orchestra playing just one clean continuous note: C. Its successor, the 1973 release *Cyborg,* was uncomplicated compositionally, but more innovative. As a result of these two recordings, a cohesive sense of identity was formed. On later recordings, such as *Picture Music* and *Timewind,* his compositions became more expansive pieces, which slowly evolved from simple drones to dramatic classical tapestries with a deep emotional ambience. Between that time and now, more than 60 album releases of his original compositions have been released.

Unlike many of his electronic music colleagues, Klaus Schulze has always been an advocate of live performance, and has toured throughout Europe frequently. Klaus Schulze's music has inspired generations of new electronic music composers.

The following interview is a candid discourse with a musical pioneer who still remains a leading influence in electronic music. Many thanks to Klaus Schulze's publisher and longtime friend Klaus D. Mueller, for arranging the original interview in the summer of

1987, and for supplying updated information and arranging a follow-up interview in February 2001.

Ben Kettlewell: How did your musical career begin, did your family encourage you to play music?

Klaus Schulze: My family actually hated the idea of me becoming a musician. I did get some help and encouragement from my brother; he played drums a little bit, mostly as a hobby. Actually, I started as a guitarist in 1953 and studied classical music from the age of 7 till I was 15. This kind of education didn't allow me to play rock music, which is what I really wanted to do. So, I switched to drums and played drums for about 10 years, although after I worked with Michael Shrieve, I would never say that I really played drums! What I got from drumming that really helped me when I started using synths and sequencers was the rhythmic feel. I think every musician should play drums for a couple of years to get a true sense of rhythm.

BK: What made you switch from drums to synthesizers?

KS: I wanted to create new music, so I chose an instrument that I had never played before. My first contact with a synthesizer, an EMS Synthi A, was in a little studio in Berlin where Tangerine Dream and Ash Ra Temple and others used to rehearse and learn a bit about technique, under the guidance of the serious composer Thomas Kessler. I still have the EMS here in my studio. The EMS was the first synth manufactured in Europe. With the synthesizer you could change the scales of a keyboard so you wouldn't be locked into the half steps of a standard keyboard. And, you could create sounds from scratch.

BK: Electronic instruments have changed a lot since you first started using them. As a composer, do you think that the advent of digital synthesis, sampling and computer music instruments have affected your musical ideas?

KS: I always try to use the latest technology. This isn't always easy. Everything changes all the time. The instruments change, the people change, the artists change, the fashion changes, the media changes, the listener changes, their views and opinions change... even the sound format changed during my career, from vinyl to digital CD, and from analogue tape to sampling, computer, and hard disk recording. One of my jobs during the '70s was to get rid of people's prejudice, especially when the majority of those people knew nothing about a synthesizer, sequencer, or computer. Of course, my way of producing music changed with the technology, but not my musical ideas.

BK: How do you use the Fairlight and your MIDI setup in performance?

KS: Using computers in live performance gives me a lot of freedom. I can program the background material and blend it in with any one of the 32 channels on my mixing console, so I have a background that can change with every situation. During performance, it is not always possible to change tonalities on the computerized instruments. That is also why I still use analog synths like the Minimoog on stage. Computers are excellent and variable tools; a chip for me is not something sacred, but a commodity. The fear of computers disappears if one works at it and works with affection.

Klaus Schultze in performance.

Photo courtesy Klaus Schultze Productions

BK: How do you compose your songs? Tell us how you develop an idea.

KS: I do not write a composition. It's in my head and during work it all comes together. Sometimes it happens in a night, and other times it takes a few weeks, even months. In the early days I mostly improvised. Little by little I learned to form my music. I do not write on pieces of paper; I play it on tape, and play it in my head.

Because I play music most of the time, I have many tapes full of musical ideas.

BK: Did you compose the music for the film *Angst* in this way?

KS: Yes. The film people cut their film to the finished music. Normally, it's vice versa.

BK: A lot of people consider your compositions as classical. You have even received an award in Paris for this. Do you consider yourself a classical composer?

KS: The Beatles are classical too. My part in the contemporary music scene is ambiguous. My records are sold on the pop market; they have to compete on the pop record shelves. But if one listens to them, they are definitely not pop music. Neither are they classical music in the sense of a Mozart or Beethoven, or a Henze or Penderecki, Actually this labeling is not my problem, but I have to deal with it. These days (1987) marketing people label this type of music, "new age" music, but I haven't met any musician who is happy with this label.

P.S. Anno 2000: Meanwhile the same people (artists, fans, companies, journalists) call the same music "trance/ambient/techno."

BK: Do you find that listeners are more sophisticated about electronic music today than they were during recent decades, and if so, what does that mean for you as a composer?

KS: Oh yes, certainly yes. But only those who always had an interest in this kind of music, and of course, musicians today know a lot more about electronic instruments than when I started. Today it is very easy and affordable to go into a store and buy a synthesizer, effects, and a cheap 4 or 8 track-recording device and make a good recording. For me all this means that I have to be better, more sophisticated. Some people today immediately hear if I use an old instrument on a new album. Fans are strange sometimes. On one hand they demand "new music," and on the other they prefer the "old Schulze."

BK: In the 18th and 19th centuries, composers spent a lot of their time working with notes, but today electronic musicians have to create the sounds as well. How much time do you spend developing sounds as opposed to getting the notes arranged the way you want them?

KS: In the days when composers had no tape recorders or MIDI sequencers, the distribution of music was quite different. To get your music played, you had to physically write down music and get it printed. Today we put a sound on a tape or disk and there it is, ready for manufacture. I have been composing electronic music now for many years, I know exactly what sound fits here or there, and how to create it.

BK: Are there any specific considerations when you are composing a part for a certain instrument?

KS: I generally do not compose a part for a specific instrument. I have a sound idea, or a theme or melody in my head, and I play it. I have my own style and this limits me a bit, if limit is the right word, because I'm happy with it. My fans would be disappointed if I suddenly would do, for example, a blues or a "normal" piece of music with a song structure, a piece of pop music.

BK: Did learning on modular instruments have a lasting impact on your work?

KS: Oh, sure. That is my greatest advantage. With modular instruments one had to learn the logic of a tone, of a sound, how it's built and what it means. It's a lot easier for a newcomer today, but how will that person know what goes into the sound the keyboard is making? These old modular analog synths are very important. Handwork!

BK: When a new instrument comes out, how do you go about investigating it? What do you look for in deciding whether or not to use it?

KS: There are always people trying to convince me to try or buy a new instrument. Sometimes I try it, and sometimes I buy it. The main feature I look for is the ability to produce my own sounds. I have no interest in preset instruments. In my career I've seen musical waves come and go. A musical fashion is short, and I'm lucky that I have never made fashionable music. I will go on.

The following is an interview that took place on May 1, 2000. Thanks once again to Klaus D. Mueller for his assistance.

BK: Since our last interview, music technology has grown at a rapid pace. How have these technological changes influenced your music?

KS: Yes of course. It's a platitude: Everything changes all the time. And of course, all this is of some influence to me, as it is to all people, music makers and music listeners. Just take for instance, that people get older and during all these years they learn a few things about music (if they are interested and open-minded). Of course, they listen to music differently when they are 50 as when they were 20 years old. (This is just one example of changes.) The influences are multiple and mutual, and quite normal.

BK: How do you view the current electronica/ambient/techno music scene, and what direction do you think the music will go in during the next ten years?

KS: Today, there is no extra branch anymore called "electronic music." Most of today's music is done electronically. Especially the more "cheap" music, but also plenty of good and interesting modern pop and dance music. Ninety-five percent of today's music is done the electronic way with samplers and computers. Music goes on. It develops, changes, old sounds and rhythms come back, vanish and come back again. A few new things or long forgotten things are added. The various fashions and the promotion by the people and companies who live from it do their part. Every few years a new generation of musicians and customers is ready to join that game. Of course, they want their very own music, different from the older people's music. This goes constantly on and on...

I have created my own music since 1972. I found my own unique style very early. Since then I've seen many musical fashions and trends coming and going. I still play "the same." Of course, I notice all the many new trends. Some I like and some I don't. And partly I consider them, but only if I like them and it fits to my own musical world. I like some of the Techno stuff, because I played this pure electronic rhythmic music for many years anyway. So I didn't have to change a lot. All I had to do was to put a bit more bass onto my music, put my rhythm a bit more in the foreground. I was a rock drummer in my early years. Since 1974 I use rhythm, drums, and sequencers in my concerts and on my albums. I remember when I used for the first time very heavy digital computer rhythms on my album *Dig It* in 1980: the hard-core Schulze fans went furious. A few years later it was accepted, and all second and third generation electronic musicians used it too. When "Techno" was new, most "electronic" fans hated it (again). Now, a few years later, solo rhythm computers and pure rhythm are the thing! Even the old-fashioned copycats try to add some modern sounding "techno" now, 10 years later.

An artist is often seen as a prophet, but I can tell you: He is in no way a prophet. I have no idea what the future will bring. It will go on, of course, and I think that for a long time the synthetic sounds and the computers will be used. Until something else will be invented or the public's taste changes drastically. Maybe the public will prefer again crooners like Bing Crosby or Sinatra? Or there will be a stark fondness for "a capella" groups? Or for strings? Or for lousy amateurs? Or belcanto? Or something that we don't know yet or just cannot imagine? If I only knew, I would be the richest person in the world.

BK: Tell me about your new studio setup, and its advantages/ disadvantages over the old one(s).

KS: The setup is given in detail in the website (**www.klaus-schulze .com**) for those interested in checking it out. The "advantages" are the normal ones: It's easier to handle, it's better in sound. After each "new" setup, the variety is larger, wider. This was so in every addition or change of equipment, be it in 1973, in 1975, in 1979, '89, and so on... A change gives also some fun. I don't believe that the public is really interested in the advantages of one of my software programs from version 4.0 to 4.1 and if they would understand a word of what I'm talking about, because this is too special (and boring) for the general public. Although it is part of my daily work, it's really the product that counts. The consumer's only concern should be what he hears and how he reacts to what he hears. No one is really interested in the stagehands used backstage at a theater play production, or the number of revisions of a book before it's in the readers' hands. I just saw in a CD catalogue a not so old CD by Stockhausen. His composition and recording and even part of the title are "...for 4 sound engineers, loudspeaker towers, and mixing desk." I wonder every time anew, how far behind the times those "modern" serious composers are. As everyone knows, the use of sound engineers, loudspeakers and mixing desks was a normality in rock music already thirty years ago, and is not really worth mentioning since today even amateurs have their virtual "mixing desk" on a monitor. It's funny that the name "Stockhausen" is regarded as a trendsetter. It is always used when it comes to "modern" music, at least by those with no knowledge and interest in real contemporary, modern music, be it Elvis in 1954, the Beatles in the 1960s, or Madonna and Prince in the 1990s. Maybe in the year 2013 those "serious" people (composers and journalists) will also discover the advent of the "sequencer," 40 years after Tangerine Dream used it for the first time.

BK: It seems that more and more, the future of getting a composer's music out there is through the emerging music formats such as MP3 and working with the web. What are your views on this?

KS: The Internet is in fashion with all the exaggerations and fears of each technical invention. There are modern movies that show in a scene: a website on a monitor, and the www address is given as xyz@abc.com. In other words, many people speak about this new media without knowing too much about it. For them it's, of course, a miracle and a cornucopia. But it's just another media. And 95 percent of the people just use it as they use the telephone: for trifle things like looking at pictures of naked girls, or writing the same nonsense they put on a postcard. We still get e-mails from people who ask us where to buy *Timewind*, regardless of the WWW's possibilities to find out very easily. Many just use it as a quicker way to send a postcard.

BK: In terms of the music industry's fear of MP3 and its eventual better-sounding descendents, you're competing with the record store, the distributor, with the large chains etc. How do you think will this impact the industry as a whole?

KS: At the moment the download of a full CD in best CD quality is more expensive (because of telephone costs) than to buy it in a shop. But download will be faster, in the future. Yes, people have to think about the changes, what it does mean for all people involved. Luckily, an LP or a CD was probably closely bound up with personal memories and still is something people want to have in its "original" form, not just virtually. No one collects Pat Boone, but they do collect John Lee Hooker, and no one collects music on his hard disk but as a nice looking product in his living room's shelves. The music business is a many billion-dollar business. Of course all involved parties want to get rich quick by the new technology. At the moment these "parties" are mainly servers who offer "free" downloads (and make money with the advertising on their sites). They don't care about other people's ownership and that music has to be produced and marketed, which costs the producer a lot of money: Money, that those people have to pay who want to have and listen to the music. At the moment we have a discussion about who gets how much of the money, because we have a new situation; people who had no access to the music business yet, ask for a share. Of course ALL want to 'make the fast buck' with the help of the new technology. Many see the new technology as a bonanza. For them it's not the art of music, it's just money. And those people will never accept the rights of a composer, a writer, and the many musicians; except if we—the creators of music—force them. It's capitalism and a fight for money.

BK: Already many existing radio stations have web radio, and this has become a big area of contention now with the passing of the Digital Millennium Act in Congress in 1999. All of the performance rights organizations and the recording organizations, like ASCAP, BMI, RIAA are all saying, gee, there's all this music being put out here, which is essentially being put out without any royalties being paid. There's a lot of piracy going on. And there's a big scramble to figure out what to do about that. Many stations have taken a wait-and-see attitude. What are your opinions on this subject?

KS: I wonder who's listening to the radio via a computer monitor, or reading a book from the monitor? I believe it's just a contemporary novelty. It was done because it could be done. I also wonder what's the use of it? Radios are in every household, and everyone can choose among 20 to 50 different stations, depending on his taste. And if one from New England wants to listen under any circumstances to a Malaysian radio station, there are easier ways: for many years there are also radios available who can fulfill such exotic desire. Many people only listen to radio in the car, anyway. I think that "web radio" is done just because it was possible to do. All too often, technicians are like that. But who needs it? Who was missing it when it did not exist? Mankind is doing many silly things, and I believe this is one of them, but at least it's a harmless one.

SOLO WORKS

Irrlicht (1972)

Cyborg (1973) 2CD set

Picture Music (1973)

Blackdance (1974)

Timewind (1975)

Moondawn (1976)

Body Love (1976), soundtrack

Mirage (1977)

Body Love Vol.2 (1977)

"X" (1978) 2CD set

Dune (1979)

"...Live..." (1980) 2CD set, live

Dig It (1980)

Trancefer (1981)

Audentity (1983) 2CD set

Angst (1984), soundtrack

Inter*Face (1985)

Dreams (1986)

En=Trance (1988)

Miditerranean Pads (1990)

The Dresden Performance (1990) 2CD set, live

Beyond Recall (1991)

Royal Festival Hall Vol. 1 (1992), live

Royal Festival Hall Vol. 2 (1992), live

The Dome Event (1993), live

Silver Edition (1993) 10CD set, limited edition, 2000 copies

Le Moulin de Daudet (1994), soundtrack

Goes Classic (1994)

Totentag (1994) 2CD set, opera

Das Wagner Desaster-Live (1994) 2CD set, live

In Blue (1995) 2CD set

Historic Edition (1995) 10CD set, limited edition, 2000 copies

Are You Sequenced? (1996)

Dosburg Online (1997)

Jubilee Edition (1997) 25CD set, limited edition, 1000 copies

Trailer (1999)

The Ultimate Edition (2000) 50 CD set

Contemporary Works (2000) 10CD set

Live at KlangArt Vol.1 (2001)

Live at KlangArt Vol.2 (2001)

With Tangerine Dream
Electronic Meditation (1970)

With Ash Ra Tempel
Ash Ra Tempel (1971)
Join Inn (1973)

As Richard Wahnfried
Time Actor (1979) with Arthur Brown and Michael Shrieve
Tonwelle (1981) with Manuel Goettsching
Megatone (1984)
Miditation (1986) with flutist Steve Jolliffe

As Wahnfried
Trancelation (1994)
Trance Appeal (1996)
Drums 'n' Balls (1997)

With others
Dziekuje Poland Live '83 (1983) 2LP with Rainer Bloss, live
Drive Inn (1984) with Rainer Bloss
Babel (1987) with Andreas Grosser

...and many more, either as guest musician, or as producer, recording engineer, label owner, doing the mix or a re-mix. A "Tribute to Klaus Schulze" album was also released (1998); it even includes a KS track under a thinly hidden pseudonym.

CHAPTER 5

The Berlin Sound: An Interview with Christopher Franke of Tangerine Dream

The first extensive creative surge of music incorporating electronic instrument technology happened in Europe. To this day, some of the most enduring names associated with synth based music are European composers/performers. The Germans were, without a doubt, the most prolific and insightful in the way they approached this new medium in the early 1970s.

Christopher Franke

Photo courtesy Christopher Franke

One name that immediately comes to mind is Christopher Franke. Born in Berlin, Germany on April 6, 1953, Christopher Franke studied classical music and composition at the Berlin Conservatory. During this time in his early career, he was most influenced by avant-garde composers such as John Cage and Karl-Heinz Stockhausen. Christopher Franke was actively involved in shaping a hybrid of rock and jazz as a drummer with the group Agitation Free, one of the pioneering bands of progressive rock and fusion. Along with his teacher, Swiss avant-garde composer Thomas Kessler, Christopher set up an impressive sound studio, which soon became a haven for young musicians dedicated to experimental music.

At this studio on Berlin's Pfalzburger Strasse, Christopher met Edgar Froese and Conrad Schnitzler of Tangerine Dream. He soon joined this seminal group to perform on their recording *Zeit* in 1972. Conrad Schnitzler quit the group a few months later and Christopher invited Peter Baumann to join the group. In the fall of 1970, Franke converted a 1930's ballroom and cinema into one of the most atmospheric recording studios in Berlin. His studio became the scene of many Tangerine Dream album and soundtrack recording sessions. Between 1970 and 1988 Tangerine Dream released 36 studio, live, and soundtrack albums, seven of which became gold records. They composed the music for more than 30 American feature films, including *Firestarter*, *Legend*, and *Risky Business*.

Christopher Franke was a pioneer of modern electronic music and was one of the first Europeans to use commercially available synthesizers. Through innovative use of sequencers as percussion instruments and tone generators, live concerts became revolutionary events. Tangerine Dream's world tours brought them to the U.S., Japan, Australia, and much of Eastern and Western Europe.

In 1988, Christopher Franke left Tangerine Dream after 18 years of intense recording and touring schedules. He felt burned out. He spent time in Spain recuperating and developing his own musical ideas. An abundance of composing work in Hollywood's growing film and television industry brought Christopher to Los Angeles in 1990 where he settled and opened a second studio in the Hollywood Hills. The following year he formed the Berlin Symphonic Film Orchestra, and released his debut solo album *Pacific Coast Highway*. In 1993 Christopher founded his own label, Sonic Images, and released several collections of his music for the syndicated sci-fi series *Babylon 5* as well as his ongoing solo projects.

The following is an interview with Christopher Franke that was conducted in March 2001:

Ben Kettlewell: I'm going to start out with the most repetitive question, but I'm sure your audience will still be curious to know. When did you first become interested in music?

Christopher Franke: I cannot rule out that musical inspiration started during my embryonic stage (chuckling). Musical consciousness and left brain activity probably awakened at the age of three, when I heard my mother teaching young students violin technique, my interest then was mainly to shut off the torturing music. But the classical string quartet music, which floated throughout the house at night, certainly stimulated my musical juices.

BK: You studied classical music and composition at the Berlin Conservatory. How did this impact your early career?

CF: It made me realize how important a good technical foundation would become, and also the paramount fact, that you must learn the rules, only to break them later. I probably started out as a rebel, but today I'm quite grateful for having had this experience, and I utilize it every day when I mix electronic classical and world music styles.

BK: Did composers like John Cage and Karl-Heinz Stockhausen have any impact upon your interest in electronic instruments?

CF: There are, of course, the Gods and Forefathers of 20th Century techniques, who paved the way very early on. To listen to their early compositions was an epiphany for me, which had a profound impact.

BK: You and Klaus Schulze both began your professional careers as drummers in progressive rock bands. What was the impetus, or the turning point between being a drummer in a progressive rock band (Agitation Free), to becoming a pioneer in creating music electronically?

CF: I started out as a multi-instrumentalist with a good dose of curiosity in music and "acoustic projections," which are new and unexplored. I was prepared to study whatever instruments were required, in order to get closer to the sounds in my dreams. The impetus was the projected vast number of different sound creations that an electronic music workstation was capable of generating. This became "louder" than life, considering the primitive and humble beginnings of synthesizers.

BK: You are one of the "founders" of what fans of electronic music call "The Berlin School." How did this term originate? What are its implications?

CF: Berlin had a larger number of musicians who used synthesizers and sequencers in a TD-ish style, than any other city in the Northern Milky Way. "School" is a noble term for describing a cluster of events.

BK: You were a member of the seminal group, Tangerine Dream, for almost two decades. It must have been difficult touring with such delicate analog equipment in the early 1970s as well as keeping all those oscillators in tune during a performance. What was a live concert in the mid-1970s like?

CF: It was Hell on Earth, but we were addicts and I was searching for the karmic constellation, which created this punishment.

BK: How did you migrate from touring and recording with TD to a career of film scoring, television soundtracks and a solo career in recording?

CF: After trying so many musical platforms I had to focus on one or two only, so I could further develop my musical skills. Film scoring seemed to me to be the ideal scenario in which the demand of musical experimentation and a positive cash flow is in harmonic balance. I was determined to find interesting projects, which still left enough room to be a recording artist. I don't rule out the possibility of special event concerts in the not-too-distant future. The "one-thing-at-a-time" method has worked well for me so far.

BK: After you left TD in 1988, you spent quite a bit of time in Spain before moving to the United States. How did you like Spain? What did you do while you were there?

CF: Spain is like a European California: Nice climate with lots of inspirations. Just the scenery I needed to plan my next big move. In Spain I composed music for the only reason of pleasure and personal growth, which revitalized my instincts.

BK: 1990 seemed to be a pivotal year for you. You moved to Los Angeles, and setup a studio in the Hollywood Hills, released one of your most critically acclaimed albums of all time, *Pacific Coast Highway,* and then went back to Berlin to give birth to the Berlin Symphonic Film Orchestra. Where did you get all the energy? What brought about these great achievements in your career?

CF: As I mentioned, I recharged my batteries between the years 1988 and 1990 on the beautiful West Coast of Spain. I read quite a few books about alternative medicine and how to stay fit both physically and mentally. Inevitably, I became, once again, very hungry and motivated to be productive in my artistic expression.

BK: In 1993 you launched your own label, Sonic Images. Can you tell me about your vision behind creation of the label?

CF: The driving force in the '90s was "independence." Modern technology enables even a cottage industry to use almost the same infrastructure as major record labels in terms of promotions, marketing, and most importantly, artists and repertoire. The majors already had a bad rap, thinking too commercially and trying to give the fans what they want, rather than what they need. So I took quite a risk to form my independent outlet, first with my own albums, then specializing in soundtracks, which was easy enough by just being in Hollywood, then branching out with other artists in the styles of world and electronica.

BK: Your music in its own way rivaled Jan Hammer and his weekly *Miami Vice* soundtracks and their popularity with your soundtracks for the hugely successful syndicated sci-fi series *Babylon 5*. Was it difficult to come up with that amount of high-caliber music each week and have it in the studio on time for the next show?

CF: At first it was a tremendous challenge, but I had the energy to work long hours and, again, technology helped a great deal to produce and record music much faster utilizing a tapeless studio and a large amount of sound modules. The vibrant Californian atmosphere also supported my strength, enabling me to make weekly delivery deadlines.

BK: What are your current projects?

CF: I'm working on an electronica/trip-hop/trance solo album, and the sequel to *The Celestine Prophecy* with world and classical influences. On the scoring side I'm finishing a remake of the Agatha Christie classic *Murder on the Orient Express* and then I'll start with a movie based on an Arthur C. Clarke novel.

BK: What do you think about the evolution of electronic music over the past 30 years?

CF: It never ceases to amaze me how big and global it has become considering that I still remember pretty well when it was hard-core esoteric with only a handful of players in the know. Now it is here to stay so I'm fully expecting you to write a new book on the subject every other year.

BK: What do you consider to be the most significant changes in music, and music technology since that time?

CF: The MTV generation is engulfed by an ever-growing media power, which is quickly exhausting its listeners and they are looking elsewhere. Every trend creates an anti-trend and that's where the music landscape becomes really interesting. Lots of independent activities create a healthier balance between boring commercial and meaningful productions. Music technology became affordable to everyone, which can be seen both as a good and a bad thing. It is definitely a liberation for the masses.

BK: How do you feel the new technologies are going to alter the way music is created, performed and accessed in the twenty-first century?

CF: The most powerful, influential new technology will be artificial intelligence. Its beauty lies in the fact that it will, again, profoundly change the rules of creation and performance of music and it is mysteriously hard to interpolate how exactly this will take effect. I expect that the degree of spontaneity and complexity will transcend to heights never before seen.

Christopher Franke, 1970s.

Photo courtesy Christopher Franke

CHAPTER 6

The Story of Don Buchla: Suzanne Ciani on the Buchla Modular System

If we look at the timetable of events in electronic music history, especially those of the 1960s, we see a type of simultaneous discovery; people isolated from each other in different parts of the world developing the same ideas and technologies along parallel lines, independent of each other. This phenomenon is certainly true of Bob Moog on the East Coast of the United States and Don Buchla on the West Coast. Of all the instrument designers of the sixties, Buchla's approach to instrument design was most different from Moog's.

Robert Moog and his associates analyzed musical events and created an instrument well suited to their production values. Buchla constructed his electronic components with no prior expectations of the end result. The Buchla, unlike Moog's designs, had no keyboard at all. Don Buchla believed that piano-style keyboards had no business being interfaced to synthesizers. Buchla used potentiometer-controlled, voltage-input and output modules that could be combined in any series to produce intricate sounds. Buchla began building and designing electronic instruments in 1960 when avant-garde composer Morton Subotnik, a member of the famous San Francisco Tape Music Center collective, commissioned him to build an instrument for composition and performance. With a grant from the Rockefeller Foundation, Buchla developed his first modular synthesizer, the 100 series Modular Electronic Music System, built in 1963.

This was a large instrument, utilizing control features such as touch sensitive and resistance sensitive plates. It operated on special modules designed to generate signals, or process particular classes of signals. Up to 25 modules could share a single power supply, to form a super-module.

There were three types of signals used in his innovative instrument:

1. *Audio signals, or sine, square, sawtooth or harmonic waves, were produced internally by a generator or externally by using tape loops, microphones or other external sound sources. These signals were then processed by being filtered, gated, mixed, or modulated at the standard level of 0 decibels, or 600 Ohms.*

2. *Control Voltages determine the parameters of frequency, envelope characteristics, and amplitude. They are generated by keyboards, programmable voltage sources, and envelope generators at the standard voltage range of 0 to 15 volts.*

3. *Timing pulses are used to trigger notes, open gates, or initiate chains of musical events. These pulses originate from keyboards, programmable sequencers, and pulse generators.*

Several inputs could be connected to a single output on this instrument. Timing pulses could be paralleled and connected to any input. The system output could come from any module and was powerful enough to drive line inputs on tape recorders or power amplifiers.

In 1970, Buchla created the 200 series Electronic Music Box, which could be configured for a variety of applications, from electronic music composition and performance, to psychoacoustic study, to special effects generation, to bio-feedback research and video synthesis. The hybrid 500 series, a digitally controlled analog synthesizer, was introduced in 1971.

These instruments could be expanded to create hybrid digital-analog systems incorporating editing and performance capabilities, programmable patching, and multiple arbitrary function generation.

Buchla's sound generators were capable of producing many types of waveforms. Sound modifiers were implemented for changing the "shape" and texture of notes.

Buchla also developed sequencers for performing a predetermined number of pulses. The pulses generated by the sequencer created different pitches and intervals, or different rhythms, depending on how the sequencer was programmed. The repeating sequences of pulses could be pre-set, and a "random voltage generator" was used to produce unpredictable pulses of different voltages. This was one of Buchla's main contributions to the field of analog synthesis.

Buchla worked closely with composer Morton Subotnick in developing his synthesizer. Buchla's idea was to build a voltage-controlled modular system that generated a number of waveforms, which included sine and square waves, and later many other variations. His concept was to include the idea of a sequencer, an analog automation device that allowed a composer to set and store a sequence of notes and play it back automatically with a synthesizer. As most inventors construct a device to do away with a tedious and time consuming function; Buchla's sequencer eliminated the need to manually splice magnetic tapes to construct a sequence of sounds.

Five-time Grammy nominee Suzanne Ciani (pronounced chah-ni) spent a number of years working with Don Buchla, building and developing new models of Buchla synthesizers and modules.

This "Diva of the Diode," as her associates affectionately call her, taught herself how to play piano, and was inspired by Bach and the composers of the Romantic era. She received her classical music training at Wellesley College in Massachusetts. After graduating from Wellesley College in 1968, she earned her Master's in Music Composition from U.C. Berkeley.

As a graduate student in Music Composition, Suzanne began working with the pioneers of electronic music. She had her roots in both digital and analog synthesis from the beginning. She studied at Stanford with Max Matthews, the father of computer music, and John Chowning, the father of FM synthesis. But what most changed her life was meeting one of the earliest designers of analog music instruments, Don Buchla, whose apprentice she became, working on the assembly line at his Oakland shipyard loft. She was to devote the next ten years of her life to exploring the possibilities of this unique instrument, the Buchla, and her mastery of it would launch her career. She says, "His designs for instruments were extraordinary. He brought the thought process of designing musical instruments right down to the origin of physical human nature and music. There is nobody like him."

Suzanne Ciani is a composer and recording artist who has released 11 instrumental recordings. After a long tenure with Private Music / BMG, Suzanne launched her own independent label, Seventh

Wave. Her New York-based commercial music production company, Ciani Musica Inc., was top in the field of sound-design and TV spot scoring, and produced award-winning work for a long list of Fortune 500 companies, among them Lincoln/Mercury, American Express, General Electric, Atari, General Motors, Columbia Pictures, and Coca-Cola. One of the most popular sound effects of this period was her creation of the sound of a Coca-Cola bottle popping open and the drink being poured, a simulation she created with her Buchla, not to mention her participation in designs for AT&T telephone company sounds.

Suzanne Ciani in her studio, mid-1980s.

Photo courtesy Suzanne Ciani

Suzanne has also done a great deal of television scoring, including the creation of a new library for the ABC Television Series *One Life to Live*. Film scores include the Lily Tomlin vehicle *The Incredible Shrinking Woman*, and the Petrie sisters' movie *Mother Teresa*, among others. Suzanne has garnered numerous distinctions, including five Grammy nominations and a *Keyboard* New Age Keyboardist of the Year award for her work as a recording artist. Her music, renowned for its romantic, healing and aesthetic qualities, has found a large audience all over the world, and her performances include numerous benefits for humanitarian causes.

The following text is from two interviews: one took place during the summer of 1987, the other was conducted in March 2000.

Ben Kettlewell: Suzanne, can you tell us about your experiences working with Don Buchla?

Suzanne Ciani: I was hoping to learn enough about the design of the instrument so that I could build one myself. The first thing I remember about the job was that I was fired the first day I began work there. I had gone down to the office to be interviewed for a job soldering for three dollars an hour. At the end of the first day, Don discovered a cold soldering joint in one of the pieces of equipment, and decided that I must be the one who did it. I refused to take that for an answer, and refused to be fired.

Ciani sets up a patch on the Buchla Modular System

We were all perfectionists. We all worked very carefully at a very long table. No talking was allowed. KPFA Radio was always on in the background, and we soldered and hand assembled the instruments there. The best part about it for me was getting to use the equipment, the very elaborate system that Don had there for himself. It was an entire room filled with a mountain of modules, and some which weren't even available outside of his studio. He was very involved in performance himself, so the systems were really designed for him. And I worked out there many, many a night; many hours spent discovering that system of his. It was wonderful.

BK: What features make the Buchla stand out from the others?

SC: The Buchla is not used as much nowadays primarily because of interfacing problems, and its non-MIDI status, but the system I have is a Buchla 200 series, and it still has functions that aren't duplicated at all in current equipment. For instance, the "white noise" is particularly wonderful. There are three types of white noise, and there is so much control over the shaping of that. It is what I used for "waves" sounds on my first album, *Seven Waves*. The envelope generators, for instance, give one the opportunity to very quickly shape the envelope of the sound. The voltage controls envelopes, so by varying voltage, one can quickly shrink and expand the entire envelope.

Another feature which I found very useful, is that one can scale envelopes, or have one envelope on top of another, for instance the effect Vangelis used a lot in his soundtracks and albums, that "ch ch ch ch" (as in chair) airy rhythmic texture. That's very hard to do with a single envelope, but with two envelopes, you simply set up one with a short shape, and then a longer one above that to produce that cascading sound. These are things that I could see usefully incorporated into current equipment, but unfortunately, you don't see much of that.

Another really useful thing is the random voltage generator. This is a voltage generator where you cannot only specify random voltage, but a rate of the random voltage, and a range for the random voltage, and then there's the frequency modulation of the filter. This comes in very handy, especially for fizzy sounds for soft drinks, etc. There is a wonderful module called the Multiple Arbitrary Function generator, or MARF, which is like a three dimensional sequencer, where one can actually sequence sequences, or "tracks" of events in any order. Rather than describe it in detail, I will just say it's wonderful. In fact, I wrote a paper about this unit under the auspices of a National Endowment for the Arts grant. Another feature that always interested Don was the control of spatial parameters, applying voltage control to the reverb, amplitude, and Doppler aspects of a sound in a quadraphonic spatial environment. This is something that became a lot more useful as stereo television developed, and the movement in time and space became more critical. But the most amazing aspect of the Buchla system was its almost human character. Every change in voltage or triggering of an event was accompanied by a correlating red light. These myriad lights gave constant feedback of exactly what was going on in this complex system and seemed to communicate intelligently. One could set up self-generating textures that would vary constantly, randomly, musically, and these could go on for weeks at a time. It was a machine of the highest order, a companion, a partner, a friend, and a lover.

IN CONCLUSION:

Suzanne's company, Seventh Wave, is a dream come true: an artist-owned and run label that combines Ciani's musical sensitivity with her sensibilities as a Madison Avenue advertising guru. Ciani launched her artistic career from Ciani Musica Studios in the early eighties, where she was enjoying unprecedented success as New York's number one advertising sound designer. This expertise gained her notoriety not just in commercials, but also in games, television, and film. However, Ciani's dreams of living solely for her art required that she break away from New York and, ultimately, from her major label relationship with Private Music/BMG. She now lives quietly in an oceanside cabin in Northern California, presiding over her own label, concentrating on her artistic work.

CHAPTER 7

The Mysteries of the Serge Modular System

Don Buchla's efforts in synthesizer design received a great deal of attention from Serge Tcherepnin (pronounced "Cher-epp-nin"), a multitalented composer and electronic designer born in 1941 at Issy-les-Moulineaux in France. He was the son of famous Russian composer Alexander Tcherepnin (1899-1977), who was an explorer, an experimenter, and a prolific and much performed composer who left four operas, thirteen ballets, four symphonies, numerous large orchestral and chamber works, and over 200 piano pieces. Serge's parents encouraged him to study music. Serge began violin instruction, and music theory at an early age and studied harmony with conductor, Nadia Boulanger, one of the most influential conductors of the twentieth century, during his high school years. Serge came to the United States to Harvard in 1958. Two well-known composers at that time, Billy-Jim Layton and Pulitzer Prize winning composer Leon Kirchner, had a great impact on his approach to composition.

Four years later, in 1962, he spent the summer in Germany at the Darmstadt Ferienkurse fur neue Musik, which fueled his interest in improvisation. His keen interest in improvisation inspired him to compose *Kaddish* for narrator and small ensemble, based on a text by Allen Ginsberg (1962) and *Figures-Grounds* for instruments (1964). Serge taught himself the art of electronic design and circuit building, and enjoyed constructing "junk electronic" components, as he loved to call them. He constructed tape compositions based upon the recording of various electronic devices constructed from old transistor radios and other electronic components.

On completion of his studies in music and physics at Harvard, Serge received a generous grant from the German government and went back to Germany for supplementary studies with Pierre Boulez, Karlheinz Stockhausen, and Herbert Eimert.

Two years later, in 1966, Serge was commissioned by the Studio di Fonologia in Milan to compose an electronic music score. From that point, until the summer of 1968, Tcherepnin was occupied in creating experimental works at the Studio fur Electronische Musik of the Koumlln Musikhochschule in Germany. Tcherepnin was employed at the BBC Radiophonic Workshop in London during the summer of 1968, helping his father, Alexander Tcherepnin, in the production of an electronic sound-effects tape for the BBC production of his father's opera *Ivan the Fool* produced by Douglas Cleverdon.

Serge continued to work with electronic circuit technology and began to design devices specifically suited for live electronic music performance. He moved to San Francisco in 1970 where he attended Cal-Arts. While there, Serge discovered that the college had several studios with Buchla modular systems installed in them. The Buchlas were very expensive instruments, and the school kept the studios locked at all times. Getting studio time in a Buchla-equipped studio at Cal Arts was a privilege available to a select few (staff members and a select number of students). While the Buchla, ARP, and Moog synthesizers were fascinating and impressed most faculty members, Serge strongly believed the designs could be improved in many ways. Two of the biggest disadvantages were price and size. They were unaffordable to most people and could easily occupy an entire wall. Serge got together with two other students and brainstormed. It was after several of these sessions that Serge Tcherepnin, Randy Cohen, and Rich Gold decided to build their own synthesizer modules.

Serge's kitchen became the "factory" for the fist modules created by the newly formed partnership. They had a great deal of success in achieving their goals, and in a short time, other faculty members and students heard about the instruments, and offered space at Cal Arts for Serge's workshop. The word was out that these guys were building some amazing synths, and they soon had clients banging on the door, willing to give them $700 -800 in advance for a custom designed six-panel synthesizer. This was not 7-800 for a synthesizer, ...this was 7-800 just for parts. A standard panel, or module filled a 4-space rack and systems varied in size from a single panel to an entire wall. Each module configuration had to be planned in advance as modules were not interchangeable, as with Moog's designs. Serge used banana jacks for inter-connecting modules instead of 1/4" plugs, which offered additional flexibility in the system. Serge and his two partners would instruct the buyers on how to build their modules by supplying complete schematics and in-house tutoring.

Morton Subotnick, already an established composer in this new medium, was a professor at Cal Arts during this time and very active with the San Francisco Tape Music Center. As mentioned earlier in the book, Morton Subotnick had already known Serge's mentor, Don Buchla, since the early 1960s. Serge was well aware of the impact that Subotnick had made on Buchla's early designs, and set out to entice Subotnick to try out his modules. Eventually Subotnick fell under the spell of Serge's unique components, and produced a number of works with the Serge Modular system.

By the early to mid-1980s, digital synthesizers such as Sequential Circuits Prophet 5, Yamaha's DX7, and Korg's Poly 61 and new technologies like MIDI were taking the music world by storm, and interest in analog systems hit an all-time low. Serge felt this depression, and in order to support his family, he became involved in doing freelance consulting for various electronics firms. In 1992, after a great deal of frustration, Serge sold his circuitry designs to an old friend, Rex Probe, and shortly after, his family returned to France. Serge modular systems are still produced today by the company Rex Probe began with Serge's designs, Sound Transform Systems.

CHAPTER 8

Michael Stearns on the Vast Capabilities of Modular Synthesis

Michael Stearns is one of the originators of a new genre of music that emerged in the 1970s. His music has been described as space music, contemporary instrumental music, ambient music, world music, new age music, and simply electronic music. Michael uses synthesizers and samplers in conjunction with instruments and sounds from other cultures, newly developed instruments, the human voice, and the sounds of nature. His works include music for television, theme parks, 17 IMAX films, and 17 solo albums.

Michael Stearns with his Serge Modular System.

Photo courtesy Michael Stearns

Previous credits include music for Disney Films, HBO, ABC's *The World of Explorers, 20/20, Ripley's Believe It or Not,* and Ron Fricke's non-verbal masterpieces *Chronos, Sacred Site,* and *Baraka.*

Michael began playing classical guitar in the early 1960s. He performed in bands playing rock and jazz, and at the age of 16 played concerts before audiences of over 7,000 people, backing up artists such as the Lovin' Spoonful and Paul Revere and the Raiders. In 1968, he created and performed his first electronic, Musique Concrete piece while studying at the University of the Pacific. He spent the next four years studying electronic music synthesis, the physics of musical instruments, and accumulating equipment for his first studio in Tucson, Arizona, which he opened in 1972.

In 1984 Stearns founded M'Ocean, a recording studio in Santa Monica, CA, especially equipped for surround sound and electronic music. In 1992, Michael moved to Santa Fe, New Mexico where he now works in his multi-channel surround sound facility, Earth Turtle.

Michael is a master of programming modular synthesizers. In the following interview he discusses the Serge Modular System, invented by Serge Terrapin, undoubtedly the most complex analog synthesizer ever invented.

Ben Kettlewell: When did you first become interested in synthesizers?

Michael Stearns: A good friend, Kevin Braheny, turned me onto the Serge Modular system. Kevin and I were working at the Continuum Studio in Los Angeles, and he had just finished building his twelve-panel Serge Modular system. This was about 1977. Kevin became my guide into the mysteries of the Serge. He is an amazing composer. I was able to use his Serge system and pick his brains for two years before purchasing one of my own. Access to Kevin's system was very important and helpful. The Serge is very complex and it's also a very personal synthesizer. Because of its modular nature, one must specify which modules and in which order the modules on a panel are built. Each panel can have any combination of oscillators, noise generators, filters, and equalizers, components that modify, mix, and distribute the sound, and controllers, which feed voltages and create feedback loops within the instrument. From four to eight separate modules will fit onto a single panel. The way a musician thinks about music, synthesis, and patching must be built into the flow of modules and panels. By using Kevin's instrument for several years, I really got into how my thought processes, as far as synthesis and patching went, were different from Kevin's. This gave me the opportunity to formulate how I would put together my own Serge System from the perspective of being thoroughly familiar with the different modules and their functions. When the time came and I could afford to build my own system, I began with nine panels. At this point, I have expanded into a seventeen-panel system.

BK: How do the controls on a Serge differ from other modular synthesizers?

MS: The Serge is a modular analog synthesizer, and it shares certain things in common with other analog modular systems. They all have modules, common in application, such as filters, oscillators, envelope generators, and mixers. Then there are modules that are unique to the Serge, specialty modules that are only found on the Serge system. The other manufacturers make their own specialty modules, so each is unique in its own way. Some of the other companies that have manufactured modular synthesizers are Moog, Buchla, ARP, Roland, Korg and Emu.

Perhaps the biggest difference that we could talk about, is the difference between modular analog synthesizers, which the Serge is, and the two other primary classifications of synthesizers that exist. They are the hard-wired analog synthesizer and the hard-wired digital synthesizer. Usually the latter has a piano keyboard, a control surface with buttons and knobs, and some form of display. All of the patching takes place through the use of the buttons and knobs, which route and control the electronics on the circuit boards inside of the instrument. The Serge also has printed circuit boards on the inside, but all the patching is done on the outside of the instrument. There are many, many combinations and ways of routing and modulating different parts of a modular synthesizer that are not possible with a hardwired analogue or digital system.

The Serge differs from the other analog modular systems, in that you have five different kinds of filters. There are also unique modules like wave multipliers, analog shift registers, frequency shifters, n division comparators, triple wave shapers and many others. As these modules are unique to the Serge system, they help you create that unique Serge sound.

BK: Tell us why you still use the Serge, even though you have a lot of other state of the art equipment in your studio?

MS: Well, I think I keep coming back to the Serge because of the complexity of a modular instrument like this. There are so many ways in and out of the instrument, so many ways to process sound, to create new types of sounds; so many subtle ways to create nuance in sound. It's really an open system, and a wonderful way to create music. Right now in the studio I have digital instruments, analog instruments, samplers, but I always come back to the Serge when there's a certain complexity and texture that I'm looking for. Because in a modular instrument you create the signal path as you are patching, if you have a large enough instrument, you can create many signals and actually create four or five instruments that are happening simultaneously. These instruments can be responding in a random manner with each other, or by feeding back different parameters, or busing different controllers they can interact synchronously. With the advent of MIDI, and more complex hardwired synths, the modular approach has become more possible within the studio as a whole. With MIDI, the musical interaction within the entire studio, between the instruments and computer controllers, is like a huge complex modular synthesizer.

Modular synthesizers are rarely used for live performance, but I usually take mine when I do concerts, to create textures that play in the background. The Serge is a constant discovery, in which the worst mistakes sometimes turn into fantastic new musical worlds to explore.

BK: Do you think those modular systems like the Serge will continue to be a creative tool for future generations of musicians?

MS: Modular systems will be around for quite a while to come. I'm certainly always discovering new things to do with mine, new ways to use it. I have a number of friends that have Serge Modular Systems and also Moog Modular Systems, Buchla and ARP Modular Systems, as well as others. They are all still using them in their studios, and I think that there is a real place for an analog modular synthesis system in any electronic music studio.

While the name Michael Stearns may not be a household name, chances are you've heard his music somewhere. Below is a partial list of albums and film scores Michael has created.

MICHAEL STEARNS SCORES

IMAX/OMNIMAX Movies
Behold Hawaii MacGillivray Freeman Films
Boar Pigs Tom Huggins
Challenge MacGillivray Freeman Films
Chronos Canticle Films
Dead Fish Working Michael Lee
Homeland MacGillivray Freeman Films
IMAX Slitscan logos Graphic Films
Indonesia Indah 3 MacGillivray Freeman Films
Island Child MacGillivray Freeman Films
Mt. St. Helens Graphic Films
Race the Wind MacGillivray Freeman Films
Ring of Fire Graphic Films
Sacred Site Canticle Films
Seasons Graphic Films
Thrill Ride N Wave Pictures
Time Concerto MacGillivray Freeman Films
To The Limit MacGillivray Freeman Films
Tropical Rain Forest Shedd Productions

8/70 iWERKS
Gunma Graphic Films
Shimane Graphic Films

RIDE/SHOW
Back To The Future, The Ride Universal Studios
Dolphins, The Ride IMAX Ride Film
Earthquake Universal Studios
Journey to Technopi Boss Films/Goldstar
Scuba Dog Boss Films/Taito
Silver Legacy Circus Circus
Star Trek, The Experience Paramount
Top Secret Catalyst Entertainment

WORLDS FAIR/EXPO
'89 Race the Wind MacGillivray Freeman Films
'91 Eureka! La Pasion Por Conocer MacGillivray Freeman Films
'93 Journey To Technopia Boss Films/Goldstar

COMMERCIALS
Isuzu (For '96 Olympics) Goodby, Silverstein and Partners
Power Gen Great Guns
Spec Savers Julian Hanford
Umbro Soccer Goodby, Silverstein and Partners

DOCUMENTARY
Advice on Lice Disney Films
LandLight Cinubia Productions
Paha Sapa HBO
Spirits of the Voyage Triton Films
The Getty Mountainair Films
Volcano Rescue BBC/Discovery Channel
World of Explorers ABC

3-D
Ahead of Time Sony Pictures
Time Out Café Kong Productions

THEATRICAL RELEASE
187 Warner Bros
A Passion in the Desert Roland Films
Baraka Magidson Films
Doe In The Headlights Mountainair Films
Sound Man Mountainair Films
Temptress Paramount
Titanic Paramount

TRAILERS
The Abyss James Cameron
Brave Heart Mel Gibson
Vampires John Carpenter

DISCOGRAPHY
Desert Moon Walk 1977 Continuum Montage
Ancient Leaves 1978 Continuum Montage
Sustaining Cylinders 1978 Continuum Montage
Morning Jewel 1979 Continuum Montage
Planetary Unfolding 1981 Continuum Montage
Light Play 1983 Continuum Montage
Lyra Sound Constellation 1983 Continuum Montage
M'ocean 1984 Sonic Atmospheres
Chronos 1984 Sonic Atmospheres (Soundtrack to Ron Fricke's Film)

Plunge 1986 Sonic Atmospheres
Floating Whispers 1987 Sonic Atmospheres
Encounter 1988 Hearts of Space
Sacred Site 1993 Hearts of Space
The Lost World 1995 Fathom/Hearts of Space
The Light in the Trees 1996 Amplexus
Collected Ambient and Textural Works 1977-1987 1996
Fathom/Hearts of Space
Collected Thematic Works 1977-1987 1996 Fathom/Hearts of Space
Desert Solitaire 1989 Fortuna/Celestial Harmonies
Singing Stones 1994 Fathom/Hearts of Space (With Ron Sunsinger)
Kiva 1995 Fathom/Hearts of Space (With Steve Roach and Ron
Sunsinger)
Dali, The Endless Enigma 1990 Coriolis
Baraka1992 Milan (Soundtrack to Ron Fricke's Film)
Deep Space 1994 Omni
Musique Mechanique 1995 Celestial Harmonies
Storm of Drones1996 Sombient
Celestial Journey 1996 Rising Star
Songs of the Spirit 1997 Triloka
Trance Planet 4 1998 Triloka
Soundscape Gallery 2 1998 Lektronic Soundscapes
Within, The Nine Dimensions 1999
The Middle of Time 2000 Earth Turtle Music
Spirits of the Voyage 2000 Earth Turtle Music
Sorcerer, (co-written with Ron Sunsinger, dedicated to the late Carlos
Castaneda.) 2000 Spotted Peccary Music
The Storm, 2000 Spotted Peccary Music

CHAPTER 9

Breathing Analog Fire: An Interview with Steve Roach

I first met Steve Roach in 1986 when he was a guest on my radio program, *Imaginary Voyage*. He had just completed an east coast tour promoting his album *Empetus*. Since that time, it has been a real joy watching his career expand and flourish.

Born in 1955, Roach is constantly searching for new sounds that connect with a timeless source of truth in this ever-changing world. Roach has earned his position in the international pantheon of major new music artists over the last two decades through his ceaseless creative output, constant innovation, intense live concerts, open-minded collaborations with numerous artists, and the psychological depth of his music.

Steve Roach in the Timeroom, 2001.

Photo courtesy Will Merkle

Inspired early on by the music of Klaus Schulze, Tangerine Dream and the European electronic music of the '70s, Steve began his musical explorations directly on synthesizers at the age of nineteen. He made his recording debut with the album *Now* in 1982. Two years later he created one of the most pivotal albums of his early career, *Structures from Silence,* one of the landmark ambient releases of the '80s, presenting a new sound that lives on today. The album was re-released in 2001 by Project. It is comprised of three long tracks featuring reflective intimate timbres and cascading lush harmonic waves. Roach sought to alter the listener's awareness of their physical surroundings by increasing the space within each of the pieces, and by extending the length between the sections to an expansive level, capturing the slow breath of the silence between the sounds.

Roach has always been a fervent collaborator, and has been involved with many well known electronic/ambient artists, including: Robert Rich, Vidna Obmana, Michael Stearns, Jorge Reyes, Suso Saiz, Michael Shrieve, Kevin Braheny, Richard Burmer, Stephen Kent, Kenneth Newby, and Australian Aboriginal didgeridoo virtuoso David Hudson to name just a few. Over the years he has also encouraged, produced and collaborated with a number of up-and-coming artists, including Vir Unis, Thom Brennan, and Biff Johnson.

Recognized worldwide as one of the leading innovators in contemporary electronic music, he has released over 50 albums since 1981, including the award-winning live-studio masterpiece *On This Planet* (1997, Fathom), the critically acclaimed *Magnificent Void* (1998, Fathom*),* the time traveling *Early Man* (2001, Projekt), and a number of albums that are already considered classics of the genre, most notably the ground-breaking double CD *Dreamtime Return* (1988, Fortuna).

All of Roach's early works have stood the test of time, drawing a new generation of fans who are only beginning to discover the vast territory of sonic innovation this artist has covered over the last two decades.

Roach's music, described by critic Dwight Loop as "techno-tribal music for the global village," blends the visceral sounds he designs on synthesizers and samplers with the primordial rhythms of ethnic percussion and other exotic instruments, including the Australian didgeridoo. He studied traditional didgeridoo techniques and made his own instrument with aboriginal didgeridoo master David Hudson during two extended trips to the southern continent in the late 1980s. Roach also scored music for a PBS documentary on the rock art of the Dreamtime (the foundation of aboriginal mythology) and recorded indigenous artists for the influential release *Australia: Sound of the Earth* (1990, Fortuna). Roach went on to produce David Hudson's solo works, *Woolunda* (1993, Celestial Harmonies), the first compact disc recording of solo didgeridoo music, and *Rainbow Serpent* (1994, Celestial Harmonies), which features Hudson in an expanded role as percussionist as well as didgeridoo virtuoso. The 1998 Roach-Hudson collaboration, *Gunyal* (Celestial Harmonies), is a visceral collection of dreamtime sound worlds combining powerful didgeridoo playing and surreal textures.

In recent years, Roach collaborated with Tibetan monk Thupten Pema Lama, blending solo prayers and chants with a subtle compliment of soundscapes created in reverence to these offerings. He also produced two recordings for the African group, Takadja (whose first self-titled album produced by Roach received a Juno Award, Canada's Grammy, for best world music recording).

Roach's music has been featured in a number of films, including 1995's *Heat*. His talent for creating atmosphere-drenched textures and surreal sound worlds has also led to increasing recognition of his work among film composers, such as Graeme Revell and Brian Keane, who brought Roach on board as a sound designer in several film and television projects. Roach's numerous artistic collaborations include two releases with Suspended Memories, the award-winning *Earth Island* as well as the group's enthusiastically received debut, *Forgotten Gods* (1993, Hearts of Space). In 1988, Roach teamed up with former Santana drummer Michael Shrieve on *The Leaving Time* (BMG). Two sonic essays of the American Southwest, *Western Spaces* (1987, reissued on Fortuna in 1990) and *Desert Solitaire* (1989, Fortuna), were highly successful group projects with artists Kevin Braheny, Thom Brennan and Michael Stearns.

In 1998 Roach started his own label, Timeroom Editions, as a compliment to his online presence represented by an extensive website. The momentum of this prolific artist built to a high point in the year 2000 with no less than seven releases and concerts in both the US and Europe and a third AFIM award for *Light Fantastic* (Fathom) in the category of Electronic/Ambient.

In 1990, the California native moved to the Sonoran desert just outside Tucson, Arizona, to be closer to this long-standing source of inspiration. Like the stark, red-rock landscapes of Australia, the American Southwest has long provided Roach with the experiential and psychological richness that imbues his work with the power and serenity of nature.

As one of the few electronic-based artists performing live consistently for over 20 years, Roach's engagements have taken him from concert halls in the United States, Canada, and Europe, to lava caves in the Canary Islands and volcanic craters in Mexico. These exotic settings have helped him further shape his style, a sonic vision that thrives in a sphere of ritualistic intensity beyond categories, national boundaries, cultural barriers, and quite often, time itself.

Ben Kettlewell: Since the early days of your career, you've enjoyed performing in front of a live audience. Back in the days of *Structures* and *Empetus*, when most of your gear was analog, it must have been difficult to represent what you achieved in the studio in a live environment. Given the complexities, and the temperament of analog synths, how did you achieve this?

Steve Roach: A typical concert for the '80s involved taking the entire studio out onto the stage every time. It was a monumental event, one that became a strange and involved ritual-obsession over time. It was like taking apart a large interconnected, living being and then rebuilding it at a location far from the safety of the my studio. I was driven to create these hyper-intense, sequencer-driven, mandala-like pieces in the moment, with the same approach as I would in the studio. There was no question as to this being the only way to present my music live.

As the concert approached, I would be creating new pieces in the studio right up to the last moment, building the energy to a high place right up to pulling the plug and breaking down all the gear. With the help of a few devoted friends, everything was packed up, transported and then rebuilt at the site. I was always required to be in the venue by mid morning for an 8PM concert. By early afternoon, I would be back up and tuning, tweaking, replacing dead cables, getting dialed into the room and sound system. I would start to work with the analog sequencers and proceed to find the qualities of the hall and start merging with the environment.

Really, the concert would start in the late afternoon. Before the audience arrived I would move through the pieces, which were built like a continuous journey. Once in the hall, I would continue to pick up from where I left off back in the studio, getting back to that place that I was carving from just the day before, but now with the expanded sense of sound and space and with the anticipation of the audience about to arrive. The raw power of these sequencer-based pieces presented a mega volume that was something to behold when it finally came together. That's what is so addicting about presenting this music live. So, by 7:30 that evening, I would essentially whip myself into an ultra high state of focus, becoming one with sound and equipment, staying with the synths and sound up until it was time to let the audience into the space. By this point I was pretty much merged with the gear, breathing analog fire. I would usually retune everything just before the doors opened. With the concert about to start, I was pretty much like a cat pacing in a cage, waiting to jump back in the sound current that had been cooking all afternoon. The pieces recorded on my *Stormwarning* CD are a perfect document of this period. The on-stage gear for these concerts was an ARP 2600, three ARP Sequencers, Micro Moog, Roland SH101, Roland SH 1000, ARP-Solina String Ensemble, Ensoniq ESQ1, OBXA, Oberhiem system, DMX, DSX, OB8, Xpander, Emulator 1, Roland Space Echo, Teac board and more stuff I can't recall. In thinking about this time, it was all a completely obsessive and compulsive state of being. I was really quite possessed with the need to create an altered state by way of analog-based, sequencer-based music. It became an important part of the development of my music at that time: in the way I would push myself and the equipment to find new places that you simply cannot access when all is warm and cozy in the studio. All of this helped to shape me as an electronic artist, right up to the present moment. I feel the same motivation now, but the methods have evolved.

BK: It sounds like preparing for a live concert was a monumental effort in those days. How has this setup changed in recent years?

SR: I have put so much time into it and experimented on many different levels. I paid a lot of dues by flying around with this massive collection of equipment for years. With my music and live presentation changing, the evolution of technology is giving more options in smaller packages. It finally made more sense to reduce the size of the setup and have maximum potential to present the music I do now.

Also, the analog stuff was getting more fragile and more valuable if it was lost or broken. Now with the smaller versions of the Oberheim gear, such as the Nord Rack and smaller more powerful samplers, I have developed a new approach to present the music live in a dynamic way. It was important for me to continue to tour without going broke and breaking my back in the process. As my music changed, and the live attitudes with it, I had to design this new system, one small enough to enable me to fly to about anywhere and hardly pay any excess baggage, to collect a couple of cases at the airport. The idea of creating my "sound worlds" live has taken on a new life for me.

The priority for my live presentation these days is to keep it moving, allowing me to focus on various levels at once within the flow of the music without getting lost tweaking out in front of an audience. This is what started to occur in the strictly analog days, more and more tweaking of smaller portions of sound, something that should be going on in the studio, not the stage. Now I am doing a lot of multi-tasking, mixing and re-mixing, live playing of acoustic instruments including didgeridoo, and the processing and looping of these, drawing from the synths and samplers, atmospheric and groove sources. Between playing instruments, I'm constantly hovering over the Mackie 24 SR Mixer like a painter would at his palette, mixing and processing the colors, so to speak, and pouring them back out through the speakers. With this approach, I'm able to focus on the overall shape. It feels like being the pilot of some kind of traveling sound-craft. The range of sonic terrain I can cover now is vast. For the future, I hope to include a laptop and the Doepfer MIDI-to-analog sequencer to the program when appropriate.

BK: The Oberheim Performance System played a crucial role in your studio and your live setup for many years. Can you tell me about the system, and what attracted you to the "Oberheim sound"?

SR: I was attracted by the potential to create these incredibly warm textures, the quality of the sound that just felt right in my ears. My first contact was an Oberheim 4 voice, which had a sound all its own. I followed the progression of the instruments and jumped in with the OBXA, then graduated to the pre-MIDI unified "Oberheim System." This was perfect for how my live approach was unfolding. Eventually this system was retrofitted with MIDI and then the CV-gate world as we knew it was changing fast. I had several friends working at the company so I was privy to what was going on in R&D and that was part of the allure as well.

It was one fine day when the Xpander was finally born. I had played with the prototype versions, starting with no graphics on the faceplate. It was an exciting time to see and hear the development of these instruments being made just a few miles from my home. It seems that the timing with the Xpander and MIDI emerging and hitting at the crossroads around the same time created a visionary instrument that still holds its own in so many ways today. It was truly a big step in the evolution of electronic instruments. Also, with Oberheim being a product of Southern California, I like the idea of using an instrument indigenous to my area as well. The Xpander and Matrix 12 are still the main stays in my system today. I have said before that I can see spending a lifetime working with the Matrix 12, and while fifteen years is not quite a lifetime, it just keeps sounding better to me over time.

BK: You were also using an ARP 2600 and ARP sequencers back in the early days of the "Timeroom" in San Diego and Culver City, during the late '70s and early '80s. How did you sync all this gear together during a performance?

SR: It was CV and Gate, S trigger for the Moog. I had a clock divider built that subdivided the various clocks for triggering the sequencers and arpeggiator. Early on the ARP sequencers and clock divider were used as the master clock, then later the Oberheim DMX Drum Machine drove the entire network.

BK: Electronic instruments have changed a lot since you first started using them in the 1970s. As electronic instruments have evolved, how have digital synthesis, sampling, computers used for music production and new forms of signal processing affected your musical ideas?

SR: I think it's clear my music has become more complex and multidimensional. Early on, in the '80s for example, I was working more directly with melody and analog sequential patterns as a strong central element in the music. It seems over time I keep changing the magnification of the lens, coming closer and closer in on the aspects of sound that are so compelling to me. Including the ethnic-acoustic elements and using the computer as a non-liner compositional tool as well as for sound design has certainly blown the lid off for me over the past four years since I incorporated it into the studio. The previous approach of carving it out in the moment is still alive in the way I capture "experiences" occurring in the studio, but now I can take those and approach the performance like a surgeon going deep into the body of the sound and finding a more complex, involved world of textures and forms that keep revealing themselves as I change the perspective.

BK: Did learning on modular instruments like the ARP 2600 have a lasting impact on your work?

SR: Indeed. In fact, I started reading the manual before I could afford the 2600. So, it first started as visualization from reading, then interacting and exploring the basics with hands on, letting my imagination configure these various complex puzzles that would sometimes offer rewarding sound worlds. The pathways this approach created are still being accessed today with my current digital-analog units and, of course, the Xpander and the Matrix 12, which offer the modular approach as well. I am sure it would have been a different story if I were to start out on the freeze-dried sample playback units that were popular for a while. I am happy to see the resurgence of modular and knob-intensive instruments again.

It's interesting having grown up with analog equipment —synths and recording equipment. For me the organic influence has created a foundation that absorbs whatever new approach comes along, while still keeping the human element alive in the machine. This was the only way to create in the "old days." With the analog gear nothing could be stored in memory, only in your own memory. I feel this created a different relationship to sound: at any moment, it could change or be rewired, never to be heard the same again—much different from calling back your favorite patch # 54. You always had to approach it in the moment with these "living" sounds. I still maintain this approach along with the evolution of new methods. I also love the process of creating living analog worlds of sounds that are cycling, ebbing and flowing, constantly changing at a minute level. I often have these sound worlds running live for days, and it seems that the longer it runs, the warmer and more melted together it feels.

BK: When a new instrument comes out, how do you go about investigating it? What do you look for in deciding whether or not to use it?

SR: I look for sound quality first, how it moves me. Then, how is the interface for programming? Is it intuitive or cumbersome? Then the basics like modulation routing and filter choices, if that applies. I will always get a hold of something for a few months and live with it over time to see how it settles into the sound relationship with the other instruments. I am very careful how I introduce a new instrument to the mix since I evolved the current system to a place that creates nice balance between the direct analog experience and the digital. After having fallen prey to techno lust a few times too many, I find nowadays that a nice quiet session with the Xpander will tell me I really don't need to be buying any new toys that are trying to do what this already does much better. It still inspires in ways that most synths never will, for me anyway.

BK: Tell me about your new Timeroom studio setup, and its advantages/disadvantages over the earlier one.

SR: Well, it's a hybrid evolution of the earliest system. It's still centered around an analog-digital synth-sequencer configuration. I see no disadvantages to the system these days. It would hold more than a lifetime's worth of exploring, even if nothing was added from this point forward.

The rundown for my set up as it has evolved is: For the MIDI sequencing I use the Akai MPC60 as the main brain that clocks the Doepfer Shaltwerk, Doepfer MAQ16, and two Korg Electribes. The sequencers can be routed to the Xpander, Proteus World, Procussion, Roland MKS-30 and all the main synths in the system. The Korg Z1 is my current master keyboard, above that is an Emu E6400, next to that, a Nord Rack 2 and just above that, the trusty Oberheim Xpander. On the other rack is an Oberheim Matrix 12 and below that, a Korg Wavestation Ex.

I also have a handful of Alesis MMT 8 sequencers, which are great for stand alone MIDI recordings of on-the-fly loops. For recording, I have two ADAT 20 bit recorders, which are not seeing much use now with the arrival of the PC 800 P3 running Vegas Pro, Acid and a variety of plug ins. For an audio interface, I am using the Layla 24-96 unit combined with the ADAT for 16 out. Then a few racks for the effects gear, PCM 70-80-500, three Jammans, Eventide, and so on.

Since I have built my sound and approach around the constant interaction of playing with the various sequencers, knobs, etc., both in a rhythmic and slow motion context, I need to have a my hands directly on knobs and sliders, and effects sends, all a part of the studio as one large instrument. For this reason I still use a Soundcraft Delta 8 analog console. Against two walls is a collection of didgeridoos, and a large collection of all sorts of percussion, drums, clay pots, pre-Hispanic flutes, shakers, rattles and strange sound making objects that all find there way in the mix at the right time.

BK: After this rundown of the contents of the studio, it seems that the Timeroom represents a lot more than just a studio full of gear. Can you tell us about it?

SR: The neutral, safe environment of the Timeroom is something that I longed to have before building it from the ground up. It was a name adopted back in San Diego. Wherever I would set up my creative space, the name would follow. Starting in 1978, I can think of six locations of the Timeroom before I built its present location here in Tucson. I wanted to create a space that was more than a room full of gear. It had to offer a sense of sanctuary during the creative process. For me, this was achieved by the shape; the big window looking out at the desert and the mountains, the color scheme, the arrangement of gear, no phones or clocks. This is a place I love to be in every day. So, in an Eastern sense it relates to having this quiet place inside yourself no matter where you are, which is a much harder task to maintain out in the world today. The Timeroom supports and encourages my desire to create these sounds that often feel just out of reach, just below the surface but always present, a place you know exists, but were unaware of until sound worlds are created that feel familiar in that strange, elusive, clearly non-verbal way. Again, the ways of a visual artist, painter or sculptor in terms of the relationship with the process of creating one's work over long periods of solitary time is at play here.

BK: It seems that more and more, the future for getting a composer's music out there is through emerging music formats such as MP3 and working with the World Wide Web, which you seemed to have mastered through your own site, **www.steveroach.com**, and your MP3 site. What are your observations on these events?

SR: As an independent artist, it's the best thing to happen since affordable-portable synthesizers, and all the tools for self-production. The Web's nervous system is a natural answer to the question that all the home-based recording gear offered as new artists started creating music on their own terms. When I released my first albums on cassette and LP in the early '80s the baby steps were taken toward this sort of do-it-yourself method. Of course, what would take weeks or months by way of snail mail and delayed print timelines happens in minutes now.

I see it as a great way to get the music to people who might not have the chance to find it due to the strangle hold that pop culture has on traditional radio, press and TV. I see a mutation that involves taking the college radio paradigm, mixing it with syndicated radio shows like Hearts of Space and Echoes, splicing this into specialized online magazines and then including the artists' sites, MP3.com, all the links and so on. Put all this in the hands of the people directly, and you have a great system to empower the individual. The best way to get the word out about the music is to hear it directly. I feel it's a great addition to the written review. There's nothing like hearing for yourself and making a direct connection. Since this music isn't advertised much, it's a great way to help get it heard beyond the ambient, electronic, music-between-the-cracks zones.

BK: Already many existing radio stations have Web radio, and this has become a big area of contention now with the passing of the Digital Millennium Act in Congress in 1999. All of the performance right organizations and the recording organizations, like ASCAP, BMI, RIAA are saying that music is, in many cases, being distributed without royalties being paid. There's a big scramble to figure out what to do about piracy. Many stations have taken a wait-and-see attitude. What are your opinions on this subject?

SR: As an artist that makes his living directly from his work, naturally I am not in favor of uncontrolled "stealing" of my work. Again, using radio, television and Film Sync use as a format, the need to find a fair way to compensate the artist who is providing the "software" to broadcast in the first place is vital for us to continue to have the freedom to create. I feel the entire controversy with Napster, and so on, is more telling of how our society has devalued music and art in a lot of ways, expecting it for free without considering what it takes to create it in the first place.

In my case, it's not a privilege. It's been hard earned at many personal costs. It's a complex situation, but for the time being, I am happy to use the MP3.com site as a way to share the music with new and established listeners. It's also a way to give the listeners some special tracks, previews of what's coming, live concert tracks and so on. In this case it is useful and feels fair. MP3.com has a pay-for-play program, which in reality has been more supportive financially than some CD's I have released on previous labels after the "Creative Accounting" occurs. At any given day on an MP3 server, I could have hundreds of listings. I know this brought some serious listens to my music after hearing their feedback at the WEB store. It still needs to be monitored, not just for the protection of the fat cats at the big labels, but for the fringe dwellers who have always had a harder time getting the music into distribution channels in the first place.

So, for now I see the MP3, net radio and so on as a great promotional tool, an alternative to print ads and other conventional modes. I am still a believer in manufactured CD's as the preferred medium for now and feel the convenience, reliability and quality control, along with the complete vision that goes into the real deal when holding it in your hand, is hard to beat. When the next obvious medium of delivering music is to the point where someone like my mom can easily download an entire CD with full artwork, quickly without any drama, then I'll feel its time has arrived. Till then, the modes we have now are just fine, along with the exploding Internet culture.

BK: Tell me about your Timeroom Editions label and how it came to be.

SR; As I just mentioned, the Web site and the online mail order service has changed things dramatically. Timeroom Editions was created primarily as an Internet mail-order series of releases. At first it was to solve the problems of too many releases competing in the mainstream. Even more, this keeps me in the flow without all the drama of timing releases. Each release simply comes out when it's ready, with just a few announcements letting the subscribers know about a new Timeroom Edition.

These discs are there at the site for those who want to go deeper into my work. The number I might sell annually is small in the eyes of a normal record company, but it's clear it's a direct-from-the-artist affair. My hard-core audience loves this and so do I. The direct feedback feeds the fire, pure and simple, no drama: Create the music and have the direct pipeline to the folks who want it. It's not a new thing for me since I have been doing my own mail order since the beginning, but the level of efficiency that the Internet provides makes it enjoyable without consuming other aspects of my life, keeping the path clear for the mainstream label releases with Projekt, while satisfying my creative drive and the fans on the inside who can never have enough. The mail order service is also filling a big hole in terms of my back catalog and the fact that a lot of stores don't carry many back titles, so this is a good feeling as well, to help people find a release they have been searching for.

BK: Let's get back to your music. Many reviewers and listeners describe your music as a transformational tool, which helps bring the listener into a deeper level of consciousness. Why do you think so many people share that vision in regard to your music?

SR: The willful intention in all my music is to create an opening, which allows me to step out of everyday time and space, into a place I feel we are born to experience directly. Many of our current social structures and material concerns shut down the opening or build a complex array of 'plumbing' to divert a direct experience we all crave in one way or another. In any case, these sound worlds can offer a place where the bondage of western time is removed and the feeling of an expanded state is encouraged. I often refer to the words "visceral," being in the "sound current," or "sound worlds," when describing my work. This is a prime area where I feel the measure of all my work—in the body. So, for me to create these sounds and rhythms, and utilize my own body as the reflecting chamber is my direct way of living in the sound current that occurs naturally when the juices are flowing. From the feedback I receive, this is something I know receptive listeners are feeling as well. Tapping into the creative process at this direct level simply feels like a birthright.

I truly feel the complexity of what makes me a human being and drives me to create this music is something that can never be measured and explained in terms conveniently reduced to a string of words. Starting with the impulses and urges of early man, deep in the collective memory up to now, I feel compelled to make sense of the chaos and beauty around me—to give it meaning, and feel more whole and alive for our time on this planet. As far back as I can remember, the realm of ineffable feelings emerging in everyday life haunted me.

When I discovered the way to express this world through sound, things just fell into place in many ways. It feels like it's enough to just say I have to create my music in the same way I have to breathe. It's not a question of whether it's pleasing or disturbing to other people, or record companies and so on. I do it for myself before anyone else. The fact that I have devoted all of my adult life to creating this music at whatever cost outside the interference of commercial concerns has allowed me to follow some tracks to places that are essential and universal at the core. I get the sense the listeners to the music feel this and respond naturally.

BK: Where do you find the inspiration and time to create such a great body of output, especially in the past four years? What inspires you? What keeps you working at this pace?

SR: It's just the natural pace for me to operate at. It's not forced. I don't feel I'm working at it rigorously. It just feels like I am in the flow. I love being in this sound current and capturing the music as I do. It's a constant feedback circuit. Over the years the momentum builds and the process becomes more rich and fulfilling for me. It's a way of life for me, not a job or a profession. It's my chosen path, being in the flow of sound and music. Looking at the flow of a visual artist or sculptor, for example, these people usually have reams of work in various stages. A constant regeneration occurs where the work helps build the momentum and energy that inspires the actual process. It's no different for me. I've always felt more connected to this process of creativity.

Somewhere along the way, the record industry set a standard to protect their own investments with an artist or group squeezing out a release every fifteen months. That system has never really made sense for the way I work. Now, with the Timeroom Editions, and the outstanding collaborative relationship with Sam Rosenthal, owner of Project Records with whom I release my above-ground work, I have found a nice flow and balance.

BK: You, Robert Rich, and Michael Stearns were among the first Americans to delve into this type of music. What was it like back in the 1970s trying to introduce your music to a new audience?

SR: It's been a long, wonderful and strange trip indeed. When I set out to live the creative life as a sound sculptor, it was a different time to say the least. In the mid-'70s, this music was still being born, especially in the States. There were almost no labels, no real radio support, a few underground magazines, like Eurock and Synapse, the latter of which I also wrote for. Compared to today, with the Internet as the hub of all things, it was the dark ages. Imagine trying to hook up with like-minded people or get your music to people beyond your immediate reach. It was also an incredibly exciting time with impending changes in the air. The frontier of consciousness expanding music was clearly growing, and this impetus was spawning many new instruments and small companies that often came and went as fast as they appeared. I set out to do electronic music against many odds, but my passion to live in the sound current was all that mattered, and this is what drove me through all the highs and lows and beyond the naysayers. At that time, only a handful of people around me knew what I was talking about when I would start on these born-again tirades about the "music of the future." There really was a feeling of being a part of something significant, in a historic sense. To witness all these changes and to meet and work with many of the people helping to bring all this together, in such a short time, was nothing short of fantastic. Just a few years ago, getting your music onto an LP or a cassette run was a major accomplishment. Then there were the tasks of gathering names from underground sources and mailing packages and letters to each and every one. It was a grassroots effort where I felt like every cassette or LP sent out was like a personal connection. I still feel this way but on a larger scale. My first release was *Now*, in 1982, followed by *Structures from Silence* on cassette. It was this release that brought me to the attention of Fortuna Records, based in California. This is about the time I met Robert Rich, who was also self-publishing his early work, like *Trances and Drones*.

It's important for me to say I have never approached my music as a career, a profession, or a way to make a living. My obsession to live in these sound worlds has eventually provided the support to keep me creating. I survived a lot of strange jobs at that time. One of the better ones was eight hours a day in a clean room at a Microbiology lab for a few years, then straight home to the Timeroom all night, living like a techno monk in a tiny one-bedroom house in Culver City, Ca. I even had a visit from Chris Franke of Tangerine Dream at one point, which for me at the time was pretty much like the Dalai Lama stopping in, at this stucco Gingerbread looking bungalow built in the '30s for the workers in the film studios nearby. Every spare penny went toward supporting the equipment habit I needed to create this music. The fact that I eventually reached the point where the music in turn supported me enough to quit my day job and live in the sound current exclusively is something I don't take for granted.

As a side bar, this is a very brief overview from my perspective of events not long ago—in the pre-internet era. The "commercial" groundswell started to build in the late '80s. The catchall term New Age was adopted for the purpose of retail and marketing. This travesty of a definition started to build momentum and swooped up many forms of unsuspecting genre-less music at the same time. Companies like Windham Hill and Private Music, backed by major label clout and greed, continued to build the fire and find a peak in the early '90s, inspiring dozens of overnight labels to spew out reams of forgettable "product." In my opinion, this glut of "product" helped to poison the well to a certain extent and turned a lot of people off to this music in the end. Still, the momentum from this time had a positive side, and thankfully, like a raging California wildfire, it burned itself out, leaving behind a smoldering, ashen heap, which fueled the natural process of survival of the fittest. The Phoenix rose up. On the 8th day, what's his name created the Internet, the Mecca for all fringe dwellers old and new, including the ones that survived the great "wildfires" of the early 1990s. These events seem like bumps in the long road when even looking back a few years later.

BK: I want to talk about your method of composition. Is there a chain of events, or a memory that conjures up a particular sonic image, or do you go into your studio, and just start exploring ideas?

SR: There are so many levels at work here. Long-term ideas that build up energy often start as spontaneous moments in the studio. Sometimes a title or a word will key me into the deeper storehouse of memories. The ongoing meditation of working on the various sound worlds will often take me to places I could arrive at no other way. I have this biological need to create certain types of zones that have become established in my music. It's something that wells up time after time, and it's a world I'm compelled to keep exploring in various ways.

The biggest influence is living here in the desert. It's a constant generator that feeds my inner life in many ways. I have no formula since every project takes on a different shape and set of harmonic sonic-mythic-rhythmic puzzles to solve and explore. In some settings, the feeling of creating a film is the best way to compare the process. Shooting the film can be compared to capturing improvisations and explorations in the moment, then telling the story by way of editing. Like the texture and grain of the film, the processing can drive it, slow it down, and sweep one away, whatever. Besides the powerful places right here in the southwest, I get tremendous inspiration from films, along with the visual arts. Since I never really do songs, the long form pieces are created from many different elements that, once woven into the fabric, serve multiple purposes in the big picture.

It is always important to remember the instruments are tools to help me express multi-leveled emotional nuances and states of consciousness. I'm careful not to let the technology take over and turn me into a more rigid, machine-like being.

BK: When you're working on a composition, molding sound, building things up, how do you sense when the piece is complete?

SR: Gut feeling. Instinct. Creating a flow and balance that just feels right. Sometimes with a piece that occurs spontaneously, it feels finished right on the spot. Other times I can work on a piece over a long period of time before it feels complete. Each piece or final CD had its own story for me on many levels. Sometimes, I put all of myself into the one I am currently engaged in, only moving forward when it feels complete. Sometimes I have several different fires going at once, and they all influence each other, maybe balancing each other as they express opposite feelings or sides of my personality. With that said, I can listen to older releases and hear them from a new perspective. This might trigger a new idea or technique and sometimes remind me of a path I traveled down for a while and want to jump back on that track and keep exploring it further and deeper.

BK: Can you tell me about the *tabula rasa* and how that affects your preparation for creating music?

SR: *Tabula rasa* means "clean slate" in Latin. It is for me a state of creative nothingness, a mindset that lets go of all preconceived ideas, habits, social mores, philosophical ideas, obligations, methods and techniques. While some of my work is influenced by the past, by feelings I've already explored and want to go deeper into, a piece created from the *tabula rasa* state has no connection to the past, no connection to time at all really. It seems to rise up from a place of pure, unformed potential that leads you into a new way of working and perceiving. I just create an opening in my mind and my heart and let it happen. Some of my best work has come from this perspective. These pieces have led me down an unexpected path, expanding my style and my scope as an artist.

BK: Your albums, *Dreamtime Return* and *Sound of the Earth*, marked quite a pivotal period in your career. Can you tell me about your meeting with David Hudson, and how your trips to Australia brought all this together?

SR: *Dreamtime Return* was certainly a culmination of my deepest desires and aspirations up to that point. I came into my own as an artist during that project. It was really an initiation for me on many levels, including the connection to my own sound that I was constantly searching out. Most of all, it was a time of intensive personal growth and understanding. I felt that I'd left a lot of the overt European influences behind at that point, integrating them in a more personal way, and my relationship to land where I grew up deepened. The expansive, breathing, warm harmonic waves of sound reflected the desert landscapes that shaped me when I was young. These sounds, and the sensations that gave rise to them, were already alive within me; I just had to wipe the slate clean of European influences to allow this deeper, personal music to come through. Around this time, the mid-80s, the feeling of a sonic and spiritual bridge between the Southwest and the Australian outback was also awakening.

I spent a lot of time in Joshua Tree, outside L.A. in the desert region. I grew up in the Southern California Deserts, Anza Borrego and others. From the bedrock of this amazing land of extremes, I began to feel a sense of spiritual expansion, which grew out from beyond the desert I grew up in and was inspired by—a much larger, less familiar landscape. This was when the Dreamtime concept started to unfold.

Around this time I also saw the film by Peter Weir, *The Last Wave*, in which I heard the didgeridoo for the first time. It was a white filmmaker's version of certain mystical aspects of the Dreamtime and Aboriginal culture in its own obviously diluted way. But still, it was a significant point in my growing fascination with Australia. I had a friend who moved to Australia in the '60s and came back with captivating stories of this faraway place. The mystery of this ancient landscape spiraled through my subconscious for years. In the mid '80s I was starting to work on preliminary pieces for *Dreamtime Return*, just gathering different impressions with no idea that I would be going to Australia. I really hadn't thought about it much more than just fascination about the different deserts out there that you could travel to in your imagination.

Knowing I was working on this project, the owner of Fortuna Records at the time, Ethan Edgecomb, sent me a book, *Archaeology of the Dreamtime*, about the time I was starting to get deeper into the project, around 1986. Probably within a month of receiving that book and reading it—which was written from an anthropological point of view of the Australian Aboriginals in the Cape York area of Australia—I received a phone call from a filmmaker who was working on a film called the *Art of the Dreamtime*. Using that very same book as a reference, he was producing a documentary for PBS and planning an expedition to that very same remote area in Cape York with a film crew from a university. One thing led to another, and I became the musician/composer on that expedition. They took care of everything for me, so I was one of the crewmembers. It was just an unbelievable turn of events. The filmmaker said he first heard my music when he was traveling to Mexico through Texas and *Structures from Silence* was playing on the radio late at night across the desert. I remember him saying that he felt like he was in a Stanley Kubrick film.

The feeling of synchronicity was overwhelming at times. Along with being in those remote Aboriginal sites for weeks, the entire project brought up so much in me that went way beyond music. Being at these sites, sleeping on the same dirt as the ancient people of the land and listening to pieces on headphones that I'd already created back in the Timeroom before I ever imagined I would go to Australia was unforgettable.

This was also when I met Aboriginal Didgeridoo player David Hudson, who I went on to produce three didgeridoo records for. He taught me to play the didg. The entire Australian-*Dreamtime Return* period was a tremendous opening for me as an artist, and as a person. It taught me to really listen with my ear very closely to the ground, a direct experience of how magical things can happen when you listen with your heart and an open mind. The influences of those events continue to spiral out, unfolding with a natural order.

I feel the uninterrupted connection still reverberating from that point—the understanding that I came to during the two years of making *Dreamtime Return*.

By 1989 I was back in Australia for a second adventure that led to the project *Australia: Sound of the Earth*. It was directly after this second trip to Australia that I moved to Tucson and started a new life with my wife Linda Kohanov.

A curious side note is that David Hudson came for a visit here in Tucson in the early '90s with his fiancée Cindy and ended up getting married in the desert behind my house. He was taken with how much Tucson felt like Alice Springs, in central Australia, the place where they met originally. They were inspired by the parallels between the two deserts and how Tucson was able to bring up similar feelings for them. Since they were on an extended holiday, they rose to the moment.

BK: You've combined the use of ancient indigenous instruments with high technology in many of your works. Can you explain the synergy you find by combining ancient and modern musical tools?

SR: I see the didgeridoo and my favorite analog synthesizer, the Oberheim Matrix 12, as both being high points in their own time, created out of a need to hear and create a sound that the consciousness was needing. The didgeridoo was a much earlier form of technology, one that created a rich, continuous drone in the same way as the most current synthesizer and computer setups. In the right hands, the Oberheim Matrix 12 Analog Synth can tap into the same timeless realm as the didg, and elaborate on this feeling with a much more intricate series of multi-layered voices, creating a harmonic atmosphere that blossoms into waves of sound, seemingly spilling forth from some other world. The rich, uninterrupted harmonic drones of the didgeridoo have an almost electronic sound that captivated me the moment I heard it. The sounds embraced each other so well, creating this electro-organic quality. I went on to explore this by extensively fusing all sorts of elemental sounds into the electric stew. The simple act of having an open microphone recording an acoustic track in the midst of a full blown electronic piece adds a since of space, injecting "air" directly into what was once a hermetically sealed world. My recordings *Origins* and the recent *Early Man* are prime examples of this synergy.

BK: Do you plan to further explore the DVD format in your future creations?

SR: This medium is a natural extension for the music, which is often quite visual on its own. I have had quite a few visual music pieces in the past on video and Laser Disk. The merging of music and images has been a part of my creative process. It appears that DVD is the mode to parallel if not replace the audio CD in future. Also the possibilities of the extended program time and surround mixes will become more available in future music. I am watching closely with sober anticipation.

BK: What are your plans for the future? Where do you see this kind of music going in the next ten years?

SR: I usually have several projects on the burner at once, usually in vast contrast to each other, so I am sharing time between these now. I find they usually feed each other in curious ways during the parallel creative process. As for a ten year projection, it's up to those making the music to meet the challenge of having all the tools anyone could ever ask for while expressing something connected to the bigger picture, something that comes from a genuine place. I have always seen this indefinable sound-art as an outlet for the innately talented—for people, who, not too long ago might never have found a way to express these worlds. This means more and more people, like myself, who didn't fit into the conformity of the academic world, or didn't give in to the bondage of creativity within the conventional matrix of the music or film business, can express their own unique visions with true independence. I feel the best qualities of this music are evolving in exciting ways, in all the sub-genres. It's a moot point to say the boundaries are dissolving; it's a big boiling pot by now. I say, just keep stirring it, adding new ingredients and trying new recipes while staying connected to the soulful qualities that move one to create in the first place. The good stuff will rise and the rest will fall away like it always has. One thing for sure is there will be more of both extremes.

A SELECTED STEVE ROACH DISCOGRAPHY:

Solo Albums

Now (1982)

Traveler (1983)

Structures from Silence (1984)

Empetus (1986)

Quiet Music 1 (1986)

Quiet Music 2 (1986)

Quiet Music 3 (1986)

Dreamtime Return—2 CD (1988)

Stormwarning: Live In Concert (1989)

World's Edge—2 CD (1992)

The Lost Pieces (1993)

Origins (1993)

Artifacts (1994)

The Dream Circle (1994)

The Dreamer Descends (1995)

The Magnificent Void (1996)

On This Planet (1997)

Slow Heat (1998)

Dreaming Now... Then: A Retrospective 1982-1997—2 CD (1998)

Truth & Beauty: The Lost Pieces Volume Two (1999)

Light Fantastic (1999)

Atmospheric Conditions (1999)

Midnight Moon (2000)

Early Man – 2 CD (2000)

Core (2001)

Structures from Silence (2001) Re-release

Streams and Currents (2001)

Pure Flow—Timeroom Editions Collection 1 (2001)

Collaborations:

Moebius (1979) Moebius

Western Spaces (1987) Steve Roach, Kevin Braheny, Richard Burmer

The Leaving Time (1988) Michael Shrieve, Steve Roach

Desert Solitaire (1989) Steve Roach, Kevin Braheny, Michael Stearns

Australia: Sound of the Earth (1990) Steve Roach, David Hudson, Sarah Hopkins

Strata (1990) Steve Roach, Robert Rich

Soma (1992) Steve Roach, Robert Rich

Ritual Ground (1993) Solitaire [Steve Roach, Elmar Schulte]

Forgotten Gods (1992) Suspended Memories [Steve Roach, Jorge Reyes, Suso Saiz]

Suspended Memories: Earth Island [Steve Roach, Jorge Reyes, Suso Saiz] (1994)

Well of Souls (1995) Steve Roach, vidna Obmana

Kiva (1995) Steve Roach, Michael Stearns, Ron Sunsinger

Halcyon Days (1996) Steve Roach, Stephen Kent, Kenneth Newby

Cavern of Sirens (1997) Steve Roach, vidna Obmana

Gunyal (1998) David Hudson, Steve Roach

Dust To Dust (1998) Steve Roach, Roger King

Ascension of Shadows (1998) Steve Roach, vidna Obmana:

Body Electric (1999) Steve Roach, Vir Unis

Live Archive (2000) Steve Roach, vidna Obmana

Circles & Artifacts (2000) Steve Roach, vidna Obmana

Vine, Bark & Spore (2000) Steve Roach, Jorge Reyes

Prayers to the Protector (2000) Steve Roach, Thupten Pema Lama

Blood Machine (2001) Steve Roach, Vir Unis

InnerZone (2002) Steve Roach, vidna Obmana

The Eternal Expanse (2002) (with Steve Roach, Patrick O'Hearn, Vir Unis and vidna Obmana)

CHAPTER 10

Invisible Musicians: Laurie Paisley on the Sequencer

A book about the first generation of synthesizers would not be complete without mention of sequencers. Composer, musician, and inventor Raymond Scott is credited with inventing the first sequencer back in the early 1950s. It was an electro-mechanical instrument comprised of stepping replays controlled by hundreds of switches, tone circuits, solenoids used to time the events, and 16 oscillators. He aptly named his invention the "Wall of Sound." It measured 6 feet high and 30 feet long. Today, a sequencer of much greater complexity could fit in the palm of your hand.

Sequencers gained international recognition when groups like Pink Floyd and Tangerine Dream began recording and touring with them in the early 1970s. The first generation of sequencers used analog technology, inspired by the same principles used in creating tape loops. An analog sequencer is capable of producing short loops or patterns of melodies or rhythms, usually not more than 12-16 steps or notes in length. These notes, or patterns, repeat in an endless cycle until the machine is reset.

Most people think of an analog sequencer as a device that can "play" a series of pre-determined notes on a synthesizer automatically. While it's true that this is the most common use for an analog sequencer, it is capable of a lot more than simply generating loops of sequenced notes. During the 1970s and early 1980s, the practical advantage of analog sequencers, such as the vintage ARP Model 1621 Sequencer, was that they could simultaneously generate a number of different voltages at each step in a pre-established sequence. By utilizing a sequencer such as the 1621 with a compatible "interfaceable" synthesizer such as the ARP 2600, by using a CV (control voltage) converter box, the user could vary not only pitch levels, but also the entire composite synthesized sound by presetting the instrument's pitch, tone color and volume at each step by use of CV and Gate procedures.

This technology became indispensable for many practical applications, particularly for live performance situations. In a live application, the sequencer was used to create polyrhythms and fluctuations in tempo by patching a sequence of control voltages into its own internal voltage controlled clock. Chris Franke (Tangerine Dream) was a master at refining this technique.

To learn more about sequencers, I visited Laurie Paisley at her home studio in New Jersey in the fall of 1986. For many years, Laurie Paisley was vice president of the IEMA (International Electronic Musicians Association) and a frequent contributor to the organization's monthly magazine, *SYNE*. She is a prolific electronic musician who has released a number of highly acclaimed innovative recordings on her own label, Metheluna Music. Ms. Paisley's path to electronic music was full of quirky twists and minor diversions.

In the following interview, Paisley focuses on sequencers, both analog and digital, and tells how many famous pioneering musicians of the '70s and '80s, such as Emerson, Lake & Palmer, Yes, Vangelis, Tangerine Dream, Kraftwerk, Morton Subotnik, Jean-Michel Jarre, etc. used them to develop their own unique style of composition. She also described the evolution of sequencers, from early analog models to the digital versions of the late '80s, and then to the software-based computer controlled sequencing packages we see used by every studio today.

Ben Kettlewell: How did you get first involved with electronic music?

Laurie Paisley: I studied classical music as a kid. I didn't listen to radio or records till I was 13 or 14. When I was 14, I dropped the keyboards and picked up the guitar, an acoustic twelve string. I played folky stuff like Jackson Browne, Dan Fogelberg, and John Denver. When I was 16, I got into rock music and I started playing in bands. Yes and Emerson, Lake and Palmer were popular at the time. Soon after that, I got back into the keyboards. I wanted to be in a band that was playing that kind of music. After being in a bunch of bands and dealing with things like leaving my instruments at a rehearsal space and not being able to work on my own stuff, or playing with bands who played all originals but none of my originals, I decided to go solo. I wrote lots of little songs on keyboards.

BK: How do you go about composing a piece for synthesizers?

LP: It starts out on the wing; I just sit down and play. When I'm playing, I get ideas, and when I come across something I like, then I stop improvising and I work on that one thing. I then develop that theme. I string a whole bunch of these little parts together. To me, the real challenge is in the arrangement. As long as I get good music, good arrangements, …good compositions down on tape, it doesn't matter whether I played it or programmed it. However, I soon began to think, …who the hell do I think I'm kidding. There is nothing that beats the mastery of an actual instrument. I guess I feel that way deep down because I was brought up as an acoustic piano player and then moved into electronic music. I want to be an excellent synthesist as well as an excellent pianist.

BK: You use both analog and digital sequencers a lot in your recordings. Can you tell us how these devices differ?

LP: The sequencer is a type of storage device that stores predetermined control voltages, which correspond to notes and pitches. In analog sequencers, the notes are programmed one at a time, by turning knobs or manipulating sliders. It is the process of fine tuning each individual note you want to incorporate into your sequence. This process is repeated until the sequencer pattern is complete. Digital sequencers can be built into keyboards, or stand-alone modules like their analog counterparts. They contain computerized circuits that store performances you play on the keyboard, or other controller. Some are stored in what is known as "step-time" which is just like analog sequencing, without having to tune each note and event of the sequence. You play the notes on the keyboard, and when the sequence plays back, the notes that playback won't have any break in the pattern unless you program in rests, or 'hold' note events. Otherwise, that just runs like an analog sequencer in that manner. It might be easier to comprehend how this process works if you understand the basic difference between a tape recorder and a sequencer. A tape recorder records only the finished product, which is sound. A sequencer records everything that goes into making the sound but not the sound itself. In other words, the sequencer records the performance information and then on playback "tells" a properly interfaced instrument what to do to reproduce the sound.

Some digital sequencers offer the ability to program in "real-time", which simply means that the sequencer records every nuance of what you played on the keyboard, just the way you played it. Every accent, every aspect of the performance will be recorded, just as if you were recording it on tape or other recording medium. A sequencer also makes it possible to save or to store your edited performance information, on a computer disk or other storage medium. This storage capability allows you to recall the data and play back any song at a later time without having to re-record the music. So, we can look at a sequencer, as a device that can record, edit, store, and play back data, which closely resembles a "photograph" of your musical performance.

In the early electronic music of the 1970s, drones, or other combinations of sound usually accompanied sequencers, and sometimes electronic percussion was also added.

These are the basic ingredients that made famous, the "Berlin School" sound, created by artists like Klaus Schulze, Tangerine Dream, and others in the early days of this genre. The advantage of digital sequencers over their analog counterparts is that you can program more than one note at a time, by that I mean simultaneously in polyphony. With analog sequencers you only have one note playing at a time, which creates rhythmic tonal patterns that loop over and over. The digital sequencers are a lot easier to work with, and can store a lot more information. You probably wonder what is the attraction to the old analog sequencers, when the digital versions are much more "user-friendly." I think both types are really important. Digital sequencers are lighter, more affordable, easier to program, and have a much greater storage capacity. For instance the classic Korg SQ-10, which I have in my studio, at most can only program twenty-four notes, where as digital sequencers can store thousands of notes; complete performances. I still think you should have both, because with analog sequencers and synthesizers, you have more control over the sound, and with their digital counterparts you have ease of use and greater memory. They both serve their purpose.

There are three varieties of digital sequencers, hardware, software, and what the industry refers to as integrated sequencers. Dedicated hardware sequencers are usually rectangular in shape, running anywhere between hand-held size to the size of a small suitcase. Their primary function is sequencing events (notes), except in some cases, where they contain their own internal sound generating capabilities (miniature synthesizers such as the classic Roland MC-80). The advantages of these devices are portability, durability, and cost. Some of the most popular hardware sequencers were the Yamaha QX-1, introduced in 1984, the Roland MC-500, introduced in 1986, and the Akai ASQ-10 in 1986.

Since the inauguration of MIDI in 1983, digital hardware sequencers commonly incorporated features such as built-in MIDI ports and an internal disk drive, like the MC-500 mentioned above or a built in SCSI port to connect to a computer for storing data.

The next type of digital sequencers that were introduced were software sequencers; computer programs specifically designed for music creation and storage. Dr. T introduced the first commercial software sequencers in 1984 by Emile Tobenfeld's company (Dr.T Software) with their KCS (keyboard controlled sequencer) for the Commodore 64. Dr T's software quickly evolved, and eventually became a software package known as Omega II, for the Atari, a sequencing pack with interactive editing, performance, and algorithmic composition features. The KCS software was ported to the AMIGA, and Macintosh platforms in 1983. Dr T's software was a grouping of several MIDI programs that sync together under a multitasking environment called the MPE (Multi Program Environment). Three years later, Cakewalk, produced by 12 Tone Systems in Cambridge, Massachusetts for the PC platform, which became very popular.

This type of sequencing became an overnight success for several reasons. Laptop or desktop computer monitors could display a lot more information than a tiny liquid crystal display on a hardware sequencer and the process of editing various parameters became much more effective and less time consuming. Also, the computer-based sequencers had more memory for note and data storage, and could be used to graphically edit and store (sounds) patches on disk, called patch librarians. They also had the ability to print out a musical score, a Godsend for composers working with ensembles and orchestras. MIDI sequencing software revolutionized the music industry.

When comparing the various types of sequencers, the advantages of using computer-based software sequencing programs were light years beyond their hardware counterparts. The only disadvantage in a computer-based performance setup is portability, although with the power and speed of the new computers, this is becoming less of an issue.

Don't ask me which one is best, because each of the types I've discussed has advantages and disadvantages. No matter which type of sequencer you decide to use, sequencing a music score is a very tedious task, every aspect of the score must be entered: note after note, variations of tempo, volume, etc.

IN SUMMARY:

Integrated sequencers were further developed in the late 1980s. They were comprised of a series of integrated digital circuits built into synthesizers, samplers, and drum machines. This integration evolved into a generation of instruments commonly known as workstations, which combined a synthesizer, effects unit, drum machine, and sequencer into one unit. The first of these to make a big impact on musicians was the Korg M1, which was introduced in January 1988. The M1 was an amazing instrument for its time. The M1 had many advanced features, including something Korg called the AI synthesis system, which used PCM samples (pulse-code modulations) to create sounds, incorporated built in digital effects, a drum machine and a sophisticated eight-track sequencer that stored up to 10 songs and 100 patterns. The M1 was the ultimate workstation of the late 1980s taking integrated sequencers to a new plateau.

Although sequencing in the twenty-first century is predominantly in the digital domain, and usually is computer based, some musicians still love to use retrofitted analog gear and new hybrids of analog digital technology in the creation of their music. A great example of these new hybrids is the amazing Polymorph synth/sequencer developed by the German electronics company, Quasimidi. Klaus Schulze uses over a dozen of these units in his "Big Wall" stage and studio setup to create amazing complex arrangements.

The analog technology discussed in the beginning of this chapter may seem antiquated to some. It still remains a vital part of music technology for the immediacy it offers the musician, who has the ability to physically manipulate actual controls and connections, resulting in instantaneous changes in the structure of a song.

Part Two

Digital

CHAPTER 11

Computers in Music: Intelligent Instruments

Over the past 20 years, the computer has transformed the world and become an integral part of our everyday lives. The consolidation of computer and synthesizer technologies was the most important musical event of the '80s, and is still one of the most explored and fastest changing aspects of current music technology.

This evolution began with the contributions of Dr. Max Matthews of Bell Labs, Dr. John Chowning of Stanford University, and Peter Zinovieff, founder of the Electronic Music Studios (EMS) in London.

Dr. Matthews played the violin and was a telecommunications engineer at Bell Telephone Laboratories' Acoustic and Behavioral Research Department. As director of the Acoustic Research Center at Bell Labs during the 1950s and 1960s, Dr. Matthews earned primary credit for the development of digital music technology. The research began when Matthews was assigned to explore the digital transmission and recording of speech patterns for Bell. The tests were carried out to judge the quality of the sound used in telephone communications lines. Dr. Mathews constructed a converter to feed an analog sound source into a computer and another one to convert it back to an analog sound. This idea brought about the birth of analog/digital conversion, and Dr. Matthews' team at Bell Labs became leaders in the field of music synthesis. MIT Press published the results of their research in the book *The Technology of Computer Music* in 1969.

Dr. Matthews' first computer synthesis program, Music 1, was completed in 1957. After much experimentation with the software code, and after realizing its limitations, Dr. Matthews created Music II in 1958. Music II ran on a faster processor, the IBM 704, and was the first software ever written to create programmable digital wavetables. Two years later, in 1960, using the faster, more user friendly IBM transistorized 7094 computer, Music III was conceived. This third incarnation of the software included features like timbral variation and computer-assisted orchestration.

In 1962, fellow Bell researcher Joan Miller worked with Mathews in developing Music 4, the first widespread computer sound synthesis program to be written in FORTRAN, which was the newest computer language at the time. FORTRAN was much more efficient code than the Assembly language used in the previous three incarnations of the software. The Music series software evolution ran on a parallel course with that of the IBM computer, culminating with the introduction of Music V in 1968. It was written in FORTRAN, and ran on an IBM 360. This new development was aided by collaborations with several researchers and composers. Composer Jean-James Tenney, who was also a member of the technical staff at Bell Telephone Laboratories between 1961and 1964, assisted Dr. Matthews in his research, as well as another pioneer and noted composer in the field of computer-generated music, Claude Risset.

In 1970, Dr. Matthews began to concentrate his efforts on the use of computers in live performance with his construction of a hybrid instrument, which combined a Honeywell DDP-224 computer system with an analog synthesizer. He appropriately called this new system GROOVE (Generated Real-time Output Operations on Voltage-controlled Equipment). This complex system was connected by an interface comprised of two 12-bit digital to analog converters designed especially for coupling analog and digital devices. This was an antecedent of SCSI and MIDI interfaces.

Musicians were presented with a choice of a QWERTY keyboard or a two-octave piano-style keyboard to control the system. These could all be connected using programs written by individual users for specific compositions or arrangements. The user could enter code for FORTRAN programs consisting of library requests and original data to interface these component modules.

Bell Labs made drastic changes in their facility during the early 1970s, and the GROOVE system was dismantled. This was the first fully developed analog/digital hybrid music synthesis system, which allowed the composer to manipulate sound in real time. Dr.

Matthews continued his research, and remained active in computer-generated music into the 1990s.

Barry Vercoe, founder of the MIT Experimental Studio, and Professor of Media Arts and Sciences at the MIT Media Lab, was one of the first researchers who extended the capabilities of Dr. Matthews' Music 4. Using the technology developed by Dr. Matthews, Vercoe developed Music 360, a modified version of the program, which led to the eventual development of Music 11. Music 11 was a complex program that was powered by the PDP-11 computer. Created by the Digital Equipment Corporation and donated to the lab, Music 11 incorporated many new features, among them the ability to display and print a graphic musical score.

Barry Vercoe went on to create and develop the CSound environment in the fall of 1985. At the time, this was a powerful language for synthesizing and compressing audio. This eventually became one of the most widely implemented software sound synthesis systems in the world. This same CSound technology is incorporated into the new MPEG-4 audio compression standard, which will soon replace the MP3 format. MPEG-4, unlike previous audio standards created by ISO (International Organization of Standardization) and the IEC (The International Electrotechnical Commission), is not focused on a single application such as real-time telephony or high-quality audio compression. Instead, MPEG-4 Audio is a new standard that applies to every software application involving the use of complex sound compression, synthesis, sound manipulation, or playback.

While Barry Vercoe was developing faster, more complex versions of the Music 4 software, John Chowning, who taught computer-sound synthesis and composition at Stanford University for more than 30 years, created (with his associate, James Moorer) another variation on Dr. Matthews' Music V, Music 10.

During his research, Chowning accidentally discovered that he could produce musically complex, harmonically interesting results by modulating one sine wave with the output from another by using high-speed vibrato signals. As a result of this discovery, in 1968, a practical application for frequency modulation (FM) synthesis was born. The concept of frequency modulation (FM) had already been generally accepted since the early 1900s, but Chowning's work developed this technology into a convenient, practical musical synthesis tool for the musician.

Dr. John Chowning is the founder and director of the Center for Computer Research in Music and Acoustics (CCRMA) at Stanford University in Palo Alto, California. Both John Chowning's research and compositions have been significant developments in computer music.

Chowning was a 29-year-old graduate student when he entered Stanford in 1962. Previously, Chowning had studied composition for three years in Paris. While in Paris, he became interested in electronic music, when he attended concerts given by the leading French and German composers of the time, such as Pierre Boulez and Karlheinz Stockhausen. A fellow student in the Stanford University Orchestra gave Chowning a copy of Max Mathews' book, *The Technology of Computer Music*, which described how computers could be programmed to create music. Chowning soon visited Bell Labs in New Jersey to investigate further. Stanford had a large computer, but at the time had no analog synthesis equipment; consequently, Chowning began researching the possibilities of digital synthesis creation.

In his article "The Synthesis of Complex Tones by Means of Frequency Modulation," published in 1972 by The Journal of the Audio Engineering Society at MIT Press, Chowning said, "FM is something I stumbled upon in the mid-1960s. It turned out that one could, in a sense, 'cheat on nature.' By modulating the frequency of one oscillator (the carrier) by means of another oscillator (the modulator), one can generate a spectrum that has considerably more components that would be provided by either of the two alone."

FM, or frequency modulation, produces sound by generating a pure sine wave, universally known as a carrier. This waveform is then mixed with a second waveform, known as a modulator. When the two waveforms are adjacent in frequency, a complex waveform is fashioned. By manipulating the carrier and the modulator, it is possible to generate different timbres, or instruments.

The Japanese electronics giant Yamaha was the first company to vigorously explore and invest in Dr. Chowning's theory. This relationship led to the development of the legendary Yamaha DX7 synthesizer, released to universal acclaim in 1983. The DX7 was comprised of inexpensive hardware capable of employing the use of FM operators in real-time. The DX7, which sold 160,000 units in 1983 alone, put commercially available synthesizers on the map.

While John Chowning's contribution changed the way music was created for many years to come, Yamaha, like many other synthesizer manufacturers, never matched the success of the DX7 with later generations of instruments.

In 1969, Peter Zinovieff, the founder and driving force behind Electronic Music Studios (EMS) in London, pioneered the use of mini-computers for musical applications. The original EMS product introduced in 1969, the VCS3 (£300 in 1969), also known as "the Putney," was one of the first commercially available compact portable synthesizers. It dramatically altered the playing field, making low cost portable electronic instruments available for the first time. Two years later, the Synthi A, introduced in 1971 as "the synthesizer in the briefcase," became very popular with recording studios, music schools, and colleges, as well as live performance ensembles. The Synthi AKS also included a touch keyboard and hosted a built-in digital sequencer, which stored up to 256 notes. Thirty of the first units produced included a black and silver Touch pad, a "spin-and-touch" random note selector and a resistive touch sensitive keyboard. In the fall of 1971, the keyboard was replaced with the familiar EMS blue capacitive touch sensitive keyboard, which included an integrated sequencer.

During the next decade, many instruments were produced by a team of very talented engineers working at EMS. They included Tristram Cary, a famous composer for film and broadcast, whose musical credits include *Dr. Who* and several classic Hammer films. Cary later became Professor of Electronic Music at the Royal College of Music, followed by a long tenure as Professor of Music at the University of Adelaide in Australia. David Cockerell, another engineer at EMS, designed many of their circuits between 1970 and 1972, later working for Electro-Harmonix in the U.S. designing most of their effects pedals. Many well-known musicians used the EMS instruments during the 1970s. They included Brian Eno, when he was in the band Roxy Music, Pete Townsend of the Who, Edgar Froese of Tangerine Dream, Klaus Schulze, Giorgio Moroder, Jean-Michel Jarre, Kraftwerk, Hawkwind, Tim Blake, and Pink Floyd.

Peter Zinovieff created the MUSYS III hybrid system in 1962 with the help of fellow EMS engineers Peter Grogono and Jim Lawson. The development of the MUSYS System actually started out as a collection of complex analog hardware, but as the circuits became increasingly sophisticated, Zinovieff devised methods of using a computer to control the synthesizer circuits. EMS designer David Cockrell, interfaced two of Digital Engineering Corporation's PDP-8 computers, introduced on March 22, 1965, with custom software designed by Peter Grogno to control an EMS Synthi 100.

The PDP-8, a very flexible and user-friendly computer, was recognized as the most important small computer of the 1960s. It was the least expensive computer on the market at the time, and the first computer sold on a retail basis. It was also the first parallel general-purpose digital computer sold in a tabletop configuration. Input to the PDP-8 was accomplished with a QWERTY computer keyboard or by a velocity sensitive piano-style keyboard. To actually have a computer monitor, when most people working with computers during that era programmed with punch cards, was unheard of at the time. In April 1995, Robin Wood, a member of EMS since 1971, acquired the company. The Synthi A, VCS3, and the EMS Vocoders are still being manufactured by EMS today.

Matthews, Chowning, and Zinovieff contributed a great deal to this rapidly expanding field. Since the publication of Dr. Matthew's highly praised book, digital music technology has expanded in many directions.

Probably the greatest impact on digital music was made by the introduction of the home computer. Affordability of systems like Macintosh, Amiga, and PC-based CPUs, as well as the venerated Atari XT and Commodore 64 computers, made electronic music a reality for thousands of musicians who could not afford much higher priced digital workstations.

Laurie Spiegel was one of the first composer/programmers to write commercial music software for the home computer. Having come from a folk music background, Laurie envisioned the personal computer as a new type of folk instrument. Spiegel began incorporating analog synthesizers into her music in 1969. Four years later, in 1973 while working at Bell Labs, she began writing interactive compositional software. Perhaps her greatest achievement at Bell Labs was VAMPIRE (Video And Music Program for Interactive Real-time Exploration/Experimentation), which was an offspring of Dr. Max Chowning's GROOVE (Generating Real-time Operations On Voltage-controlled Equipment) mentioned earlier in this chapter.

Spiegel later founded New York University's Computer Music Studio, and became well-known for her music software for personal computers, especially Music Mouse, a fun to use program, where the user creates musical arrangements by movements of the mouse, using mathematically generated algorithms to produce the music. This program made it possible for musicians to generate music in either tonal or atonal styles by hitting the computer's keys and moving the computer's mouse. Her albums, *The Expanding Universe* and *Unseen Worlds,* have become classics in the genre of electronic music.

The first generation of professional commercially available computer music instruments, or workstations as some companies later called them, were very sophisticated elaborate systems that cost a great deal of money when they first appeared. They ranged from twenty five thousand dollars to over two hundred thousand dollars depending on the extra frills available for each system. The two most popular CMI (computer musical instruments) were the Fairlight and The Synclavier.

Cameron Jones received two patents from the U.S. Patent Office for two devices, the *high-resolution musical note oscillator* and the *partial timbre sound synthesis method and instrument,* were integrated into the Synclavier Digital Audio System. Cameron Jones and his partner, Sydney Alonso, along with composer Jon Appleton, who was hired as a musical consultant for NED, developed the first Prototype of the Synclavier at Dartmouth College in 1975. It was updated and refined the following year and marketed by the company they founded, New England Digital, as the Synclavier ll.

During that era, the Synclavier was the first truly portable digital system to offer a vast amount of programmable control. It weighed less than a Minimoog, and a touring musician could tuck the keyboard unit under one arm, and carry the CPU that controlled the instrument in a small snare drum case. The Synclavier II was available in several configurations that offered customers a choice of 8, 16, 24, or 32 voices. It featured harmonic summing, real-sound sampling and manipulation, multi-voice sequencing and editing, a 16-track digital sequencer, and unlimited sound storage. The amount of storage depended on the size of the hard drive(s). Everything a musician needed to operate the Synclavier ll was located within easy reach. Computer memory was very expensive at the time and a fully equipped Synclavier II cost more than $200,000 in the early 1980s.

Four of the most well known musicians who used the Synclavier were Pat Metheny and Lyle Mays of the Pat Metheny Group, performance artist/composer Laurie Anderson, and Frank Zappa, each a pioneering innovator in their own way.

Both Pat Metheny and Lyle Mays incorporated a Synclavier system into their live performances as well as many Pat Metheny Group and solo project albums recorded after 1984. One of the most original guitarists of the past three decades, respected by millions of musicians, Pat Metheny is an exploratory guitarist who has achieved immense success. Metheny's numerous releases with the Pat Metheny Group are sometimes difficult to pigeonhole as a genre but are always comprehensible and original. These albums consistently stretch the boundaries of jazz.

Pat Metheny began using the Synclavier on the album *First Circle*. It featured Pat's "Synclavier guitar," which was a souped up Roland GR303 guitar with custom onboard electronics to control Pat's Synclavier II. "Forward March," the opening track, has a lot of out-of-tune sounds, a result of Metheny exploring the Synclavier's microtuning function. There are more Synclavier II solos on this album than any other Metheny Group album. As of mid-2002, Metheny has recorded 24 records in the past 23 years. Metheny earned fourteen Grammy Awards, and three gold records during his long career. Pat Metheny's extraordinary approach to arrangement and music composition has been documented in many musical settings, and he will be remembered in musical history as one of the greatest contributors to modern jazz.

Frank Zappa started his musical career in high school as a drummer in garage bands in Baltimore. Zappa first gained national popularity in the mid-1960s as guitarist/composer in the band, The Mothers of Invention. Although he has become a rock music legend, he was also a very serious composer. Zappa recorded several albums with electronic music pioneer, composer, Pierre Boulez and the London Symphony Orchestra. His first attempt in merging synths into his music was with a one-of-a-kind instrument designed for Zappa by Bob Easton at 360 Systems in California. They jointly named the instrument the Electro Wagnerian Emancipator. Because of poor sound quality, it never made its way onto a recording.

Zappa discovered the Synclavier in the mid-1980s. Besides playing a major role in the creation of his albums, *The Perfect*

Stranger, Thing-Fish, Francesco Zappa, FZ Meets The Mothers Of Prevention, Civilization, and the posthumous album *The Lost Episodes—The Grand Wazoo*, the Synclavier II was also the primary instrument on his critically acclaimed *Jazz from Hell* album, released in November of 1986. On the albums, *Thing-Fish*, and *Francesco Zappa*, he used only the synthesizer portion of the instrument without the sampler. Zappa used a Modulus Graphite guitar controller at first, but eventually input all his notes to the instrument with the computer keyboard. He began to work with the instrument's sampling capabilities on *Frank Zappa Meets the Mothers of Prevention*. He once said that the main advantage for him in using the Synclavier in his music was that it helped him to imagine rhythms that human beings had difficulty contemplating. He used original samples that were created in his New York studio in order to get high quality isolated digital tones. The culmination of this original sampling is represented on the seminal album *Jazz from Hell*. After his untimely death from colon cancer in 1993, Frank Zappa's musical legacy continues with his daughter, Moon Unit Zappa, and his son, Dweezil Zappa.

Another composer to bring the Synclavier to the public spotlight was Laurie Anderson, one of the most noteworthy performance artists of the last two decades. Poet, writer, visual artist, sculptor and social commentator, Anderson was best known as a musician. When her song "O Superman," based on the 19th-century hymn *O Souverain* from Jules Massenet's opera *Le Cid* and its refrain "O Sovereign, O Judge, O Father!" reached the #2 spot on the British pop charts in 1981, her reputation as one of the most eccentric performers in pop music was affirmed. Subsequent releases, like *Big Science, Mister Heartbreak, United States live, Strange Angels*, and *Bright Red*, won both critics and listeners praise. Laurie has created various types of performances, ranging from simple spoken word oratories to highly sophisticated multimedia events, which she has performed throughout the world.

In October 1999, the Next Wave Festival at the Brooklyn Academy of Music premiered *Songs and Stories from Moby Dick*, an original stage production written by Anderson, inspired by the Herman Melville book. She composed a score and performance piece based on the life of Amelia Earhart in 2000, for the American Composers Orchestra. Besides being one of the first people to work with the Synclavier and the Vocoder, she is recognized worldwide as a leader in incorporating technology with performing arts. Anderson was actively involved in the creation of the "Talking Stick" with engineers Allen and David Liddle. In 2000, author Roselee Goldberg published a biography on the life and career of Laurie Anderson.

Many other great musicians composed with the Synclavier during the 1980s and 1990s, including Suzanne Ciani, a brilliant composer/musician and electronic music pioneer. Suzanne Ciani used the instrument on her early albums for the Private Music label, and on many other scores and commercials she produced during the 1980's. In the following discussion, Suzanne unravels some of the mysteries behind this complex instrument. Some of you may remember the Coca-Cola commercials where someone opened a bottle of coke and poured it into a glass. These sounds were created in Suzanne Ciani's studio.

Ciani says, "The Synclavier is a completely digital instrument. The software allows timbre design through FM synthesis. Another program called re-synthesis analyzes timbres by breaking them into a number of frames. A very powerful tool is digital sampling, allowing the recording of a sound from the real world into the memory for later manipulation. There is music printing program, which is useful for compositional feedback when you're in the creative stages of writing or for creating professional scores, or printed out parts for musicians to play at sessions. Sequencing, or the recording of patterns into the digital recorder, is multi-track.

"FM synthesis is one of the ways of creating a sound. The way the actual Synclavier is set up gives me four simultaneous FM possibilities to work with, called partial timbres. So I can set up a timbre on partial timbre one and enrich it further by adding two, three, and four. That's one way of creating sound on the Synclavier.

"Another way of creating a sound is via sampling. Sampling might include a sound from a tape recorder, a sound of a real musician playing a note, or a sound of anything you want. We've recorded anything from a champagne bottle opening to glass breaking. Once these sounds are recorded, you get to manipulate and edit them in the system. For instance I recorded some coins in a bag, shortened the sample, and now it sounds like a tambourine, and I can incorporate this sound pitched in a track to use as a rhythm element. Other sounds that I use are composite sounds made of five or six elements that I create and store in the sample library. I tend to use the storage system to file the sounds that I've created so that I have immediate access to them when I'm playing the keyboard.

"The third way of creating sound on the Synclavier is resynthesis, which is actually a blend of the first two methods I've just described. In fact it usually starts out with a sampled real sound. Then the resynthesis program analyzes the sound and breaks it up into a number of frames. These frames work in the way a film works, where the persistence of vision and multiple frames make up a single motion in the film. In sound synthesis, and especially in the resynthesis program, I have maybe up to twenty frames in a single sound, and each one will have a different component of the sound. They all happen rapidly after each other to produce the complete sound. The sound itself depends on all those elements being merged together.

"Your imagination is the only limit in a system like this. You can record any sound and then modify and edit that sound. So by editing, I mean you can mix sampled sounds together or splice and re-combine sections of a sound with digital splicing. I can record a sound and change the attack or the final decay or easily modulate the pitch via the keyboard."

The Synclavier was matched in power and performance only by one other instrument during that era, the Fairlight CMI, produced in Australia. It was one of the top digital workstations of the 1980s.

Two Australian engineers, Peter Vogel and Kim Ryrie, established the Fairlight Company in Rushcutters Bay, New South Wales, Australia, in the spring of 1975. They began their enterprise by manufacturing and selling video special effects boxes for television and film companies and electrical components for radio stations. Their objective was to produce a digitally controlled musical instrument that would provide an alternative to the analog synthesizers that were popular during the 1970s.

In 1976, they built their first synthesizer, the Qasar M8. It was an eight-voice synth based on Motorola consultant Tony Furse's dual-processor computer chip. Furse, previously an engineer at the Canberra School of Electronic Music, had already designed and built a system with many of the Fairlight features, notably the light pen used for entering information and editing scores, and the display monitor.

Vogel and Ryrie wanted the Quasar M8 to be capable of producing realistic sounds. After extensive research and refinement, they developed a means of recording authentic sounds (samples), which became a library of rudimentary samples that could be altered and modified electronically. The Fairlight Computer Musical Instrument was ready to be introduced to the public in 1979.

The first models of the Fairlight included a sample library. Soon, owners of these instruments began creating their own unique samples and offering them to Fairlight for use in their libraries. One of the most famous samples produced for the Fairlight, which was soon ported to other sampling platforms, was the breathy vocal pad that Klaus Schulze constructed. This pad, this single sampled sound became famous over the next decade, and could be heard in many of Jan Hammer's episodes of *Miami Vice*, as well as dozens of other albums and soundtracks. Thus, the Fairlight CMI's popularity soared mainly due to its sampling capabilities.

The Fairlight's only competitors in price and performance during the mid to late 1980s were the Synclavier from New England Digital, mentioned earlier, and the AudioFrame, produced by the WaveFrame Corporation in Germany. The Fairlight II series retailed at $25,000 or more, and the Fairlight Series III started at $40,000 and with add-ons could go up to a couple hundred thousand dollars. Fairlight discontinued the Series III in 1991. After the Series III, the company concentrated its efforts on the creation of hard-disk recorders. There are many famous artists who used the Fairlight, among them are Peter Gabriel, Stevie Wonder, Thomas Dolby, Howard Jones, Jan Hammer, Pet Shop Boys, Tears for Fears, Frankie Goes to Hollywood, Jane Child, The Art of Noise, Mike Oldfield, and Alan Parsons.

Larry Fast (Synergy), an esteemed electronic music composer and performing musician who played keyboards with Peter Gabriel's band Genesis in the studio and live from 1977 to 1986, brought the Fairlight's unique sound into Gabriel's music. Gabriel broke new ground by combining the high-tech ambience of electronic music with various forms of world music, which is best illustrated on the first album released by Real World, *Passion*, which is Gabriel's film score for Martin Scorsese's *The Last Temptation of Christ* (1989). That year Gabriel walked away with a Grammy for Best New Age Recording, although the album could hardly be considered New Age by any stretch of the imagination. The album was also nominated for

Best Original Score of 1989. The Fairlight Series II played a major role in its production.

During the 1980s, the Fairlight and the Synclavier were the high-end option for state-of- the-art synthesis and sampling, and both were way beyond the reach of all but the most up-scale studios. Both the Fairlight and Synclavier, because of their hybrid construction, were also complete multi-track digital recording studios, something most musicians have come to take for granted with digital mastering and hard disk recording available on home based computers at a fraction of the cost.

These instruments provided precise control over all the music that was programmed into them. The composer had the ability to watch the notes appear on the screen in notated form as the notes were played. The composition could then be altered; any aspect of the musical parameters could be changed by using a light pen to scroll onto the screen, or by using the standard computer keypad, which was included. These instruments were perfectly suited for television and film, because they were the first musical devices to accept time code (SMPTE), which was recorded on the film and allowed the composer to score the musical events in sync with the film.

As hardware processing speed increases, and the memory capabilities multiply, software developers write new, more powerful, and imaginative programs, for sequencing, recording, notation, and mastering. The new millennium saw the introduction of very fast processors, such as the AMD Athlon, Intel Pentium, as well as Apple G4 technology, with excellent software for MIDI and audio recording, scoring, mastering CDs, film work, and producing music for the Internet, along with applications for streaming audio, MP3 recorders, encoders, players. The list goes on and on.

CHAPTER 12

Affordable Sampling Technology Emerges

In Chapter 11, we covered the use of computers in music, culminating in the high-end computer music instruments (CMI), the Synclavier and Fairlight, which introduced state-of-the-art digital sampling technology in the early 1980s. Next came the advent of complex, reliable, and affordable digital synthesizers and samplers such as Ensoniq's Mirage and Akai's S612 sampler.

Digital samplers, which were introduced during the 1980s, have become one of the most significant tools of the music industry. They store high-quality sound samples digitally, and then replay these sounds when a musician plays a note to trigger the sample. These samplers can then alter the recorded or sampled sound using various techniques. The most common technique is called looping, where a small recording can be played back for long periods of time in a continuous loop, saving valuable memory space. Then there is pitch shifting, which raises or lowers the original pitch of a sound. Cross-fading is another very useful feature achieved by fading out one sound while another sound fades in, leaving no space between the two sounds. Other features commonly used are interpolation and filtering. These editing processes are useful in economizing on memory required to store a sample.

What eventually became known as "sampling," in many ways, had its roots in Musique Concrète, which originated in France over 50 years ago. Pioneers such as Pierre Henri and Pierre Schaeffer, Louis and Bebe Barron, and Tod Dockstader all worked with tape manipulation—what we now refer to as "sampled sounds"—in the 1940s. In the early 1960s, the Mellotron used tape loops of pre-recorded sounds for playback *(discussed in Chapter 2)* and was the first commercially successful forerunner of sampling devices. In 1966, the Beatles expanded their musical palette when they used a

Mellotron on *Sgt. Pepper's*. That album that took over 700 hours of studio time to record and launched the Beatles into a whole new musical realm. Another English group, the Moody Blues, followed the Beatles' lead, making a big impact when they used the Mellotron extensively on their first seven albums. The Mellotron was the primary instrument favored by the European progressive bands of the 1970s, such as Yes, Gong, Minimum Vital, Cyrille Verdeaux, and Hawkwind. Over the next 12 to 15 years, the Mellotron made a profound impact on many genres of music. (See Artistpro's *The Mellotron Book* for the complete history of this unique and much-loved instrument.)

A California-based company, EMU Systems, was the first company to introduce affordable sampling technology. They introduced the 8-bit Emulator I in 1981, and a refined, much better sounding version, the Emulator II, in 1984. The Emulator II listed for $8,000. This brought down the price of samplers from the $25,000 range to under $10,000, but it was still out of reach for many musicians.

In 1983, inventor Raymond Kurzweil, who had developed a revolutionary reading machine for the blind that could scan written material and read it aloud in a synthesized voice, developed the first ROM-based sampler. Stevie Wonder, a customer for Kurzweil's reading machine, asked Kurzweil to create an electronic instrument that blended the richness of acoustic sound with the control and sound modification of electronics. In 1983, Ray and his team of engineers put their heads together, and the result was the K250, an instrument that effectively reproduced the full complexity of acoustic instrument sounds. Kurzweil continues to be a major contributor to current sampler technology, with the enormously successful K2000, K2500, and K2600 series. Samplers like the Emulator and the Kurzweil quickly began appearing in the keyboard arsenals of well-known musicians on major labels. In the early 1980s, this technology, although more affordable, was still beyond the budgets of most working musicians.

In the mid-80s, the long wait for working musicians around the world was over when the first truly affordable sampler became available to the masses. In 1986, I bought my first sampler, an Akai S612, on the advice of Bill Rhodes, then working as a sound designer and product clinician for Akai *(see interview in Chapter 14)*.

The Akai S612 wasn't the company's first excursion into the world of musical instruments; Akai had already released the AX73 and AX80 analog synths. However, this instrument, designed by David Cockerell, formerly with EMS and Electro-Harmonix, launched the name Akai as a serious musical instrument manufacturer. For its retail price of $895, this was an extraordinary value. For that period in time, the specs were remarkable: a 12-bit architecture, with a maximum of one second's worth of sampling at a 32kHz sampling rate. The S612 had a built-in disk drive for external storage to 2.8-inch "Quick Disks" (apparently named by someone with a peculiar sense of humor since it took several minutes to load a disk). It did, however, establish Akai as one of the leading players in the sampling technology field, a position it has maintained to this day.

Around the same time, in the mid-1980s, electronic instrument manufacturer Ensoniq produced the hugely successful Mirage sampler. Oberheim released the Oberheim DPX-1, and the large Japanese electronic instrument manufacturers Korg, Casio, Yamaha, and Roland quickly joined the sampler market.

Sampling technology and synthesis soon merged with the introduction of wavetable synthesis. Companies like Korg, Roland, EMU, PPG, and Kawai created synthesizers that played looped waveforms from stored digital memory, known as ROM (Read-Only Memory). These were then combined with various types of synthesis engines, such as additive synthesis, subtractive synthesis, and vector synthesis to create extremely rich hybrid sounds. Some of the most popular synth/sampler hybrids of this generation of technology were the Sequential Circuits Prophet VS, Wolfgang Palm's PPG Wave 2 computer, the Korg M1, and the Kawai K5. My favorite was the Korg Wavestation, because it could sequence waveforms to create unusual rhythms and textures. The Wavestation, introduced in 1990, was based on the 1986 Sequential Circuits Prophet VS. Sequential sold the technology to Korg after discontinuing operation in 1988.

In their effort to reach a broader market, Kurzweil developed the first ROM-based sample playback machine, the K1000, in 1987 ($995 list). Two years later, EMU introduced the Proteus 1 ($995 list), which became a big seller. The Proteus has gone through many incarnations, which have gained immense popularity among musicians. Both the K1000 and the Proteus derived their sounds from the libraries of their high-end parents, the K250, and the Emulator II.

The creative applications of samplers have also evolved a great deal over time. Back in the 1980s, artists such as Johannes Schmoelling (Ex-Tangerine Dream), Jan Hammer, Jean-Michel Jarre, and Klaus Schulze created dramatic textures with samplers, using them as integral parts of their innovative compositions.

Most people were content to use pre-recorded samples, usually supplied by the manufacturers or third party software companies. The true innovators like Johannes Schmoelling, in his opera score *Wuviend REIT* (recorded on the Erdenklang label), created amazing aural tapestries with complex layers of original samples. This use of sampling became very popular with composers of ambient music in the 1990s. Composers such as Jeff Greinke, Vidna Obmana, Robert Rich, Jeff Pearce, Steve Roach, Mark Rownd, and others reinvented ambient music by creating dreamy layers of indistinguishable timbres creating beautiful atmospheric albums.

During this period, bands such as the Orb, William Orbit and others began to incorporate layers of samples with percussive loops creating trance, house, dub, and many new forms of energetic dance music.

One of the biggest developments of this technology that edged its way into popular music culture was the advent of rap and hip-hop in the early 1980s. The turntable became an innovative way of playing samples. The man who actually began this sensation was known as Grandmaster Flash, who used technology as a channel to broaden the scope of hip-hop culture. Grandmaster Flash was one of hip-hops founding fathers and the creator of what became known as the "Quick Mix." He was the first person to re-arrange the structure of songs by using duplicate copies of records and manually editing/repeating the best moments, which he later dubbed (no pun intended) the "break" by rubbing the record back and forth. This became known as "cutting" and was later called "scratching." His DJ style became a rage in his hometown, the Bronx, and within months, it was huge around the world. Grandmaster Flash paved the way for many of today's DJs on their road to stardom.

Flash was the first to develop live performance stunts like mixing records behind his back or down under tables, and kicking mixing faders with his feet. In the late 1980s, Flash was also the first DJ to develop and market his own DJ device, aptly named the Flashformer.

A whole new generation of sampling devices, and synth loop modules especially designed for rap and hip-hop, House, Acid, and Trance have sprung up since the mid-1990s. The music has continued to grow in popularity, and as a result, companies like Emu, Korg, Roland and others, continue to explore more innovative technologies geared to this genre. A great example of these devices is the EMU Orbit, named after William Orbit, which sequences break beats, drones, and samples to create live mixes.

Nearly every recording studio now is totally digital and most are controlled by personal computers. Most samplers and synthesizers now have a SCSI port, fire wire optical bus, or some type of communication port feature to access and share information with computers and other digital recording devices such as hard-disk recorders, ADAT machines and automated mixers. With suitable digital audio editing software, like Sound Forge or BIAS Peak, samples and patches can be loaded directly into the computer or the sampler from almost any source. There are also many software-based samplers, or "virtual instruments" on the market, like the Unity DS-1 and Gamma, which duplicate their hardware counterparts exceptionally well. Virtual synths are also becoming more and more popular. Software like Waldorf's PPG Wave 2.0, Native Instruments Pro-52, the Roland virtual sound Canvas, and others are showing that software-based synthesizers can actually equal or surpass their hardware counterparts. One drawback is that software-based samplers and "virtual instruments" require massive amounts of memory (RAM) and CPU usage to function properly.

The new generations of digital samplers are capable of reproducing and manipulating sounds in ways never possible before. Over the past two decades, samplers have changed the face of modern music by creating entire new genres of music that would never have been possible without this technology.

CHAPTER 13

The Introduction of MIDI

Let's travel back to the 1970s and early 1980s for a moment and try to picture the studio or stage setup of your favorite keyboard player: Keith Emerson, Jan Hammer, or Joe Zawinul, for example. The performer usually had at least four to six devices on stage, because back in those days, you had to have a separate keyboard or synth module for every tone type you wanted, and none of them could communicate with one another.

There were notable exceptions, such as the Oberheim "system" comprised of the OB8 eight voice polyphonic keyboard, OBX sequencer, DMX drum machine, and Oberheim Xpander. The Xpander was one of the most flexible non-modular analog synths of all time. This sophisticated hardware communication protocol developed by Tom Oberheim, allowed these instruments to communicate perfectly in sync within the confines of a pre-MIDI environment.

In June 1981 at the National Association of Music Merchants (NAMM) convention, a small core group of electronic instrument manufacturers discussed a proposal for establishing a standard for digital communication between electronic music devices called MIDI (musical instrument digital interface). Tom Oberheim, founder of Oberheim Electronics, along with Dave Smith from Sequential Circuits and I. Kakehashi from Roland Corporation opened the door to this new technology. In November 1981, Dave Smith submitted a proposal, the "Universal Synthesizer Interface" (USI), to the Audio Engineers Society. Several Japanese manufacturers who had been working on their own proposal, which was more complex than Smith's USI. At the January 1982 NAMM show, representatives from these Japanese manufactures met with Dave Smith and Tom Oberheim, and within the next six months a standard had been established and several companies began production of MIDI capable instruments.

They revealed their amazing new discovery at the first NAMM show in Los Angeles in January 1983.

In this demonstration, two "incompatible" synthesizers, a Sequential Circuits Prophet 600 and a Roland JX-3P, were connected by two MIDI cables. A spokesperson from Sequential played a few bars on the Prophet 600 and the audience heard both the Prophet 600 and the Roland JX-3P create music simultaneously. Next, the process was reversed to demonstrate the shared protocol of this revolutionary communication. Other types of MIDI information were transmitted, and thus, a whole new revolution in music technology began. The technology was standardized and became known as the MIDI 1.0 specification, which was formally published in August of 1983.

Since the advent of the first commercial synthesizers in the late 1960s, performers and composers had been exploring methods to "layer" their music created on synthesizers and samplers to be able to play more than one sound simultaneously. This technique, made possible for the first time by the use of MIDI, is now commonly known as a "stack." With the introduction of MIDI, an entirely new vocabulary was introduced, enabling a solo performer to produce the sound of a full ensemble.

The first keyboard commercially produced with a MIDI interface was the Prophet 600, made by Sequential Circuits in 1982 ($1,995). It was comprised of six voices, a sequencer, and arpeggiator. Almost overnight, nearly every synthesizer being manufactured included MIDI ports, and by the spring of 1984, the author of this book used MIDI to sync up a Sequential Circuits Six Trak keyboard (the first commercially produced multi-timbral synth) with a Commodore 64 running Dr. T's amazing newly developed "KCS" sequencer software.

By 1985, all of the musical manufacturers supporting the new MIDI protocol had brainstormed and decided to establish a new organization, the MIDI Manufacturer's Association. Their task was to generate and disseminate all the documents pertaining to the MIDI standard, and it was through the MMA that new changes to the original MIDI specification were created. A prime example of this collaboration and standardization was the music software company Opcode, who created the MIDI File Format specification and gave it to the MMA. As a direct result, every music software company began creating MIDI sequencer software that could read and write each other's data files. Another software developer, Digidesign, created MIDI Time Code. The musical tower of Babel had disintegrated.

Since the 1980s, as the personal computer developed and became more refined, it became the ideal system for utilizing the potential of MIDI, with the diversified fundamentals of electronic music creation. The emergence of the MIDI standard in 1983 in many ways brought back the functionality of modular synthesis to the new, quickly evolving digital domain. A vast consumer market developed for software packages such as MIDI sequencers and librarians. The personal computer had suddenly become a fundamental part in the electronic musician's studio.

MIDI wasn't originally considered for use with microprocessors like the home computer. It was originally designed as a practical means of interconnecting musical instruments as explained above. By being a creation of the digital domain, the obvious logical progression of interfacing MIDI equipped hardware with personal computers immediately became self-evident. IBM compatibles, as well as Atari, Commodore, and Macintosh computers had the capacity to connect to MIDI devices by means of a small hardware "patchbay," the MIDI interface. Generally this device provided one or more MIDI in and MIDI out ports, and occasionally a MIDI thru port, so that information could be exchanged with up to sixteen independent sound sources, from keyboards, or rack-mount modules to a computer. On PC based computers, the MIDI interface was generally in the form of an internal soundcard, or an add-on card that plugs into an expansion slot in various PC based systems. On the Macintosh platform, it is always a device that connects either to an external serial port, parallel port, USB port, or FireWire port.

Two of the pioneering computer companies who were forerunners in MIDI software and hardware interfaces were not Apple or IBM, as one might expect, but Atari and Commodore. Unfortunately, even though technically superior at the time, Atari and Commodore couldn't compete with larger companies like IBM and Macintosh, who had gained widespread acceptance, saturating over 90 percent of the market. As a result, by the early 1990s both Atari and the

Commodore AMIGA had vanished like the dinosaur, although AMIGA reincarnated itself once again in the winter of 2000/2001, and is now back on the market after many years of digital obscurity.

The majority of synthesizers and samplers manufactured since 1983 feature built-in MIDI capabilities that allow the user to cultivate compelling MIDI environments without ever having to connect to a computer. In the past ten years, the power and potential of home computers has expanded exponentially. As a result, thousands of MIDI musicians and recording studios are using software-based tools such as Cubase, Pro Tools, Logic Audio, and Opcode's Vision to manage their MIDI setups. The MIDI protocol presents a stable, efficient set of rules for transmitting musical performance data.

Some universally accepted varieties of MIDI software applications include music instruction software, MIDI sequencing software, music notation software, hard disk recording/editing software, patch editor/librarian software, computer-assisted composition software, and virtual instruments. These are software-based synthesizers, samplers, and effects modules, which perfectly emulate their hardware counterparts. Although MIDI specifications have not changed much since 1983, current and future developments in computer hardware and specialized software for MIDI applications make the frontiers appear infinite for an ongoing music revolution.

CHAPTER 14

Bill Rhodes on MIDI and Sampling

Bill Rhodes wears a lot of hats in his multifaceted musical career. Formerly a Professor of Music at Monmouth University in New Jersey, with a Master's degree in Composition, Bill has been an educator for over thirty years and has an extensive knowledge of electronic musical instruments. He's currently a composer-pianist working for the Music Industries Corporation as a product specialist and consultant. From the early 1970s until the mid-1980s, Bill worked for many pioneering synthesizer and sampler manufacturers, which included Music Technology, Inc. (Crumar) as well as Korg, Kawai, Akai, and others.

Bill Rhodes

Photo courtesy Jazzical Records

Bill has six CD releases on the IC label (Hamburg, Germany) and two CDs on the Jazzical-Digital label. Bill was also featured with Rick Wakeman from the mega-group Yes on a recent double CD. His latest release, *Concerto for the New Earth*, was issued in the winter of 2000.

Rhodes discusses two of the most important events in non-acoustic music of the twentieth century: MIDI and sampling technologies.

Rhodes defines MIDI, its development, and its functions on many levels of music production. As we already know, the Musical Instrument Digital Interface (MIDI) protocol provides the user with a uniform and proficient means of conveying musical performance information as electronic data. MIDI information can be seen as a set of instructions, which tell a synthesizer or other MIDI equipped piece of gear how to "perform" a piece of music. The synthesizer or sampler receiving the MIDI data generates the actual sounds.

Rhodes also discusses sampling: what it is, how it's done, and the many applications for sampling, including today's sophisticated hard disk recording studios, which use sampling to record albums. (All CDs, DVDs, and other forms of digital recording are produced with sampling technology).

Bill fills in the technological gaps and shares insights into future innovations in music technology in this interview presented in two parts. The first part was conducted in late 1987, and the second part in the fall of 2000.

Ben Kettlewell: Bill, can you tell us a little about MIDI and how it functions?

Bill Rhodes: MIDI is an abbreviation for Musical Instrument Digital Interface. It's the ability of one MIDI instrument to communicate with another, or a computer to talk to a keyboard, or a computer to talk to another computer through a keyboard. Basically what MIDI is used for is in real-time situations where people are playing live, they can perform on one MIDI instrument, and control a bunch of other keyboards, samplers, or sound modules at the same time, playing off the output of the master keyboard. There are MIDI mixdown boards which are capable of automated audio mixdown through MIDI. MIDI is also used for echo machines, delay machines, multiple effects units. Let's say you want a certain sound or patch on your synthesizer. Say, you want a slap-back echo on patch 30 of your synthesizer and you have a MIDI controlled FX device such as a Lexicon PCM70. You can have that patch assigned to a patch on the reverb unit which will recall that specific setting on command. The implications of MIDI are incredible in their scope. For instance, a guitar, drum kit, violin, or a host of other instruments can control a MIDI keyboard or other MIDI modules if the instrument\is fitted with a MIDI pickup. For a keyboard player, MIDI is indispensable. Instead of lugging around a bunch of keyboards, a musician can take one controller and a couple of modules, which can fit under your arm to a gig. This saves a lot of wear and tear. It saves a lot of time. Another thing about MIDI also is that it has the capability of transmitting all sorts of data such as pitch bend, and program change.

BK: Since its inception, MIDI technology has developed at an incredible pace. Where do you see it going in the future?

BR: It will be a lot more accessible to non-musicians. Let's say musicians that are not accomplished …neophyte musicians, MIDI will help them out as far as playing. This is especially true when we think of the implications of computers, and programming to assist in music production. Using a computer to edit or program a performance is really helpful, because you can see all the parameters of the performance, and function that the synthesizer performs on your computer screen. As far as playback, and sequencing etc. MIDI software makes it easy for a synthesist to play and get a good sound using MIDI instead of doing everything in real-time. You can correct timing errors, change the dynamics of individual notes, or build carefully controlled crescendos or diminuendos. Some of the advanced MIDI sequencers offer an onscreen mixing console for adjusting the volume, pan position, and other variables for each track individually. The computer display mixer adjustments can then be recorded and played back as part of the sequence itself, a process called "mix automation," normally found only in high-end recording studios. Best of all, MIDI sequence data is compact, so it can easily be stored on a floppy disk or other removable media. That is an interesting aspect of MIDI, …it takes on an individual personality according to the composer.

BK: You also do programming for AKAI. Can you tell us a little about that?

BR: Craig Anderton, who was the first editor of *Electronic Musician* magazine, and a genius in the electronic world as far as things he writes for *Keyboard*, *Guitar Player*, and different companies he works for. He did the programming on the Akai AX60, and I did the programming on the Akai AX80, which is the synthesizer, not the sampler. It was a regular analog synthesizer with digital functions.

BK: Tell us about sampling. Earlier in the book we discussed the sampling capabilities of high-end instruments like the Fairlight, the Kurzweil K250, and the Synclavier II. What do you see for the future of sampling keyboards?

BR: Sampling on the three instruments you mentioned is cost prohibitive (in 1987) to most musicians because they are so expensive. When the Akai S650 was introduced with a price well under a thousand dollars it drastically changed this scenario. With the Quick Disk loader, which is the sample loader, it can create and store samples on floppy disk. It's a lot more limited than the other instruments in that it has much greater memory and uses multi-sampling, which is where you can sample different pitches and nuances of an instrument separately, then combine them and get a great sound. But for the money, the Akai was phenomenal because it was cost competitive and had good sound. Sampling is heard in 90 percent of the CDs being released, whether it's commercial music, top 40, jazz, or what have you. There's so much sampling going on these days, it's incredible! Sometimes you can't really tell if it's a sample or not, because the sample quality is so good. The thing about sampling is that you can sample anything, even non-musical sounds. You plan play a "C" scale on a drinking glass, or you can have dogs barking in a chromatic scale. You can sample any sound you want. The sampler, with MIDI, is the wave of the future as far as electronic music is concerned.

BK: Software has become a big part of this technology. How will it affect the musician?

BR: When we talk about programming, MIDI is making everybody a better programmer, because with the computer, the musician can see and edit every aspect of his or her musical performance. MIDI sequencers could be thought of as "tapeless" tape recorders, except that they record and play back MIDI data (numbers that describe which notes are to be played, when they are to be played, and with what expression) instead of a audio signal. Secondly, MIDI sequencers provide numerous tracks into which data can be recorded. A multi-track tape recording in a professional studio is constructed from a series of overdubs where each instrument is recorded on its own track, usually one at a time. Likewise, a MIDI sequence is constructed from a series of tracks, each addressing a different sound within a synth or sampler, or any number of MIDI keyboards or modules connected to your computer with a MIDI interface. Now, not only do you have to be a musician or synthesist, you have to be a computer operator too, and have a good knowledge of software.

FALL 2000 INTERVIEW UPDATE

Bill Rhodes: Well, here we are in the new millennium, and as I predicted almost 14 years ago, MIDI now dominates the musical world as we know it. MIDI has become so commonplace now, that when a new technology appears, whether it's musical or computer based, we automatically assume it is MIDI controlled.

With the advent of MIDI files, the musical communications highway has been connected to a myriad of on-ramps and off-ramps, like a digital Autobahn. Instead of mixdowns from multi-track recorders mastered onto tape, we now can store sound files on CD or DVD, and edit them, copy them, or email them at will. Most advanced MIDI sequencing programs integrate digital audio capabilities, giving you the best of both worlds. With these programs, you can create a backing track with MIDI sounds from synths and samplers and then overdub vocals and/or acoustic instrument solos, with both kinds of data playing back in perfect synchronization with each other; and this scenario will only improve as technology continues to advance.

At the moment, I have just signed a product endorsement for the GigaSampler Piano (Nemesis Systems). This is a "virtual" Yamaha 9-foot grand piano in virtual sonic reality. This sense of reality is a crucial point for "piano purists." In the old days, of 8 bit or 12 bit or less bandwidth for piano samples, musicians thought they could create incredible sonic impersonations. That was really nothing! Now the bandwidth for piano samples is DC to Light Speed, with little or no digital sideband, "digital noise," and a sampling time that could use "suspended animation" for the musician to complete his compositional journey. Orchestral, soloing bass and brass instruments, and incredible pipe organ realities are also available. You can hear the "virtual" Yamaha 9-foot grand on my new album, *Bill Rhodes—The Piano Album*, that was released in the fall of 2000.

When I participated in your 1987 interview series, I mentioned that sampling was on the cutting edge of technology. Now it has "morphed" a thousand-fold. It is now virtually (pun intended) impossible to decipher the difference between an "organic" sample of a real instrument from a digital recreation. However, all this technology is only as good as the musician's abilities and application of the human element and his or her brain and fingers.

A SELECTED BILL RHODES DISCOGRAPHY:

Jazzical Records
Tropicsphere 1978
Spheres of Influence 1979
Ruprechts Werke 1982
Bill Rhodes -self titled 1990
Concerto for the New Earth 2000
Piano Album (Out of Print) 2000
Rhodeworks Vol.1 2001
Me Helix, You Axis 2001

Innovative Communications Records
Twilight Zone 1991
Burning Faith 1991
Mindbreak 1991
Sculptures 1991
Music for the Next Century 1992
Eclectic 2002

Arcade Records
Stardancer 1993
Sampler (Best of) 1994, with Rick Wakeman, Tangerine Dream, Ryuichi Sakamoto, Yellow Magic Orchestra, and others.
Bill Rhodes—The Piano Album

CHAPTER 15

Alternate MIDI Controllers

Musicologist, author, and music journalist Curtis Roads, in his book *The Computer Music Tutorial*, said "a main question in designing an input device for a synthesizer is whether to model it after existing instruments." In this chapter we will explore the many implications of that proposition.

Most of the companies that produced the first generation of commercially available synthesizers, during the 1960s and 1970s, designed the instruments to be played on a piano style keyboard. The keyboard was not by any means the only predictable MIDI controller for the synthesizer. In fact, since the early 1980s, a great deal of time has been devoted to eluding the many inadequacies of keyboard controllers.

Back in the 1970s, engineers from companies like ARP, Buchla, and Serge created complex instruments without keyboards. Musicians created their compositions by turning knobs, switching levers, and plugging and unplugging a maze of patch cords. Essentially, if you were not a keyboard player, this is the method you would employ in creating music. In the early to mid-1970s, several synthesizer designers utilized non-keyboard controllers, while the majority of synthesizer manufacturers continued to use organ keyboards on their instruments, because they were generally inexpensive and easy to interface.

The non-keyboard instrument designs of that era shared one fundamental component to trigger notes, which was the capacitive touch plate. Prominent synthesizer designers going as far back as Leon Theremin, and more recent developers such as Don Buchla and Serge Tcherepnin preferred capacitive touch plate controllers, ignoring the commercial appeal of keyboard traditionalism. Suzanne

Ciani, who worked with Buchla, says, "Don absolutely despised the use of keyboards on his synthesizers." Don Buchla was resolute in his belief that a controller such as a keyboard would be very restrictive to a musician's imagination, and in two recent conversations with the author (2001) Don still maintains his commitment to alternate controllers. Acclaimed composer and electronic music pioneer Morton Subotnick said, "Don is easily among the most advanced and imaginative of the instrument builders of the 20th century." Buchla's design was simple, reliable, and significantly adaptable. Many of the early synthesizer interfaces developed by Buchla and Serge used capacitive touch pads, mainly because they had no moving parts to break down, a very good choice considering the reliability of many instruments of the 1970s.

From my own experience, one of the first rays of hope for musicians who played non-keyboard, pre-MIDI instruments appeared in 1977. That year Korg introduced the X911, a small very affordable pitch-to-voltage synth, which had twelve keys on one side that selected one of six presets: tuba, electric guitar, violin, horn, distorted guitar, and flute. It also had a synth section that had five keys, which produced five different synthesizer waveforms buttons. It was capable of producing an automatic "wah" sound, envelope follower, and a very interesting form of waveform distortion. The unit had one standard quarter-inch input jack, and one standard quarter-inch output jack, CV/in and out Gates, VCF and FM 1/4" jacks. It was available as a monophonic synthesizer designed to create the tonal characteristics of several instruments, which could be triggered from any monophonic source. In a 1977 advertisement for the unit, Korg stated, "Any or all of these may be mixed together to produce 2047 different tone color combinations." This was definitely a wild stretch of the imagination, but it was still a low-cost synth that was a lot of fun to play around with. All the musician was required to do was to plug in a guitar or other instrument that used a standard quarter inch cable, and presto, when you played a note, or a lead riff, the instrument would output the note as a violin, etc. According to the manual, which was loosely translated from Japanese to English, it was primarily designed for use with electric guitars. Being a lead guitar player, and an big fan of guitar effects pedals, etc., I ran to my nearest music store and grabbed one up. I was amazed that it could produce bass lines that followed my leads simultaneously. The amazement soon wore off, because the nature of this pre-MIDI contraption made it nearly impossible to track any melodic pattern in real time. Anything beyond a slow 4/4 shuffle was too much for the unwieldy beast. I would have to wait ten years before I made my next venture into the realm of alternate controllers.

Even though most of the early synthesizer interfaces were very large, awkward, and costly, the ability to alter adjustments and parameters made the process of creating a sound from scratch simple, although sometimes time consuming.

During the 1980s and 1990s, methods of designing synthesizer interfaces for editing sounds in real-time became standardized. This generation of synthesizers and samplers employed a few stereotypical buttons, and in most instrument designs, a couple of control knobs, and almost always, a rectangular menu-driven LCD panel to navigate the various parameters of the operating system. This homogeneous scheme of organization can be exasperating to say the least. Fortunately, a lot of this tedious activity is now simplified by connecting the instrument with a MIDI cable to a computer operating various types of music software. While this may not be as intuitive as the hands-on modular approach, it is much more efficient to navigate than the multi-layered complex menu driven LCD panel on most current synthesizers and samplers. A trend, which emerged in late 1990s music technology, was the "retro" look, building new instruments with old-fashioned interfaces. This new equipment combines the best of analog, digital and sampling technologies. Instruments like the Nord Lead 3, the Waldorf Q16, and the Korg MS2000 have lots of knobs and sliders, like their predecessors of the 1960s and 70s, to bring real "physical" control back to state-of-the-art instruments.

In the following paragraphs we will examine some of the various types of alternate controllers to learn how they were developed for their role in musical evolution.

These include guitar controllers, stringed instrument controllers, percussion controllers, wind controllers, vocal controllers, wearable interfaces, etc.

GUITAR CONTROLLERS:

For over three decades, synthesizer interface designers have been frustrated in their efforts to use a guitar or other stringed instrument to control a synthesizer. As a result, the evolution of guitar synthesis has been slow and tedious, and disappointing to many guitarists who wanted to explore new means of expression.

Guitar synthesis began with the advent of monophonic "pitch trackers" such as the Korg X911, (mentioned at the beginning of this chapter) where only one note could be played at a time. The Korg, as I can tell you from personal experience, was a futile attempt at guitar synthesis. In 1977, the ARP Centaur polyphonic guitar—like Howard Hughes' "Spruce Goose"—never left the factory due to design problems (all units tested couldn't operate more than two hours before breaking down). After the Centaur research was discontinued, the instrument evolved into the monophonic ARP Avatar, another prototype guitar synthesizer manufactured between 1977-79 that had a list price of $3,000. The ARP Avatar project ran way over budget, and after two years of poor sales created an operating loss of over half a million dollars in 1979, contributing to the closing of the ARP manufacturing company.

The hexaphonic pickup was introduced the following year in 1980. This was the first really significant ray of hope for guitarists. This pickup made guitar synths a practical reality. The hexaphonic pickup was essentially six pickups in one, hence the prefix. Each string had its own isolated magnetic coil, resulting in six separate analog outputs. The pickup was mounted 2-3 mm from the strings and placed very close to the bridge. This research quickly initiated the development of the first generation of polyphonic guitar synthesizers. California engineer Bob Easton built the 360 Systems synth guitar, which was made popular by fusion guitarist John McLaughlin and the Mahavishnu Orchestra on the album *From Nothingness to Eternity* (1973). It sounded like a hybrid of a Minimoog and a vacuum cleaner. It was actually the 360 Systems guitar controller driving a bank of six Minimoogs; one synthesizer was dedicated to each string.

Guitar synthesizers evolved at a snail's pace into the 1980s. The conversion from pitch to voltage and then into synthesis was still too slow for any practical application. Japanese electronics giant Roland, which was already heavily involved in the production of keyboard synthesizers, became very interested in guitar controllers during this period. Their first attempt at guitar synthesis, 1978's GR500/GS-500 combo, utilized a GS-500 guitar controller controlled by a hexaphonic pickup on a well-constructed solid-body guitar, built by Ibanez, and was similar to a Les Paul. It was connected to the GR500 synthesizer module with a dense cable containing 24 wires. The GS500 also contained a conventional humbucking pickup so that the instrument could also be used as a standard electric guitar, or the player could combine synth tones with straight guitar signals. There were five sections in the GR500 synth. The first section was the direct guitar section, which controlled the output from the normal pickup through an active equalization circuit. The second section, called the poly-ensemble, was used for wave shaping, attack, decay and sustain controls. The sustain control was capable of creating infinite sustain by a mechanism that fed the divided signal from the hex pickup back to the string that created it. Under the strings, near the point where the neck joined the body, a magnet was installed that alternately repelled and attracted the string, producing a controllable feedback form of sustain. Ibanez later patented this feature in their "Sustanic" line of guitars. The third section of the synthesizer was called the bass section. This section was used to divide individual string frequencies, producing a note one octave down from the original note. The fourth section was called the solo melody section (or lead section), which was basically a standard mono synth containing a voltage controlled filter (VCF) and a low filter oscillator (LFO). The fifth section was called the external synthesizer section. This basically served as a controller for an external 1-volt per octave analog mono-synth. After a bit of adaptive technique by the player, it tracked quite well for an instrument of that period, and became very popular.

Roland was pleased with the reception of the GR-500, and introduced the GR-100 series in 1980, quickly followed by the GR-300. The choices for guitar controllers for both the GR-100 and the GR-300 also multiplied. Roland introduced three types of guitar controllers in 1981. The GR-505 was a Fender Stratocaster copy; the GR-303 was a Gibson SG offshoot; the GR-202 was a Strat-shaped hybrid of the GR-505 / GR-303; and the GR-808 was a top of the line version of the GR-303. Even though the GR-300 was slow in tracking and unpredictable in performance, artists such as Pat Metheny and Robert Fripp (King Crimson) endorsed them. Fripp demonstrated his virtuosity on the Roland GR-300 with King Crimson on several albums, as well as recording with other artists including Brian Eno, Andy Summers, David Bowie and Peter Gabriel.

Pat Metheny still uses his GR-300 synth for its unique tonal qualities. Pat uses a Roland GR-303 guitar, modified with onboard electronics to control his Synclavier II, and the GR-300. A great example of the GR-303's ability to control the Synclavier II is featured on the track *Forward March*, from the album *First Circle*.

Roland's next contribution to the evolution of guitar synths was the GR-700synth/G-707 guitar combination, introduced in 1984. It was the first guitar synth to incorporate MIDI in its communication protocol. The G-707 guitar had an angular alder body, with a maple neck, rosewood fingerboard, and a stabilizer bar constructed with expanded ABS resins, which connected the headstock and body. The stabilizer bar was added due to problems with previous guitar controllers, on which the open G-string was usually much quieter than the other five strings. While awkward in appearance, it performed very well.

The GR-700 synth module used a pedalboard, which included a ROM memory chip containing 64 different patches, and a MIDI out jack. The unit contained the same circuit boards as the Roland JX-3P, (the "3P" translates to: Programmable Preset Polyphonic) a six voice, two DCO per voice, polyphonic synth. This was a major step up from earlier guitar synth models. Since then, Roland's main efforts have been focused on developing increasingly faster tracking pickups.

In the mid-1980s, a new type of guitar synthesizer technology, known as "fret-wired" guitars, was developed when other companies noticed Roland's huge success in the guitar synth market. The first and probably the most famous of this type of controller, the SynthAxe, was designed by British engineer Bill Aitkens and retailed for $11,000 when it was introduced in 1986. It was a strange instrument for guitarist to adjust to because there were two independent sets of strings at different angles. Every fret was evenly spaced, whereas normal guitar fretboards have spaces that decrease from the nut on the headstock to the body. One short set of strings was mounted on the body and solely intended for picking or strumming. The second set of strings ran along the fretboard activating sensors, which indicated what note(s) were being played. Because of the instruments quick response, several well-known fusion jazz guitarists quickly embraced the SynthAxe as a new voice.

One of these, Alan Holdsworth, known as an uncompromising virtuoso in redefining the potential of the electric guitar, used the SynthAxe extensively on his landmark 1986 release, *Atavachron*. This recording was a rousing showcase for Holdsworth's performance capability, using a SynthAxe guitar controller driving an Oberheim Matrix-12. Holdsworth loved the SynthAxe and devised a method of attaching a breath controller to it to create fluid textures and nuances in his leads. Holdsworth received a Grammy nomination in 1984, and went on to win five consecutive awards (1989—1994) from *Guitar Player*'s Readers' Poll as "Best Guitar Synthesist."

Another well-known SynthAxe musician is Roy "Futureman" Wooten, whose highly modified Synthaxe, which he calls the "Drumitar," is used to provide the drum and percussion samples for the Grammy-winning band Bela Fleck and the Flecktones. Wooten uses the instrument as a drum kit, among other things, and is amazing to watch in live performance, especially during his highly complex "drum solos."

Because of its exorbitant price, the Synthaxe was short-lived. This technology evolved into more inexpensive controllers, like the Suzuki XG and Casio DG series synth guitars, which directly sensed finger pressure on the stringless "fretboard," and descended from Leon Theremin's filmstrip fretboard on his Theremin Cello. This short-lived generation of controllers featured additional means of generating MIDI event data such as input from touchpads, sliders, and assorted function buttons.

The Beetle Quantar and Yamaha G10, two other guitar controllers introduced in the late 80s, employed yet another technique for tracking notes. An ultrasonic pulse was generated and sent through each string from the bridge to the headstock. When the musician pressed a string against a fret, an electrical contact was made and a pulse was sent back to the bridge, which then sensed the fretting position. A second optical sensor was placed on each string to detect lateral (pitch bends) position. As a result, slurs and bent notes like blues leads could be tracked reasonably well.

Another synth guitar that used optical pickups was the 1986 "Photon" guitar made by a company called K-MUSE. This instrument used an infrared light sensor that was capable of detecting string vibrations, replacing the customary magnetic pickup. John

McLaughlin used the Photon on several albums between 1989 and 1992. It was reported to track sixteen times faster than MIDI.

The Ztar, produced by Starr Labs, is a similar instrument, which sold at a price range between $2,900 and $3,300. The Ztar featured a 6-string 24-fret "stringless fingerboard," a "trigger array," which was comprised of sensors triggered either by the picking hand or the fretting hand, an on-board drum pad array and a joystick. It was probably the most un-guitar-like MIDI controller in appearance. From a few yards away, it appears to be a guitar, but on close inspection, it doesn't have strings. In their place, the "guitar neck" has a rectangular array of push-button bars, positioned into rows and columns that relate to their real life counterparts; strings and frets, functioning as triggers for MIDI notes and chords.

Jazz guitarist Stanley Jordan, an avid promoter of the Ztar has used this instrument for many years in his music. The instrument seemed a perfect choice to compliment Jordan's "tapping technique" of guitar playing, where Stanley places both hands on the neck using his fingers to hammer on the notes.

Roland once again took the lead in the guitar synthesizer revolution with the introduction of the rackmounted GM-70 in 1987. It was the first Roland guitar converter that did not have built-in sounds of its own. Another first was the pickup, the GK-1 Synthesizer Driver, which was especially designed for the GM-70. The GK-1 was similar to a single coil pickup that could be surface-mounted on a standard electric guitar, with a blend control for balancing synth and guitar levels. It was followed by the GR-50, which was a single rack space guitar synthesizer combining the GM-70 guitar converter with the sound engine of the Roland D-110. Roland introduced an improved version of the GK-1 Synthesizer Driver, the GK-2 hex pickup, with a new cable consisting of 13 conductors and a smaller DIN connector. This cable continued to be used with the next generation, the thinner GK-2A pickup, which delivers audio and MIDI information through the same cable. In 1996, the GR-30 was introduced, followed by the GR-33 in 2000. The Roland GR-33 system tracks extremely well, something guitarists had been waiting on for many years. Another great benefit is cost; the GK-2 is very affordable.

Currently Roland seems to be dominating the playing field, while there are at least half a dozen other guitar manufacturers making instruments using implanted Roland electronics. These include the Gibson Les Paul and Explorer models, the Fender Stratocaster, the Steinberger GL2-GR and GL2T-GR, the Hamer A7 Phantom, the Zion Turbo Synth, the MV Pedulla MVP-S, the Modulus Graphite Blackknife, and Godin, a company that began with the Multiac Nylon, the first assembly-line guitar designed from scratch to optimize the potential of the Roland GR synthesizers. Most of these instruments are not mass-market items, and are only available by special order or through large mail order firms like Musician's Friend.

STRINGED INSTRUMENT (ORCHESTRAL) CONTROLLERS:

A company called Zeta Music also developed some very interesting guitar, bass, and violin controllers beginning in the late 1980s. They produced solid body guitars with a built-in multi-mode MIDI interface. The instruments used a "wired" fretboard to determine pitch. The first commercially released version was called the Mirror 6. It incorporated an active touch detector on each string to determine acoustic damping by the player's hand, along with a series of hex pickups for reading pitch bend and amplitude.

Zeta discontinued production of MIDI guitars in the early 1990s, and the company is now owned by Gibson. It continues to produce other MIDI string instruments such as the Performer and Educator series of violas, cellos, standup bass, and a series of beautifully crafted violin controllers, including the Strados Modern ($2,295). These instruments all utilize a special pickup that allows each individual string's digital output to drive a separate MIDI channel for maximum MIDI controller capabilities. The violin synthesizer's real potential, according to users like Jean-Luc Ponty and Eileen Ivers (Riverdance) is the fact that as an electric violin, the instrument can be transposed down well into the cello range without any pitfalls. Zeta also produces the world's only dedicated MIDI controller for bowed strings, violin, viola, cello, and upright bass, called the Synthony II. It is capable of translating the unique dynamics produced by bowed string instruments into MIDI signals. The Synthony II contains 480 built-in General MIDI and XG MIDI sounds, each of which can be fully customized by the user, and saved into one of 256 user presets.

PERCUSSION CONTROLLERS:

When we look back at the history of alternate forms of synthesizer controllers, the first commercially available exodus from the existing keyboard interface was the drum machine. It gave percussionists and other musicians the ability to create sound with synthesized timbres. The manufacturing of percussion synthesizer interfaces began in the late 1960s in the form of simple magnetic acoustic pickups, which were attached to surfaces that were struck with the hand, mallets, or drumsticks. The signal produced was then transferred through a chain of envelope followers to one or more analog synthesizer modules to create a tone.

In 1973, Bob Moog designed the first commercially available drum interface, which he called the 1130 Drum Controller. It consisted of an impact-sensing resistor attached to the drumhead, which transmitted trigger signal and note velocity information to a monophonic synth. Progressive, or "art rock" bands—as they were called in those days—such as Emerson, Lake & Palmer, King Crimson, and Pink Floyd, were immediately captivated by this new technology, and so were their concert audiences, who in 1974 had never experienced anything like this before. Many affordable drum pads, each with its own trademark sounds, were manufactured by several companies and available on the market by 1976.

Similar devices, most featuring some variety of built-in synthesizer, followed suit in the pre-MIDI era between 1978 and 1983, and these instruments became the mainstays in much of the dance/disco and early techno-pop music of the late 1970s and early 1980s. Two of the most popular units of this era were the LinnDrum and Linn 9000, developed and produced by Roger Linn's company, Linn Electronics. Introduced in 1979, the first LinnDrum, the LM-1, inspired a revolution in 1980s popular music. The units originally sold for $5,000 each, and only about 500 were produced. The LinnDrum used sampled acoustic drum sounds instead of synthesized timbres. This made the unit one of the most popular drum machines of the 1980s. It included twelve drum sounds, sampled at 28kHz, which included snare, kick, three toms, and hi-hats. It was capable of producing patterns in real or step time. The Linn 9000, which followed in 1984, contained a multi-track sequencer, added sampling capability, and increased the number of sampled drum sounds to 32. It had 18 touch sensitive drum pads, a built-in mixer, and a large LCD display. It also had an improved 8-bit sampling rate of 40kHz, almost CD quality, which was radical for 1984. Some of the groups that used the unit were Phil Collins, Sting, the Thompson Twins, Art of Noise, Stevie Wonder, Gary Numan, Depeche Mode, and the Human League.

A great attraction to the sound of disco and techno music was the loud thumping bass and pulsing beat produced by instruments designed by companies like the long-established drum manufacturer, Pearl, who built some of the best pre-MIDI synthetic drum kits on the market. Another company, Synares, built drum pads ranging from one to four "pads" per "drum kit," such as the Syndrum and Syndrum CN. At the low end of the market, there was the stomp box king from New York City, Electro-Harmonix, who manufactured a whole line of inexpensive synth drums.

Electronic percussion technology began to accelerate rapidly in the early 80s when analog devices moved quickly towards the digital realm. This generation of drum pads, like the ones created by KAT, who built innovate percussion controllers such as the DK-10 and the DRUMKAT 3.8, and Dave Simmons, who combined new innovative timbres with easy to play, flat-surfaced, elastic drumpads, like the Simmons SDS-7, became popular with drummers around the world. Bill Bruford used the SDS-7 on many tours with King Crimson in the early 1980s. For a number of years, the Simmons Company defined the state-of-the-art in electronic drums, with innovations like percussive hits on the drum pad being capable of controlling and varying intensity in different parts of the same pad trigger, creating multiple timbres and MIDI events. This was revolutionary technology for 1981.

The earlier method for utilizing sensors had gradually evolved to the use of pads with transducers and force sensitive resistors, to produce a new generation of more reliable and more resilient percussion pads.

As MIDI developed, these percussion devices were fitted with a MIDI output for driving external synthesizers, like the Korg Wavedrum, and the Roland Octapad. One of the most versatile percussion controllers of that era was Don Buchla's Thunder, introduced in 1990. It had a large assortment of pads and sensors, which picked up numerous aspects of the touch from a musicians hands on its playing surface, and transmitted the resulting information with the MIDI protocol to an external MIDI instrument. Don Buchla described it like this: "Thunder is an alternative controller. Making no attempt to emulate the appearance or playing techniques of existing acoustic instruments, Thunder introduces new concepts for defining musically interesting relationships between performance gesture and modern electronic vocabularies."

For melodic percussion there were instruments like the Simmons Silicon Mallet, and Don Buchla's Marimba Lumina, which presented marimba and vibes players with an extended vocabulary and range of expression. It retailed for just under $2,000.

As with everything else, new technology is always emerging. Two good examples of this new generation of electronic percussion are Roland's designs, the HPD-15 Handsonic Percussion Controller, and the V-Drum series introduced in 2001. At MIT in Boston, Todd Machover, Joe Paradiso, and a team of engineers at the MIT Media Lab have constructed one of the world's largest percussion interfaces, the "Rhythm Tree." According to Paradiso, "It is an array of over 300 smart drumpads constructed for the Brain Opera, a big, touring, multimedia installation that explores new ways in which people can interact with musical and graphical environments."

WIND CONTROLLERS:

After percussion controllers emerged, the evolution of alternate controllers continued, and by the late 1970s wind controllers soon began to appear. The Lyricon Wind Synthesizer Driver was the first to reach a wide market and gain acceptance. A new line of controllers soon followed with inventor Nyle Steiner's Electronic Woodwind Instrument (EWI), which featured the fingering protocol of a saxophone, and the Electronic Valve Instrument (EVI), specifically designed for trumpet players. In 1988, after seeing the attention Steiner's instruments were attracting, Akai began producing these instruments as a "bundle." They sold the controller, together with an analog synthesizer (Yamaha TG77 module), and a MIDI interface.

Another Japanese company, Yamaha, has contributed a great deal in development of digital wind interfaces. In 1985 Yamaha introduced the breath controller, a device that dynamically senses breath pressure when connected to a port on Yamaha's highly successful DX series synthesizers. This device offered more articulate expression on the keyboard, in much the same manner as the earlier ribbon controllers. Three years later, Yamaha introduced their first MIDI wind controller, the WX-7, which used fingering switches ergonomically positioned along the instrument, resembling that of a saxophone. This became extremely popular with wind players, and has evolved into the WX-5 and the WX11. Yamaha's pioneering techniques in physical modeling and wave-guide algorithms that are incorporated into their VL-series synthesizers are designed to work faultlessly with controllers like the WX-5 and the WX11. Other manufacturers and researchers have introduced many other wind controllers since that time.

On the low end of the price range, Casio produced the "DH" series of horn emulative controllers, and at the other end of the economic spectrum, Martin Hurni, an engineer and designer at a company called Softwind Instruments manufactured a sophisticated brass controller called the Synthophone, introduced in 1986. This was identical to an acoustic sax, (it actually used the brass armature of a Yamaha YAS-23 alto sax) but since it was a controller, produced no actual sound. It had one great feature called "Dynamic Harmony," which is a basic harmonizer that can create up to five harmony parts.

VOICE CONTROLLERS:

Since 1980, many signal processors have been specifically designed for altering the human voice. Some useful applications of this type of device were reverb, echo, pitch shifting, chorus, ring modulation, harmonizing, and vocoder effects to the voice. First came the Fairlight VoiceTracker, a $2,500 box capable of flawlessly tracking almost any sound. The IVL Pitchrider was also very popular with wind players and guitarists for a number of years. A major drawback of the Pitchrider was the lack of any sort of expression control, other than pitch and volume. On the other hand, you could use it with any sound source, including the human voice. The DigiTech Vocalizer series and the Eventide Harmonizer are two of the most popular pitch-to-MIDI converters optimized for the human voice, although the Eventide ($3,500) is cost prohibitive for most musicians.

WEARABLE CONTROLLERS:

Another type of alternate controller combines technology and clothing, such as MIDI gloves, ties, belts, shoes, or dance costumes. This technology is known as Non-Contact Gesture Sensing (NCGS). Since the early 1970s many NCGS technologies have been explored to create wearable devices, which respond to the performer's body movement.

In 1971, composer Gordon Mumma was the first to explore this new avenue of expression, when he placed 'accelerometers' and wireless transmitters into dancers' belts. Sensors can be placed inside the clothing of dancers or performers, transmitting information to computers, which then translate the data into a sonic sketch of the performance. This process creates intricate audio events controlled entirely by body motion.

Brian Eno often uses these systems in performances incorporating elements of dance and choreography in his public interactive installations. Wearable controllers were used frequently by the New York performance artist, Laurie Anderson. She removed the triggers from a set of electronic drums and sewed them into a body suit. By moving around and tapping on her body in the locations where the sensors were placed, she created a multi-dimensional performance. Anderson, enamored by that concept, went on to design a MIDI keyboard built into a necktie. Her performances employ a fascinating variety of media, which incorporate the use of film, electronic and acoustic music, slides, and interactive costumes.

In 1997, MIT engineers used conductive thread to implant touch-sensitive MIDI keyboards inside suit jackets, which they called "musical jackets." Other wearable innovations from MIT's Media Lab include "expressive footwear," comprised of dance sneakers fitted with 16 sensors that measure various movements of the dancer's feet. Teresa Marrin, another engineer at the MIT Media Lab, constructed the "Conductor's Jacket," a vest with a massive amount of bio-sensors built into it's lining. These sensors were used to measure the heart rate, respiration, temperature, skin conductance, and electromyography (EMG), which then translated these events into musical data. Many devices, like the ones developed at MIT, are now being commercially marketed. Don Buchla has also introduced a revolutionary controller, which enables control of MIDI-enabled instruments and machines using two handheld wands. The device, known as the Lightning, was first introduced in 1991. An upgraded model, the Lightning II, was first produced in 1996.

The Lightning senses the position and movement of the wireless wands that are held by the performer, and then that information is converted into MIDI data. Lightning also comes with its own built-in synth engine so it can be played without external MIDI devices. They are tracked by using infrared transmitters built into the handles of each wand. Buchla, in his own words, describes them as "an easily mastered, musically oriented interface language that allows the user to define relationships between various gestures and potential musical responses." Buchla suggests using the wands to train orchestra conductors, whose gestures and physical nuances actually direct the music. According to Buchla, the Lightning has a feature that analyzes a conductor's gestures and is capable of indicating quirks in performance, such as missed beats and tempo variations. Fellow synthesizer pioneer, Bob Moog had this to say about Buchla's instrument: "Lightning is as musically intuitive as it is theatrically powerful. Buchla continues to roll back the frontiers of innovative real time control." Besides being a powerful MIDI controller, Lightning II, along with its built-in 32-voice synthesizer, is a comprehensive instrument.

In the early days of archaic technology we were presented with an opportunity to analyze and synthesize sound. As time passed, the technology evolved, creating a potential to build digital control mechanisms into existing instruments, as well as creating new devices for exploring music.

CHAPTER 16

Neil Nappe on Alternate MIDI Controllers

Neil Nappe, a pioneering MIDI guitarist and well-known studio musician/recording artist, has worked with Larry Fast and many other New York area-recording artists over the last 20 years.

Neil Nappe and his MIDI-equipped Les Paul guitar.

In 1986, Neil Nappe was one of the first people in the world to record an album with MIDI guitar. He was one of the first artists signed to the prestigious electronic music label Audion, which also featured recordings by such luminaries as Wendy Carlos, Gary Hughs, and Larry Fast (Synergy). Neil's album *July* won critical acclaim from radio and press. He records his music on a guitar with a special pickup and MIDI converter, sending the notes he is playing to a combination of synthesizers and samplers, to create fully orchestrated sound, which can be layered to produce fully scored tracks. *July* is a great example of what an "alternate" MIDI controller can do. Neil performed live with his MIDI guitar, various synth modules, and two computers running sequencer and voicing software. This enabled him to sound exactly the same live as he did on his recording. Neil talks about his early mentor, Dr. Emile Tobenfeld, a Massachusetts engineer who developed the first commercially available music software for sequencing, storing sounds, and algorithmic composition.

In the first of two interviews conducted in 1986 and 2001, Nappe discusses the evolution of various aspects of software based sequencers, and non-keyboard controllers such as violin, woodwinds, guitar, drums, etc. As greater realism evolves from wavetable synthesis, and as newer, interactive applications were developed, MIDI-driven synthesizers will continue to be an important component for sound generation devices and multimedia applications.

Ben Kettlewell: Neil, can you tell us how you incorporate MIDI into your music?

Neil Nappe: I actually use two systems at the moment (1986). One of them is the system that is run from the computer, which does most of the sequencing chores and rhythm parts, the other part is controlled from my guitar in real-time. The sequenced system consists of a Roland TR707 Rhythm Composer, which covers most of my drum and rhythm parts, a Korg DW6000, which handles most of the bass parts, and a Roland JX3P, which is used for arpeggios and chord arrangements. The other system starts off with the strings of my Les Paul, goes through a pair of Roland GR systems, the 300 and 700, through an Oberheim Expander, and eventually winds up at a Casio CZ101. The MIDI implementation of this whole mess is pretty straightforward actually.

I started out in 1985 with a Roland MSQ700, which was one of the first hardware-based MIDI sequencers you could buy. It was highly overpriced in relation to what you can buy today, which can do six times what that unit could do for one-tenth the price. I'm not knocking the unit, because it was great when it first came out, it was unprecedented in compositional freedom in its day. You could extensively tweak an arrangement before having to commit anything to tape. That's probably one of the main reasons why I became involved with MIDI in the first place. Here, you can sit and work out a composition down to its finest details, and you don't have to worry about generative tape losses and things like that. I found the MSQ to be a bit limited in its editing capabilities, and that's what led me to get involved in software based sequencers.

I sequenced all the tracks on *July* mainly with a pair of Commodore 64 computers, although the MSQ700 is still in there too. A gentleman up in Boston, Massachusetts by the name of Emile Tobenfeld, also known as "Dr. T," wrote the software I used in this recording, and I just can't say enough about the software. Suffice to say that *July* would not have been possible without it. The software is, in my personal opinion, by and large, the most comprehensive piece of MIDI software written for an 8-bit computer. I think it's about time. We're starting to see some good software out there for Macintosh, and the IBM compatibles, as well. There is a growing availability of MIDI utility software, such as generic arpeggiators, MIDI channelizers, and various kinds of "housekeeping" tools, which anyone out there who is using a large MIDI setup, meaning a number of different synthesizers on different channels, would find of great value. Running around pulling out patch cords, changing programs, loading voices, etc, in a live performance can get to be a real pain in the neck after a while. It's so much nicer to be able to route MIDI signals by computer, which is what a lot of these newer types of software are enabling musicians to do.

BK: How do you use the software in a live performance?

NN: I find that the software that I'm currently (1986) using is very well suited to live performance. A small example of this would be that I'm able to transpose pitch up and down in real time without affecting the meter. Or, by the same token, I can transpose the meter up or down, meaning the song can be sped up or slowed down without affecting the pitch. You certainly wouldn't want to try that with a cassette recorder. The reason why I'm using a pair of computers, and I've been asked this quite a lot, is that the Commodore's disk drive is not known as one of the fastest disk drives in the business. It might sometimes take upwards of 20-30 seconds to load a song from disk. I find audiences are not very tolerant of "dead air" space between tunes, and I've got enough to do without worrying about trying to cover that silence. An interesting observation is that, in its own way, the computer is becoming a new kind of music instrument, or I would be more accurate by saying a live compositional instrument, because here you have the capability of starting and stopping individual sequences in real-time simultaneously from the computer keyboard. Say, for example, that you have a song which consists of your typical intro, a verse, a refrain, a bridge, etc. You can actually control when these particular events are going to happen, what their duration will be, and so forth, from the computer keyboard. It really gives you this tremendous amount of flexibility in terms of compositional choices. For instance, there is a song that I do called "Pickupstix," which has a well-defined structure that repeats four times. The fourth refrain will continue indefinitely until I instruct the computer to move on to the conclusion portion of the song, which enables me to tailor the song to a specific live application.

MIDI has already brought in the age of polyphonic component synthesizer systems. When you think back to the early days of synthesis when systems were based on control voltages, filters, gates, and triggers, you had a standard system that used a one-volt per octave control voltage scale that would be fairly compatible with any module out there. It was a standard that allowed synths and modules from different manufacturers like Moog, Serge, Oberheim, etc. to "talk" to each other. Of course, the big difference with MIDI is that you now have polyphonic sequencing capabilities as well. This may seem like not too big a deal by comparison to a lot of the other incredible things that MIDI is capable of doing. There was a time, where if you wanted to do any kind of polyphonic sequencing, the equipment would cost you a second mortgage. And it would still have been crude by comparison to what you can pick up now for a week's pay or less. I think that's one of the great realities of MIDI, and the fact that there is also, once again, a standard in which anything that has MIDI ports on it will work with nearly 100% with anything else that has MIDI ports. All in all, I would say, in my opinion, and that of a lot of other people in the music industry, MIDI is probably the single most important development to happen in music since the advent of the multi-track tape recorder. I think that MIDI will be an integral part of every recording studio in the world, for the simple reason that there is so much you can do without ever having to commit a note to tape.

2000/2001 FOLLOW-UP INTERVIEW:

BK: Guitar synthesis has always seemed to lag behind other forms of controllers, due to the inherent problems with tracking. Do you think things have changed much in the past ten to fifteen years? Where do you see guitar synthesis going?

NN: Difficult question for two reasons. In any type of device that attempts to convert an acoustic signal to a "control" signal, like a gate, trigger, CV, etc, which will be used to direct another sound source, such as VCO/DCO, etc., there are known difficulties.

It's difficult to talk about this without getting into the tech details. A picked guitar string has a complex envelope, from a pitch, amplitude, and harmonic standpoint. Guitarists take this for granted, even take advantage of it in order to develop unique playing styles & sounds that capitalize on the way an electric guitar responds to "English," so to speak.

For a guitar synthesizer to really "play" like a guitar, it would need to be able to convert the guitar signal in such a way as to decode these subtleties of technique and apply them to the synthesized sound source in meaningful and, probably, analogous ways.

This is, in a lot of ways, a software issue, and faster, cheaper processors will help. There have been slight, but noticeable improvements in the pickups, etc. that have made some of the more recent units more playable to some extent, at least in that they make less errors in detecting and converting the pitch and amplitude of the guitar signal.

However, I've yet to experience a guitar synth that converts the variations in the harmonic structure over time into meaningful control structures within the synthesized sound source. This leads us to the second issue: MIDI. MIDI, while a truly wonderful protocol, compared to the Gate, Trigger, and CV of days past, is not the ideal protocol for guitar synthesizers. This is because, in my opinion, it is simply too slow to be able to transmit the amount of continuous controller, and most likely, SYSEX data in real time to accurately describe the pitch, amplitude, and harmonic envelopes of a guitar signal in a way that would enable a synthesizer to make use of them.

This is not to say that the current crop of guitar synths is unusable, far from it. They have circumvented some of these problems by driving sound generating circuitry internally, which bypasses MIDI and its limitations. My gripe is that the "onboard" synthesizers—I would assume in order to keep the units affordable— are somewhat limited in their programmability for my tastes. The ideal guitar synth, for me, would have the programmability of the Oberheim Xpander, with 36 voice polyphony, stackable multi-timbral voices with dynamic voice allocation per string/channel, extensive per-string options, and the previously mentioned pitch, harmonic, and amplitude envelopes available as modulation sources within the matrix. Now that would be an instrument to be reckoned with.

I have left out "guitar-like" controllers like the SynthAxe, and other devices with wired frets, etc, because they are something of a different category of controller. Ironically, the GR300, one of the earlier true guitar synthesizers, was infinitely more playable and "guitar like" than anything that has come along since its creation. Its sonic palette, however, was quite limited, even compared with the GR700, which, while much less playable, was a pretty decent synthesizer in its own right. But there are always new designs on the horizon, and its good to keep one's ear to the wall...I've had a chance to play Roland's most recent offering, the GR33. It is a perfect example of a trend within the industry that saddens me. The playability of the unit, with the "Roland-ready Stratocaster" that the demo unit was matched with, was significantly better than its predecessors. The out of the box sound is quite impressive, with a huge assortment of useful, musical pre-programmed sounds. Roland has opted to make this unit as "guitarist friendly" as possible, and they have succeeded, to a high degree. What saddens me is that from my viewpoint, as a synthesist/sound architect as well as a guitarist, the unit's greatest strength is it greatest shortcoming. The playability of the unit is largely due to the avoidance of the limitations of MIDI in the onboard sound generator, as I have mentioned previously. Unfortunately, the onboard synthesizer is crippled. Yes, it has a large collection of sampled waveforms to choose from. You can mix and match these to some degree, control their relative volumes over time. But from the standpoint of being a "real" synthesizer, there are no LFO's, no modulation capability, no filters, minimal envelope generation, etc. Even the MIDI implementation, compared with the modified GM70, which I currently use, is very limited. Some might argue that the extensive onboard effects fill some of this void.

Sonically, the unit does sound great, the effects are superb, and it is very easy to use. But what I see in general is that ease of use has become paramount in the minds of the manufacturers, and the cost of this is flexibility/versatility/complexity. I don't fault the companies. They are merely responding to market pressure. Features are expensive. The truth is that 90 percent of the market for a guitar synthesizer doesn't want or need the ability to intricately edit or create their own synthesizer patches. Once again we see that there is sometimes a huge difference between the terms, "musician" and "synthesist." I like to think that there is a happy medium, a combination of the two, but in the real world, that is comparatively rare. Then again, maybe that's not such a bad thing after all, in a world where "alternative" is no longer alternative at all, but I digress.

BK: Has the technological evolution of synthesis inspired you, or affected the way you create music since our last discussion?

NN: I find it a bit ironic that the current big buzz in synthesizers seems to be digital recreations of classic analog instruments from the 1970s and 80s. I've always felt that synthesizers have been a divided camp in some ways. There are those who see their main purpose as the replication or replacement of real acoustic instruments that would otherwise be impractical or expensive to employ in a studio or live environment. This is certainly a valid use, and in my opinion, is the reason why samplers and sampled digital waveform synths have achieved the success that they have. They are "practical". The other camp, the one a little closer to my heart, are those who use synthesizers to explore sonic realizations not achievable through acoustic means. It seems to me that the majority of the new hardware is tailored toward the first school, and the digital audio workstation type keyboards are the flagship of this genre. The main advantages of the newer hardware, in my opinion, are that they allow a significant studio or live setup downscaling physically over their predecessors, with increased bang per buck, greater integration, etc. On the other hand, certain software based synthesizer programs, such as *Reaktor* from Native Instruments, boggle the mind. They are, for all intents and purposes, Lego Sets for virtual synthesizer creation.

The downside is that they require a fair amount of computing horsepower; the upside is that computer hardware is getting more inexpensive every day. The greatest change from my standpoint, or I should say the improvements in technology which have had the greatest impact on me and my music are those related to software technology. Computer based recording/mastering/signal processing, etc. is something we dreamed of a decade ago. It is a very exciting time for "old" music, as well as new projects. I'm really psyched to dig out a ton of old live tapes, clean 'em up digitally, and in general, see how much I'm able to fix in the "digital" domain.

BK: Tell me about your new studio setup, and its advantages and disadvantages over the old one.

NN: I don't use the Commodores much anymore. They were replaced by an Amiga 3000 with Dr. T's software and a number of PC clones running a variety of software. The hardware tends to change a bit, but the synths of old remain, as well as a Yamaha TX81Z, Roland D550, and Alesis HR16. A Mackie 1604VLZ mixer, Event 20/20 monitors, and a bunch of outboard gear still live there, Roland SRV2000 Digital Reverb, SDE3000 Digital Delay, Yamaha SPX90, Digitech IPS33 Intelligent Harmonizer, Alesis Quadraverb, a pair of Simmons SPM8: two programmable mixers, Roland GP8 Guitar Processor, Line6 POD, A/DA Stereo Tapped Delay. I still use the Cooper MSB+, as well as the Yamaha MEP4 MIDI Event Processor and a Digital Music MX8 MIDI router/processor.

The heart of the system is a modified Roland GM70 Guitar to MIDI Converter. I transplanted the guts of a Roland 202 guitar into my 1974 Les Paul Custom back in 1985, and then proceeded to make some major modifications to the circuitry, added a few additional mapable controllers on the guitar, etc. The mods are ongoing. Seems like my soldering iron never gets a chance to really cool off. This combination still works very well for me. I'm considering a GR33, only because it tracks a little better, but it is a big step back in terms of programmability and flexibility. We'll see. What are the advantages of the "new" setup? More knobs to twiddle. The disadvantages? More knobs to twiddle. Seriously, though, the biggest advantages have been in the recording capabilities. Direct to hard disk multi-track is a beautiful thing.

BK: The 1970s and 1980s seemed to be a good time to get into electronic music. What was that time like for you?

NN: I feel that 1975-1985 was in many ways the Golden Age of electronic music. It's where I heard the most magical things being accomplished with often very finicky equipment and promising technologies in their infancy. These guys were the pioneers. Oddly enough, though, what initially inspired me was the likes of Jan Hammer, Larry Fast, Lyle Mays, Eddie Jobson, Patrick Moraz, Rick Wakeman, Tony Banks, Rick Wright, and a long list of other keyboardists who were mainly using synths in the progressive bands and music that, I guess, was my roots. I had always longed to have that kind of a sonic palette at my disposal, but having no keyboard skills, I watched from the sidelines. I got on the bandwagon in '83 or so after seeing Ryo Kawasaki and King Crimson and what could be done with guitar synthesizers. The next seven years also saw some great strides, but the equipment was also maturing, so in effect, EM had become "accessible to the masses." It was a great time. There was a thriving electronic music scene, lots of radio shows, frequent concerts, just a lot of camaraderie in general.

BK: How do you view the current new electronic music scene, and which direction do you think it will take in the future?

NN: I've always tended to think of electronic music more in terms of Ambient and what has been called "New Age." So a lot what is being called "electronic" by the mainstream industry these days is a bit alien to me. I suppose that it's "electronic music" in that it was created electronically, so I guess that definition flies. I tend to be possibly a little jaded in a sense, because when I hear the term "electronic music," the genre that always comes to mind is that personified by Synergy, Wendy Carlos, Tangerine Dream, Don Slepian, et al. While the list of keyboard players I list as my influences are great musicians, and in most cases, synthesists as well, I would not call Genesis or Yes "electronic music." It's just my subjective take on the genre. But it is more "electronic" to my way of thinking than some of the really current stuff being billed as such. It is hard to say what effect the popular characterization of what is now considered to be electronic music will ultimately have on the genre at large. It makes me wonder what anyone who is not familiar with my material, for example, would think if they were to show up at a concert I was playing merely because it was billed as "electronic music." In my opinion, I barely qualify in comparison to the more established ambient/new age acts out there, but I have practically nothing in common with some of what is now commonly referred to as "electronic." Guess we'll see.

Music on the Internet and Future Trends in Music Technology: An Interview with Joel Chadabe

The Internet is the fastest changing aspect of information technology in the world today. Music, graphics, video, navigation tools, site layout, and every other aspect of what we know as the Web is constantly evolving, and constantly being refined.

In the late 1930s, English logician Alan Turing made an extraordinary discovery while exploring the basic mathematics of digital computing. Computers, Turing realized, are capable of emulating any other machine on the planet, including imaginary machines that exist only as ideas in people's minds. Turing believed that if it can be described, the computer can simulate it. Soon, Turing quietly put this fantastic idea to an historic test. Cautiously, at a top-secret lab in Bletchley Park, England, Turing supervised the construction of a machine that simulated the Nazis' best cipher machine, Enigma. His creation, called the Bombe, was an electro-mechanical device, developed by Turing with help from another mathematician, W. G. Welchman. It was modeled after an earlier code-breaking machine, the Polish 'Bomba.' Basically these code-breaking machines would emulate the ones used by the Germans to create the codes. By enabling British strategists to read enemy messages within hours after they were intercepted by radio, Turing's code-breaking computers helped to win World War II.

Modern personal computers are being used in a similar fashion, not to break secret military codes but to mimic many other kinds of audio and video machines. Given the right software and a fast Internet connection, an ordinary desktop computer can simulate the functions of telephones, jukeboxes, CD players, DVD players, short-wave radios, color TVs, synthesizers, studio effects, etc. Promoting this impetus to emulate every traditional medium, are new software programs, faster, more powerful computers, and the ever-increasing speed, or bandwidth, of Internet connections. Together, these trends are transforming the personal computer into a new kind of appliance, a multipurpose multimedia machine. The changes also pose threats as well as new opportunities for the music industry and other traditional media.

THE INTERNET:

What is required to access this new technology? Nearly every new computer on the market, Windows-based PC or Macintosh, has enough power to play multimedia files, combined with specialized software, which comes bundled with the system or available free of charge on the Web. The only hardware you may wish to add is memory, or RAM, the more the better, as multimedia applications become more sophisticated and memory hungry.

There are several ways to create or listen to audio on the Internet. Three of the most popular and useful multimedia software programs, called plug-ins, come as standard items with browsers like Netscape's Navigator and Microsoft's Internet Explorer. These are Apple Computer's QuickTime, Macromedia's Shockwave, and Thomas Dolby's Beatnik.

QuickTime, which is available for both PCs and Macs, lets browsers display standard and panoramic images and play pre-recorded clips of audio and movies. ShockWave can display animated images and interactive games that often include rich graphics and sound effects. Depending on how it's coded, a Shockwave program may even solicit interaction from viewers: for instance, various buttons to click, puzzle pieces to assemble, virtual instruments to play with. Thomas Dolby's Beatnik creates and plays back high quality audio using complex compression ratios for quick loading and streaming the audio signal.

With each program, there is generally a short time delay or buffer, which is created by the computer downloading information before it begins playback. Typically, a QuickTime file won't show up on your screen or speakers until your computer has transferred most or all of it. With a 56K modem, a two-minute QuickTime movie may take several minutes to download, whereas quickly expanding transmission technology, such as DSL, wireless, and cable modems reduce the download process to a matter of seconds.

Several other methods of downloading and listening to music on the Internet are rapidly gaining popularity. Streaming audio is one of the most common methods used to create, listen to, or download CD quality compositions. RealPlayer, made by Macromedia, and the Windows Media Player from Microsoft, are the two most commonly used programs available for experiencing streaming live video and sound.

With over 60 million copies of RealPlayer installed in home computers, and a constant flow of enhancements and extensions, this plug-in by RealNetworks has swept the Web and made its name synonymous with live or so-called "streaming" media. You can download the "lite" version of RealPlayer without charge from the Website (**www.real.com**). For a minimal fee, you can get RealPlayer Plus, which delivers better sound and images and includes add-ons like a graphical audio equalizer and color and contrast controls to fine-tune the video screen.

Thousands of websites now offer audio, video, and other types of multimedia programming for playback with this type of software. Hundreds of radio stations around the world deliver live program-ming across the Web. In fact, one of the most intriguing experiences on the Internet these days is pulling in foreign radio stations. In addition, there are a growing number of Web-only stations, often specializing in alternative forms of music.

The free version of RealPlayer provides links to a variety of preset channels, from classical stations to outlets for country and rock music, and RealPlayer Plus lists even more. For more complete listings, check websites such as **www.broadcast.com.**

As with all emerging communication technologies, RealPlayer faces increasing competition. Microsoft offers an alternative called Windows Media Player, available for Windows PCs and Macintosh computers, at no charge from the company's Website. The software plays the same streaming audio and video files as RealPlayer and handles other image and sound-file formats.

Apple's QuickTime, available free at **www.apple.com**, helps Macs and Windows PCs play streaming audio and video programs with impressive fidelity. To explore the future of audio on the Web, you may want to check out iQfx, a program that provides enhanced stereo and synthesized three-dimensional sound. The software is available for download from RealNetworks' website, and can turn mono sound into stereo and boost bass for easier low-level listening, or a more complete "live" experience.

MIDI files first began to popup here and there on the Internet in mid-1995, although at the time, you would need a "stand-alone" application to listen to the files. Plug-ins that we take for granted today in browsers like the popular Netscape Communicator and Microsoft's Internet Explorer did not exist until 1997.

The tremendous advantage MIDI has over other Web audio formats like Real Audio and MP3 is its small file size. Because notes are represented by numerical values, lengthy pieces can be down-loaded in seconds. But, the downside in using General MIDI is that it is restricted to 127 preset sounds and can't transmit real or sampled sounds. The 127 standard MIDI preset sounds in most personal computers predictably sound like a soundtrack to a kid's game, because you lose all sense of tonal quality and are left with the low-quality sounds your computer's built-in chips provide, although this is improving in new generations of home computers.

In order to hear two computers replicate the same MIDI file or song, with the same instruments, the MIDI files must always use the General MIDI protocol. Modules, sound cards, and music generating software such as Macintosh's cross-platform QuickTime plug-in, which are General MIDI compatible, have specific types of sounds, or programs stored in specific numbered memory locations. This allows you to call up, for example, program 25 and have total confidence that it will play the sound you want, because program 25 will always be a nylon string acoustic guitar sound on any General MIDI synthesizer, or computer. Sending program changes on web-based MIDI files will only provide anticipated results if they are General MIDI compatible.

The General MIDI system provides the musician with a collective set of characteristics and a common patch map for high polyphony, and a multi-timbral synthesizer, which provide composers and multimedia application developers with a common generic platform for synthesis. GM instrument sounds are achieving greater authenticity by incorporating wavetable synthesis, and as newer, interactive software/hardware packages come along, MIDI powered synthesizers and computer software will continue to be an important component for sound generation devices as well as multimedia applications.

Another method of storing music on the internet that has gained widespread popularity is a format called MP3 and MP4 or MPEG, which compresses the size of an audio file by as much as 80 percent. In 1987, the German Company IIS and Prof. Dieter Seitzer of the University of Erlangen devised a very powerful algorithm that became standardized as ISO-MPEG Audio, commonly known as Layer-3, or MP3.

Without any type of data reduction, digital audio signals typically consist of 16 bit samples recorded at a sampling rate more than twice the actual audio bandwidth (e.g. 44.1 kHz for Compact Discs). So you end up with more than 1.400 MB (the memory size of a floppy disk) to represent one minute of stereo music in CD quality. By using MPEG audio coding, it is possible to shrink down the original sound data from a CD by a factor of 12, without losing sound quality. Compression factors of 24 and even more still maintain a sound quality that is significantly better than what you get by just reducing the sampling rate and the resolution of your samples. Basically, this is realized by something called perceptual coding techniques, which address sound waves as they are perceived by the human ear.

Not surprisingly, this multimedia revolution on the Web is upsetting the music business. Viewing the technology as a threat to its control of copyrighted material, the commercial music industry is concerned about the use of MP3 format. To decode and play back the compressed music files, there are numerous "freeware" and shareware programs available on the Web (MP3.com has a list), or you can use Real Networks' Real Jukebox program. My current favorite is Sound Jam. It's like the Swiss Army Knife of digital music players. You can also play MP3 cuts on a new line of solid-state portable stereo players such as the Diamond Rio, or the Panda Player, which are just a little larger than a box of matches. There are also portable Discman-type CD players on the market that will play a standard CD, which has been "burned" with a CDR drive. A standard 640 MB CD can contain up to eleven hours of MP3 formatted songs.

It takes a few minutes to download an MP3 file on the Internet, which generally average between three and five MB per song. There are exceptions. Long electronic pieces and classical works, for example, can consume as much as 50-60 MB, even when compressed in MP3 format.

The arrival of MP3 on the Web has made a vast array of music available in a high-quality format that's easy to transport. Predictably, bootlegs of copyrighted songs are widespread. Although some recognized artists are beginning to make selected MP3 cuts available for promotional purposes, a larger share of the legitimate MP3 tracks on the Web are from local, unsigned bands, not the big stars. But stay tuned: This looks like the direction the music business is destined to follow, whether the major labels like it or not, and there are competing technological schemes proposed by IBM, Sony, Microsoft, and others that would protect copyrighted material while still delivering it over the Web.

Sony Music, home to artists ranging from the venerable Bob Dylan, and Bruce Springsteen to upstarts like Rage Against the Machine, and Macy Gray, was the first major label to start accepting dollars for downloads. And so it appears that the old, "if you can't lick' em, join-em" cliché has gone into action with the big labels.

The highly controversial Napster, was ordered to cease business in the spring of 2001, and its many offspring host virtual sites containing over a quarter-million songs, easy to locate via built-in search components and downloadable for free. One can easily imagine the impact actions like this will have on musicians and the industry as a whole. It's still a wild frontier out there in Cyberspace. The Internet was in its infancy in the mid-1990s. Who can imagine what it will be like five years from now? Today, there are approximately 220 million people online, and according to statistics, that number will double by 2003, and double again by 2005, and today's 600 million e-mail accounts will triple in that same five years.

How will this virtual intrusion of data affect the audio industry? The first indication will be a dramatic increase in bandwidth and reduced cost of Internet service. The concepts behind LAN (Local Area Networks) will eventually spread to WAN (Wide Area Networks). Another important development just beginning in the US is FTTH (fiber-to-the-home), which translates to all glass, extremely fast connections all the time. As fully optical networks mature with 10-Gigabit connections, real-time high fidelity, multi-channel audio and video will become a reality.

Along with these new technologies for data transfer, desktop and laptop computers are advancing at an extremely accelerated pace. 64-bit microprocessors operating at over 1 GHz are becoming readily available, and more and more affordable. The major OS (operating systems) will provide complete multiprocessor services, increasing the speed of native DSP operations for audio applications. Audio on the Web has taken three distinct paths: traditional digital music download and distribution, web-based radio stations, and wireless streaming applications and devices. The public's acceptance of Internet audio by consumers has confirmed the future of nonphysical music delivery. The Internet is quickly becoming another facet of our work and leisure, so acquaint yourself and embrace the technology.

PHYSICAL MODELING:

One of the current frontiers in music synthesis is physical modeling, an attempt to avoid the static nature of canned samples by generating complex, dynamic audio from computational models. As one might expect, when properly controlled, physical models of acoustic instruments are much richer and closer to their original sound. "Physical models" of artificial systems have no counterpart in nature, but can still exhibit the rich, dynamic sound qualities of real instruments, or in some cases, the old analog synthesizers, which are again prized in some studios because of their warm gritty, dynamic texture.

If your computer has enough speed and power, you can compute the sound that is emanated, based on typical inputs, such as breath pressure on an oboe reed or the bow pressure and speed on a cello string. Although the first physically-modeled instruments, like Yamaha's VL series, introduced in 1994, were derived from the efficient Waveguide parameterizations developed by Julius Smith and colleagues at Stanford's Center for Computer Research in Music and Acoustics (CCRMA), there are many other ways to model complex systems, leaving much room for exciting new developments like Roland's VG-8. This is a floor unit for guitarists that models various types of guitars, pickups, speakers, and amps by incorporating high-powered DSP processing chips.

Another great modeling instrument was Korg's Prophecy, a modeling keyboard introduced in 1996. Recent entries into this exciting new form of synthesis are the Waldorf Q16, and the Korg MS2000.

SOFTWARE SYNTHESIZERS:

General-purpose personal computers are rapidly becoming powerful enough to sustain the power of musical synthesis. Essentially, all current computers arrive equipped with quality audio output capability, and capable software synthesizers are readily available for PC or Mac without requiring additional hardware.

There are currently quite a few very powerful software based synthesizers and samplers that rival their hardware counterparts in every way, even surpassing the limitations of many existing hardware based synths and samplers. For instance, the Mac version of the Roland SC33 Sound Canvas has close to a thousand patches built-in, …approximately three times the amount of its hardware counterpart; and makes it easier to edit patches and other parameters.

Over time, the software synthesis capabilities of desktop computers will expand even further, and dedicated hardware synthesizers will become more and more applicable for niche applications.

To take a closer look at the future of music technology, the following is an interview with Joel Chadabe, composer, author of the highly acclaimed book *Electric Sound* and founder of the Electronic Music Foundation. Joel Chadabe is an internationally recognized pioneer in the development of interactive music systems. As composer and performer, he has performed in concert worldwide with percussionist, Jan Williams, and many other musicians since 1969. His articles on electronic music have appeared in *Computer Music Journal*, *Contemporary Music Review*, *Electronic Musician*, *Perspectives of New Music*, *Electronic Music Review*, *Melos*, *Musiqué en Jeu*, plus many other journals and magazines, and several of his articles have been anthologized in books by MIT Press, Routledge, and other publishers.

His book *Electric Sound: The Past and Promise of Electronic Music* was acclaimed as the first comprehensive history of electronic music.

It has been praised by leaders in the field as "*wonderful and compelling*" (Robert Moog) and "*By far the finest history and overview of the last 50 years of electronic music that I have read*" (Max Mathews) with exceptional reviews in Keyboard Magazine, Computer Music Journal, Leonardo Music Journal, and many other publications.

As president of Intelligent Music, he was responsible for the publication of innovative software, including M and Max. His music has been recorded on the following labels: Deep Listening, CDCM, Centaur, Lovely Music, Opus One, CP2, and Folkways. He has received awards, fellowships, and grants from the National Endowment for the Arts, New York State Council on the Arts, Ford Foundation, Rockefeller Foundation, Fulbright Commission, SUNY Research Foundation, New York Foundation for the Arts, and other foundations.

Ben Kettlewell: Instruments have evolved tremendously since you first started making music yourself. How have these advancements affected your personal musical evolution?

Joel Chadabe: They have helped enormously. First of all, I have always carried equipment to perform in concerts, and as I've gotten older and weaker, the instruments have gotten smaller and lighter. Maybe even more important, the cost-to-power ratio has greatly improved, and this has been a great benefit to me as well as everyone else. You can now buy far more powerful equipment and it's much more affordable than it was years ago.

BK: What do you think about the evolution of electronic music in the 1970s and 1980s?

JC: These were the early formative years. In the late 1970s, there was the first development of digital synthesizers and a major expansion of the field to include many companies and entrepreneurs, all of whom had original ideas. It was a very exciting time. The 1980s, in particular because of MIDI, saw a major growth in the market and drops in pricing due to microprocessors and other advances in electronics. The technology was developed in the 1970s, then expanded, improved and made affordable in the 1980s.

BK: It seems that more and more, the World Wide Web is emerging as the medium for composers to launch their music. Do you think there will be some future evolved form of MP3, maybe

MP6, or MPEG-4, the scalable codec from Germany? Also, in terms of the music industry's fear of MP3 and its eventual better-sounding descendents, the musician is competing with the record store, the distributor, the large chains, etc. How do you think this will impact the industry as a whole? Already a lot of existing radio stations have Web radio, and this has become a big area of contention now with the passing of the Digital Millennium Act in Congress. All of the performance right organizations and the recording organizations, like ASCAP, BMI, and RIAA, are acknowledging that there is all this music being released without royalties being collected. Piracy has become rampant, beginning with online organizations such as Napster, and its descendants, and there's a big scramble to figure out what to do about that issue. What are your opinions on this subject?

JC: There is little question that as download times get fast enough, all digital media will be distributed by download. MP3 and other compression schemes will certainly continue to be developed, and we can hope that they will improve to the point of non-compressed high-end audio, but as download times get fast enough and memory gets cheap enough, compression will be unnecessary, at least for reasons of download efficiency. With compression or without, music will be distributed by download and homemade CDRs (or other disk-based storage mediums) will be used to store these downloads.

For distributors and stores, the game will seriously change from distributing physical objects to marketing in the sense of attracting attention to particular items to download. It could be that stores will change the nature of their operations to become download centers, publishing a CD on demand, but most of the business will be through downloads at home. Certainly many distributors and stores will go out of business. There is no question that modes of distribution will change to the benefit of consumers and lower prices.

Composers may benefit in self-publication by not needing to make CDs. But there will be problems for composers and performers. One major problem now, which exists because digital copies are as good as the originals, is how to find a way to protect composers' intellectual property in copyrights. We have not yet found a way to combat piracy. It could be that we should take a different approach altogether and pay composer's general "creativity" fees. There may be other ideas in the air. But the world will certainly change and hopefully we will find reasonable ways of making change workable for artists in digital media.

BK: How do you feel the new technologies are going to alter the way music is created, performed and accessed?

JC: Technologies will become more interactive. In the not distant future, musical compositions will allow members of the listening public to perform by interacting in various ways with music given to them by composers, and that music will be accessed through download.

IN SUMMARY:

Joel Chadabe has been an icon in the electronic music community since 1969. I highly recommend listening to his music.

The following is a suggested discography:
After Some Songs (1987-1994)
Rhythms: Variation VI (1982)
Modalities (1988)
Rhythms (1980)
Settings for Spirituals (1977)
Flowers (1975)
Echoes (1972)
Ideas of Movement at Bolton Landing (1971)
Street Scene (1967)

Afterword

In closing, everything we have talked about developed on a large scale during the last third of the twentieth century. Synthesizer and electronic instrument development has changed radically, and as a result, electronic instruments have created their own niche industry.

What lies ahead? Computer software that is capable of emulating any synthesizer? Virtual Synthesis DSP modeling and sampling techniques certainly have a lot to offer in that respect.

At the AES (Audio Engineering Society) Convention, held in Los Angeles in 2000, the theme or "buzz" was centered around two quickly emerging technologies; surround sound and new 'codecs' for audio on the Internet. A Codec converts data between uncompressed and compressed formats, reducing the bandwidth an audio segment consumes.

A representative from the German based Fraunhofer Institute turned heads with a presentation of MPEG-4 audio software for computers and DSPs. The technology incorporates a Codec that is light years beyond what MP3 and current popular streaming media protocols such as Liquid Audio (Microsoft) and Real Audio are capable of producing. It uses scalable coding, which can deliver three separate bit-rates of audio in real time. This is something Internet audio has needed for quite a while, since the person encoding the audio doesn't know the speed of the processor and modem of the person on the other end downloading the file.

This technology compensates for all popular bandwidth rates. The technicians from RealAudio unveiled a similar technology, called Sure-Streaming, where you can encode a single clip that can be utilized on up to six bandwidths. Mark Yonge of Solid State Logic wowed the crowds with a demonstration of SC-06-01, the proposed standard for network and file transfer of audio. This will revolutionize the way samplers, and workstations transfer audio.

While computer-based software, and bigger, better synths and samplers have received a lot of attention at AES and NAMM during the past two years a radical innovation in guitar technology also has garnered enthusiastic responses from guitarists and press alike. Fusion guitar legend Frank Gambale has designed a radically new guitar for Yamaha, breaking a 50-year tradition in guitar design concepts. With unique features such as a rear-mount pickup/neck system, Fretwave tuning system, and a skillfully sculpted body shape, this signature guitar ranks amongst the worlds finest electric guitars. I spoke to Frank, and David Cervantes, (the luthier who built it for Yamaha) about this instrument recently and they told me how the guitar evolved.

What appears like a glued on neck is in fact a cleverly designed bolt-on. Frank said it took a while to get the rigidity of the neck-to-body joint, leaving enough space for adjustments of the pickups and other components, so it was quite complicated. Frank said the only place they could attach the tremolo spring claw was at the end of the neck and to the best of his recollection, in 50 years of electric guitar construction nobody has ever done that before. This innovation created extraordinary sustain and brightness. Even the highest notes had the resonance and clarity of a piano. I was amazed at the tone and sustain the guitar produced, as I sat next to Frank, watching him play the instrument.

Another radical innovation incorporated into the Yamaha AES FG model is the Fretwave system designed by Australian musicians from Camberra, Ian (Gunther) Gorman and Nic Ward. I met Gunther on one of his recent trips to the US in late January 2002. He explained that if you do the mathematics for standard guitar fretting you will find that fifths are out of tune by about 1.3 percent and thirds are out by as much as 2.5 percent. This is what causes chords to 'go out of tune' as you change positions on the fretboard. The problem is especially noticeable with 'first position' chords played between the nut and the 3rd fret. The Fretwave system is a new and remarkably simple fret structure that corrects this in standard guitar fretting.

In a short discussion with designer/luthier David Cervantes, he explained the evolution of the Yamaha AES FG. Cervantes built Frank's guitar and engineered its many innovations. He also created the Drop 6 and AEX 500 N for Yamaha, both of which are new and original concept instruments.

Ben Kettlewell: What are the advantages of the Frank Gambale model over standard electric guitars?

David Cervantes: The Yamaha AES FG is a better instrument all around sonically and musically. The sonic properties of the instrument are more pronounced. We've brought the instrument to a point where the way it resonates, the way its parts interact with each other is towards one common goal. In a lot of other designs that isn't the case. The continuity is more complete than in any other fretted instrument, I would say.

BK: You are working with Fender now so, as a luthier, you can look back at this as a real objective milestone.

DC: Yes. The main two technological advances are the Fretwave system and the way the bridge couples directly to the butt end of the neck. This enhances the way the strings generate sound. The vibration of the neck "lights up," because the neck is where all the tone originates, and now the sound cycles from the neck to the body and back again. The body and the bridge are working together because they are vibrating together as an integral unit. The springs that connect at the bottom of the bridge are connected right to the butt of the neck, so it allows for a complete cycle of resonance. This has never been done before and you can tell because the notes at the top of the register are a lot louder and significantly more pronounced than on any guitar made today.

There are other subtleties like the design and placement of the tuners, which allow for a straight string-pull from the back of the nut to the tuners with a three on a side configuration. This is primarily for tuning stability with the tremolo. The jack is an acoustic jack ergonomically mounted into the front surface of the guitar. The inlay motif is art deco and it has the FG initials subtly inlayed at the twelfth fret. We wanted to achieve that subtly, because most people don't want to buy a guitar with someone else's name on it.

The ergonomic placement of the knobs and switch is another innovation. Because of the way we carved the body we had to come up with a way to place the knobs and switch in a way that they would not break the line of the design. We achieved this by creating a bubble on the rear control plate, so the knobs do not protrude on the top of the body.

The Fretwave system, the body neck construction and the ergonomics are the three main innovations in this instrument. It's a bolt on neck. Traditionally the neck bolts on from the front of the body, into a recessed pocket, i.e. neck pocket. In this guitar, we really don't have a neck pocket. Ours bolts from the back of the body and the neck becomes an integral part of the body, like a spine. Frank came to me knowing exactly what he wanted and that made it very easy to accomplish in pinpointing the direction.

The thousands of people who attended the 2002 NAMM show clearly indicated that in the scramble to keep up to date with technology, talent wins out every time, and that's one factor that never changes.

In this book, I've attempted to introduce you to the diverse history of electronic instruments and some of the fascinating people who have brought them into prominence. As always, new tools for music creation will be a result of technological advances, and talented musicians will find artistic ways to incorporate them into their music. Keep in mind that today's constantly evolving digital technology is the most unpredictable medium that musicians have ever tried to master. I hope that this book will bring each reader a greater understanding of the exciting age music has entered. All the people interviewed in this book are still very active explorers of new musical frontiers, and their stories are far from finished.

The End

Glossary

Access Time: Access time is the time from the start of one storage device's access to data to the time when the next access can be started. Access time consists of latency (the overhead of getting to the right place on the device and preparing to access it) and transfer time. The term is applied to both random access memory (RAM) access and to hard disk and CD-ROM access. Access time to a hard disk or CD-ROM is usually measured in milliseconds.

ADAT: The ADAT (a registered trademark of Alesis) is an eight-track digital tape recorder that caught the recording industry by storm when it was first released in the early 1990s. Today, with over 100,000 ADATs in use in recording facilities around the world, it is the most widely used professional digital recording system. The ADAT was the first product in the category now known as modular digital multitracks (MDMs).

Additive Synthesis: The process of constructing a complex sound using a series of fundamental frequencies (pure tones or sine waves).

ADPCM: This is an audio compression algorithm for digital audio based on describing level differences between adjacent samples.

ADSR: Acronym for Attack, Decay, Sustain, and Release. These are the four parameters found on a basic synthesizer envelope generator. When a key is pressed, the envelope generator will begin to rise to its full level at the rate set by the attack parameter, upon reaching peak level it will begin to fall at the rate set by the decay parameter to the level set by the sustain control. The envelope will remain at the sustain level as long as the key is held down. Whenever a key is released, it will return to zero at the rate set by the release parameter.

Aftertouch: Control data generated by pressing down on one or more keys on a synthesizer keyboard after they have reached and are resting on the keyboard.

AGC: Automatic Gain Control

AIFF: Audio interchange file format. This is a common Macintosh audio file format. It can be mono or stereo with sampling rates up to 48kHz. AIFF files are QuickTime compatible.

Aliasing: Aliasing is the term used to describe the unwanted frequencies that are produced when a sound is sampled at a rate which is less than twice the frequency of the highest frequency component in the sound.

Algorithm: A set of procedures designed to accomplish something. In the case of computer software, the procedures may appear to the user as a configuration of software components.

Algorithmic Composition: This is a composition in which the large outlines of the piece, or the actions to be used in generating it, are determined by the human composer while some of the details, such as notes or rhythms, are created by a computer program such as Laurie Spiegel's Music Mouse by using algorithmic processes.

Alternating Current: The type of electrical current, which continuously and regularly alternates its direction of flow from one direction (positive) to the other (negative), supplied by utility power lines, and thus found in ordinary electrical wall sockets: as distinct from direct current.

Ambience: All of the "natural sounds" of any environment. The ambience of a tavern for example might consist of conversation, laughter, clinking of glasses, music in the background, electrical hum, etc.

Amplifier: A device with electron tubes or semi-conductors that is used to increase the strength of a signal.

Amplitude: Amplitude is a term used to describe the amount of a signal. It can relate to volume in an audio signal or the amount of voltage in an electrical signal.

Amplitude Modulation: A change in the level of a signal. For example, if a Low Frequency Oscillator (LFO) was modulating a Voltage Controlled Amplifier (VCA), the result would be a periodic increase and decrease in the audio level of the signal. In musical terms this would be referred to as Tremolo. The abbreviation of Amplitude Modulation is AM.

Analog: Data (signal) presented in a non-digital, continuous form.

Analog Synthesizer: A synthesizer that uses voltage controlled analog modules to synthesize sound. The three main voltage controlled modules in an analog synthesizer are Voltage Controlled Oscillator (VCO), Voltage Controlled Filter (VCF), and Voltage Controlled Amplifier (VCA).

Aperiodic Waveform: A waveform that does not have a repeating pattern.

ARP: American Recording & Performance Co, a company that introduced some amazing synthesizers in the late seventies and early eighties.

Arpeggiator: A device or computer program that sequentially moves a pattern of notes over a range of the keyboard.

Attack: The first parameter of an envelope generator which determines the rate or time it will take for the event to reach the highest level before starting to decay.

Attenuator: Attenuate means to reduce in force, value, or amount. An Attenuator is a device that reduces the value of something, usually the amplitude of a signal.

Audible Range: The range of frequencies that the human ear can hear. A healthy young human can usually hear from 20 cycles per second to around 20,000 cycles per second (20-20,000 Hz).

Auto Correlation: A process that determines optimum start and ending loop points to produce minimum discontinuity.

Auxiliary Controllers: These are external controlling devices used in conjunction with a main instrument or controller. Some examples of such controllers are foot pedals, pitch bending and modulation wheels.

Band Pass Filter: A filter, which allows only a selected band of frequencies to pass through while rejecting all other frequencies above and below the cutoff point.

Bandwidth: The available space through which information can travel. In audio, the bandwidth of a device is the portion of the frequency spectrum that it can handle without significant loss of quality.

Bank: A set of patches, or any related set of items, such as a filter bank, comprised of a set of filters that work together to process a single signal.

Baud Rate: The speed at which digital information is passed through a serial interface expressed in bits-per-second. MIDI data is transmitted at 31.25 KBaud or 31,250 bits per second.

Bend: To change pitch in a continuous manner, usually using a pitch-bend wheel or lever. Also see pitch-bend.

Binary: Of or based on the number two or the binary numeration system (base 2). Digital computers use this form of numbering because an open or closed switch can easily represent the values of 0 and 1.

Bit: A Bit is a single piece of information assigned a value of 0 or 1 as used in a digital computer. Computers use digital words, which are combinations of bits. A Byte is a digital word consisting of eight bits.

Boot: Starting up a computer by loading a program that allows it to run other programs. The term comes from bootstrapping, which means that the computer "pulls itself up by its own bootstraps."

Bounce: When recording or sequencing, to bounce tracks means to combine (mix) several tracks together and record them on another track.

Brick Wall Filter: A lowpass filter at the input of an analog-to-digital converter, used to prevent frequencies above the Nyquist limit from being encoded by the converter.

Buffer: An area of computer memory that is used to temporarily store data.

Bug: An error in a computer program that causes it to work incorrectly.

Byte: A computer word made up of eight bits of data.

Cardioid: A directional microphone with a heart shaped, narrow pattern, which picks up from directly in front of the mic.

Catalog: A list of all files stored on a disk or in a bank. Sometimes called a directory.

CD-ROM: Compact disc read-only memory. A compact disc format that can store data other than just standard CD audio. Many programs, sound sample libraries, and graphics are distributed on CD-ROM because each CD can store hundreds of megabytes of information, yet costs about the same to manufacture as a floppy disk, which only stores about 1 megabyte.

Cent: Unit of pitch equal to 1/100 of a semitone. One hundred cents equal one half-step.

Center Detent: A notch in the center of a modulation wheel or lever, which allows the performer to find the home position.

Central Processing Unit (CPU): A microprocessor or computer, which is used to perform complex task-related functions. Within an electronic musical instrument, it is a dedicated computer system for handling the many performance and control-related messages and commands that must be processed in real time.

Channel messages: These are messages that are assigned to a specific MIDI channel within a system or device.

Channel-voice messages: These are used to transmit real-time performance data throughout a connected MIDI system. They are generated whenever the controller of a MIDI instrument is played, selected, or varied by the performer.

Channel: Output the circuitry through which an instrument outputs individual notes. In analog audio (such as a mixer) each channel consists of separate wired components. In the digital domain, channels may share wiring, and are kept separate through logical operations. MIDI provides definitions for 16 channels, which transmit not audio signals but digital control signals for triggering synthesizers and other devices.

Channel, MIDI: An information pathway through which MIDI information is sent. MIDI provides for 16 available channels, each of which can address one MIDI instrument.

Channel, MIDI Control: A MIDI Channel also contains information about which controllers are being varied.

Chip: An integrated circuit.

Chorus: A voice doubling effect created by layering two identical sounds with a slight delay (20-50 ms) and slightly modulating the frequency of one or both of the sounds. The simplest way to achieve chorusing is to detune one synthesizer oscillator from another to produce a slow oscillation between them.

Click sync/click track: this refers to the metronomic audio clicks that are generated by electronic devices to communicate tempo.

Clock: A steady pulse from a generator, which is used, for synchronizing sequencers, drum machines, etc. Common sequencer timing clock rates are 24,48, or 96 pulses-per-quarter note. MIDI timing clocks run at a rate of 24 ppqn.

Clipboard: A temporary holding place in RAM for what you last cut or copied.

Close Miking: A microphone placement technique which involves placing a microphone close to the sound source in order to pick up mainly direct sound, and avoid picking up reverberant sound.

Computer Interface: Hardware, which enables a computer to communicate with other devices. A common example is a MIDI interface, which allows a computer to communicate with a musical instrument.

Condenser Mike: A microphone which converts sound pressure level variations into variations in capacitance and then into electrical voltage.

Continuous Controller: Refers to Midi information other than notes. For example, volume, pitch bending, modulation (vibrato). These parameters can change continuously over time and allow electronically generated music to sound more expressive.

Contour: See Envelope Generator

Controller: A device which let's you enter or change events into a computer or other digital device. Examples include keyboards, pitch, and modulation wheels and wind controllers.

Copy: To make a copy of something, either a sound or segment, by selecting it and choosing the copy function from the module menu. What is copied is placed on the clipboard.

Crossfade: To gradually fade out one sound while fading in another so that a seamless transition is made between the two sounds.

Cursor: A visual indicator showing the position of the next entry.

Cut: To remove something, either a sound or a segment, by selecting it and choosing the cut function from the module menu. What you cut is placed on the clipboard.

Cutoff Frequency: The frequency above which a low pass filter will start attenuating signals present at its input. Abbreviated Fc.

DAT (machine): See Digital Audio Tape recorder.

Data: Information a computer needs in order to make decisions or carry out a particular action.

Data Wheel: A knob that allows you to scroll through Programs and change parameter values. Usually used when a keypad is not available or for fine tuning and scrolling through infinite variables.

dB/Octave: The unit typically used to indicate the slope of a filter, or how fast the frequency response rolls off past the cutoff frequency. Example: A 24 dB/octave filter would attenuate an input signal by 24 dB one octave above the cutoff frequency, by 48 dB two octaves above the cutoff frequency, and so on.

Decay: The second stage in an ADSR type envelope generator. See ADSR.

Decibel (dB): A reference for the measurement of sound energy. The minimum change in volume that the human ear can perceive. Named after Alexander Graham Bell. A decibel is 1/10th of a Bel.

Delay: A controllable time parameter giving the ability to start an event only after a predetermined amount of time. The Delay function on the EIII allows you to delay the start of a sound from 0 to 1.5 seconds from the time a key is pressed.

Depth: The amount of modulation. Sometimes called Amount, Width, Intensity or Modulation Index.

Digital: Equipment that uses quantities represented as binary numbers. In a digital synthesizer every aspect of the sound generation is handled as a numeric calculation. The digital information is not audible and so must be converted to analog form by a DAC before it is output.

Digital to Analog Converter (DAC): A device that interprets Digital information and converts it to Analog form. All digital synthesizers, samplers, and effects devices have DACs (rhymes with fax) at their outputs to create audio signals.

Digital Audio Tape (DAT): The medium that a machine that records sound digitally uses. They generally use a spinning drum similar to those found in VCR's as opposed to the record and playback heads found on regular analog tape recorders.

Digital Signal Processor: See Signal Processors. Most signal processors these days are digital. They allow the instant recall of all the parameter settings of the device without having to manually reset all the controls every time a different sound effect is required.

Direct time lock (DTL) and enhanced time lock (DTLe): A synchronization standard that allows Mark of the Unicorn's Mac-based sequencer, Performer, to lock to SMPTE through a converter, which supports these standards

Display: A device that gives information in a visual form.

Distant Miking: A microphone placement technique which involves placing a microphone far from the sound source in order to pick up a high proportion of reverberant sound.

Drum Machine: A sample based digital audio device that makes use of the playback capabilities of ROM (read only) memory to reproduce carefully recorded and edited samples of individual instruments which make up the modern drum and percussion set.

Drum Pads: The playing surface buttons, which are designed into a drum machine and played with the fingers.

Drum-pad controller: Such a controller offers the performer a larger, more expressive playing surface that can be struck either with the fingers and hands, or with mallets and drum sticks for full expressiveness. Additionally, a drum controller will often offer extensive setup parameters.

DSP: Digital signal processing. Generally speaking, all changes in sound that are produced within a digital audio device, other than changes caused by simple cutting and pasting of sections of a waveform, are created through DSP. A digital reverb is a typical DSP device.

DVD: The two most two common definitions for DVD are Digital Versatile Disc or Digital Video Disc. DVD is a format based on the audio CDs, comprised of a disc 4 3/4 inches in diameter that can have two layers on each side. DVD technology squeezes all the data onto a normal CD by putting its tracks closer together with the pits in each track being smaller. In addition the data compression technology is highly efficient. The second layer on the CD is read by changing the focus of the laser. A standard DVD disc can hold 4.7 gigabytes per side, that's seven times the capacity of an ordinary CD. It gives you 133 minutes of video, which is sufficient to handle over 90 % of all feature-length films. The dual layer DVDs can hold 8.5 gigabytes on a single side, which leads to a very impressive 17 gigabytes on dual sided DVD CDs—26 times the capacity of a standard CD-ROM.

Dynamic Allocation: On the EIII, Dynamic Allocation defeats any pre- assigned output channel assignments and assigns the output channels according to a modified circular algorithm.

Dynamic Mike: A microphone in which the diaphragm moves a coil suspended in a magnetic field in order to generate an output voltage proportional to the sound pressure level.

Dynamic Range: The range of the softest to the loudest sound that can be produced by an instrument. Or the range of the low and high signal levels obtainable by a velocity sensitive keyboard. The greater the Dynamic Range, the more sensitive the keyboard.

Edit: To change or modify information. To change parameters or alter existing data.

Envelope Generator: A circuit, usually triggered by pressing a key on a keyboard that generates a changing voltage with respect to time. This voltage typically controls a VCF or VCA. An AHDSR and ADSR are two types of Envelope Generators. See ADSR.

Equal Temperament: A Scaling system where the octave is divided into 12 equal parts. The ratio of the frequencies between any two adjacent notes is exactly the same. Most keyboard instruments are scaled in this manner.

Equalizer: A device that allows attenuation or emphasis of selected frequencies in the audio spectrum. Equalizers usually contain many bands to allow the user a fine degree of frequency control over the sound.

Error Message: A message shown in the display to alert the user that an error of some type has occurred.

Fast Fourier Transform: A computer algorithm that derives the Fourier spectrum from a sound file.

Fc: See Cutoff Frequency

Filter: A device used to remove unwanted frequencies from an audio signal thus altering its harmonic structure. Low Pass filters are the most common type of filter found on music synthesizers. They only allow frequencies below the cutoff frequency to pass (Low Pass). High Pass filters only allow the high frequencies to pass, and Band Pass filters only allow frequencies in a selected band to pass through. A Notch filter rejects frequencies that fall within its notch.

FireWire: This is Apple Computer's version of a standard, IEEE 1394, High Performance Serial Bus, designed for connecting external devices to your computer. FireWire provides a single plug-and-socket connection on which up to 63 devices can be attached with data transfer speeds up to 400 Mbps (megabits per second.) With a computer equipped with the FireWire socket and bus capability, any device (for example, a DVD recorder) can be plugged in while the computer is running.

Flange: An effect created by layering two identical sounds with a slight delay (1- 20 mS) and slightly modulating the delay of one or both of the sounds. The term comes from the early days of tape recording when grabbing the flanges of the tape reels to change the tape speed created delay effects.

Floppy Disk: A thin portable disk used to store digital data.

Fourier Spectrum: The description of a sound that is in terms of its distribution of energy versus frequency rather than its amplitude versus time (waveform).

Free MIDI: A Macintosh operating system extension developed by Mark of the Unicorn that enables different programs to share MIDI data.

Frequency: The number of cycles of a waveform occurring in a second.

Frequency Modulation: The encoding of a carrier wave by variation of its frequency in accordance with an input signal.

FSK: Frequency Shift Keying. An audio tone (frequency) modulated by a square wave, which is used both for data transfer and also for sequencer and drum machine synchronization.

Fundamental: The first, lowest note of a harmonic series. The Fundamental frequency determines a sound's overall pitch.

Gain: The factor by which a device increases the amplitude of a signal. Negative gain will result in the attenuation of a signal.

General MIDI (GM): This is a set of requirements for MIDI devices designed for ensuring consistent playback performance on all instruments bearing the GM logo. Some of the requirements include 24-voice polyphony and a standardized group and location of sounds. For example, patch #25 will always be a classical guitar sound on all General MIDI instruments.

Glide: Also called portamento; a function which enables pitches to slide smoothly from one note to the next instead of jumping over the intervening pitches.

Glissando: A rapid slide through a series of consecutive tones in a scale like passage. On a Korg Poly 6 arpeggiator for example, when two notes are played with glissando on, every note in between the two notes will be played in a sequential order. Similar to portamento except that the pitch changes in semitone steps.

Ground Loop: Hum caused by currents circulating through the ground side of a piece of equipment or system. This is due to grounding it at points of different voltage potential.

Hard Disk: A storage medium for digital data.

Hard disk recorder: A computer-based hardware and software package specifically intended for the recording, manipulation, and reproduction of the digital audio data that resides upon hard disk and/or within the computers own RAM.

Hardware-based sequencer: Stand-alone devices for the sole purpose of MIDI sequencing. These systems make use of a dedicated operating structure, micro-processing system, and memory that is integrated with top-panel controls for performing sequence-specific functions.

Harmonic Distortion: The presence of harmonics in the output signal of a device, which were not present in the input signal.

Hertz/Hz: A unit of frequency equal to 1 cycle per second. Named after Heinrich R. Hertz.

High Pass Filter: See Filter

Initialize: To prepare a disk to receive data. A hard disk or a floppy disk must be initialized before it can be accessed.

Interactive sequencer: A computer-based sequencer that directly interfaces with MIDI controllers and sequenced MIDI files to internally generate MIDI performance data according to a computer algorithm.

Internal sequencer: A sequencer designed into an electronic instrument that directly interfaces with the instrument's keyboard and voice structure.

Just Intonation: A system of tuning in which the distances between pitches are based on the natural harmonic series instead of the octave being equally divided.

K: Abbreviation for Kilo or 1000

Keyboard Assignment: The assignment of specific sounds to an area of the keyboard. For example, the lowest octave could be drum sounds, the next octave could be an electric bass, and the rest of the keyboard could have various piano samples assigned to it.

Keyboard controller: A keyboard device expressly designed to transmit performance-related MIDI messages throughout a modular MIDI system

Layering: The ability to place or stack two or more sounds on the same area of the keyboard to create a denser sound.

LFO: Low Frequency Oscillator. An oscillator used for modulation whose range is below the audible range (20 Hz). Example: Varying pitch cyclically produces vibrato.

Loading: To transfer from one data storage medium to another. This is generally from disk to RAM memory or vice-versa, as opposed to saving from RAM to disk.

Lock: To prevent data from being edited discarded or renamed, or to prevent entire banks or disks from being altered.

Longitudinal time code: (LTC): Time code which is recorded onto an audio or video cue track. LTC encodes the biphase time-code signal onto an analog audio or cue track as a modulated square-wave signal

Looping: Looping is the process of repeating a portion of a sample over and over in order to create a sustaining sound. The looped sound will continue as long as the key is depressed. A sound is usually looped during a point in its evolution where the harmonics and amplitude are relatively static in order to avoid pops and glitches in the sound.

Low Note Priority: When more than one note is played on a monophonic synthesizer, only the lowest note will sound.

Low Pass Filter: A filter whose frequency response remains flat up to a certain frequency, then rolls off (attenuates signals appearing at its input) above this point.

M: Abbreviation for Mea or million.

Memory: Used for storing important internal data, such as patch information, setup configurations, and digital waveform data.

Merge: To combine or unite. To Merge means to combine sequences, sounds, tracks, MIDI data, etc.

Modeling Synthesis: A type of sound synthesis performed by computer models of instruments. This technique emulates the impulse patterns of real-world instruments using a software model. These models are sets of complex equations that describe the physical properties of an instrument (such as the shape of the bell and the density of the material) and the way a musician interacts with it.

Musical Instrument Digital Interface (MIDI): A digital communications language that allows multiple electronic instruments, controllers, computers, and other related devices to communicate within a connected network. MIDI is an asynchronous, serial interface, which is transmitted at the rate of 31.25 KBaud or 31,250 bits per second.

MIDI Clock: Allows instruments interconnected via MIDI to be synchronized. The MIDI Clock runs at a rate of 24 pulses-per-quarter- note.

MIDI Continuous Controller: Allows continuously changing information such as pitch wheel or breath controller information to be passed over the MIDI line. Continuous controllers use large amounts of memory when recorded into a MIDI sequencer. Some standard MIDI Continuous Controller numbers are listed below.

PWH = Pitch Wheel
CHP = Pressure
1 = Modulation Wheel
2 = Breath Controller
3 = (Pressure on Rev. 1 DX7)
4 = Foot Pedal
5 = Portamento Time
6 = Data Entry
7 = Volume

8 = Balance
10 = Pan
11 = Expression Controller
16-19 = General purpose controllers 1-4 (High Res.)
64 = Sustain Switch (on/off)
65 = Portamento Switch (on/off)
66 = Sustenuto (chord hold)
67 = Soft Pedal (on/off)
69 = Hold Pedal 2 (on/off)
80-83 = General purpose controllers 5-8 (Low Res.)
91 = External Effects Depth
92 = Tremolo Depth
93 = Chorus Depth
94 = Detune
95 = Phaser Depth
96 = Data Increment
97 = Data Decrement

MIDI echo: The selectable MIDI echo function is used to provide an exact copy of any information received at the MIDI in port, and route this data directly to the MIDI out/echo port.

MIDI filter: A dedicated digital device, onboard processor, or computer algorithm that allows specific MIDI messages or range of messages within a data stream to be either recognized or ignored.

MIDI implementation chart: A standardized that easily relates information to all of the MIDI capabilities that are supported by a specific MIDI device.

MIDI in: This port receives MIDI messages from an external source and communicates this performance, control, and timing data to the device's internal microprocessors.

MIDI interface: A device used to translate the serial message data of MIDI into a data structure that can be directly communicated both to and from a personal computer's internal operating system.

MIDI mapper: A dedicated digital device, onboard processor, or computer algorithm that can be used to reassign the scaler value of a data byte to another assigned value.

MIDI messages: These are made up of a group of related 8-bit words, which are used to convey a series of performance or control instructions to one or all MIDI devices within a system.

MIDI out: This port is used to transmit MIDI messages from a single source device to the microprocessor of another MIDI instrument or device.

MIDI thru: This port provides an exact copy of the incoming data at the MIDI in port and transmits this data to another MIDI instrument or device that follows within the MIDI data chain.

MIDI time code (MTC): A system for easily and cost-effectively translating SMPTE time code into an equivalent time code that conforms to the MIDI 1.0 Specification. It also allows for time-based code and commands to be distributed throughout the MIDI chain to devices or instruments capable of understanding and executing MTC commands.

Mixer: A device that allows combination of different audio signals together and outputs them in mono or stereo. Mixers come in many sizes and are referred to by the number of channels (different audio inputs) they have. Most software sequencers also have a mixer onboard, which lets you control the volume levels of the individual parts of your song.

Modulation: The process of one audio or control voltage source influencing a sound processor or other control voltage source. Example: Slowly modulating pitch cyclically produces vibrato. Modulating a filter cyclically produces wah-wah effects.

Modulation Index: The depth of modulation when performing frequency modulation.

Module Identifier: The screen that displays information about what module is currently activated.

Monophonic: A musical instrument that is only capable of playing one note at a time. The term monophonic traditionally has a very specific musical meaning that describes a type of musical texture that consists of a single melodic line with no accompaniment. The term has a different meaning in electronic music. Here it means that an instrument can only play one note at a time. If you simultaneously press down two different keys on a monophonic keyboard you will hear only one note.

Multi-timbral: The ability of a musical instrument to produce two or more different sounds or timbres at the same time. For example, a multi-timbral synthesizer might be able to produce drum sounds while also producing bass, piano, guitar, etc.

Multi-track: A way to record a complex musical piece by dividing it into simple tracks, and combining the tracks during playback.

Module: Same as tone module or sound module or tone generator. See tone module.

Monitor: This word can mean at least two different things. A computer screen or a studio stage speaker system

Multitasking: The ability for many of the faster, more powerful personal computer's to process more than one program and/or task at a time.

Normalize: A digital processing function that increases the amplitude of a sound file until the peak amplitude of its loudest sample reaches 100% of full scale.

Oscillator: An electronic circuit that produces an alternating output current determined by the characteristics of the circuit components.

Overload: Distortion that is caused by exceeding the dynamic range of a circuit.

Pan: Refers to moving an audio signal left or right in the stereo spectrum. Also called the balance control. All stereo audio mixers have panning, and most software sequencers allow you to set and change panning.

Parallel Interface: A computer interface in which data is passed simultaneously over many wires. A Parallel Interface is usually much faster than a serial interface. The SCSI Interface on the Emulator III is an example of a Parallel Interface.

Paste: To put a copy of the contents of the clipboard (whatever was last copied or cut) in at the specified insertion point.

Patch: A synthesizer sound that is stored in its computer memory. Usually refers to a sound, which can be altered, i.e. its stored in RAM memory. Sometimes also called preset, program, or sound. Comes from the use of patch cords on the original modular synthesizers.

Patch editor: A software-based package used to provide direct control over a compatible MIDI device, while clearly displaying each parameter setting on the monitor screen of a personal computer.

Patch librarian: A software package capable of receiving, transmitting, and often organizing patch data between one or more devices and a personal computer system.

Percussion Controller: Same as a drum controller, except that there are many percussion controllers which are configured like mallet instruments and thus are very adept at playing pitched parts.

Pitch Bend: A continuous controller that can be applied to synthesized note(s), usually from a joystick to the left of the lowest keyboard note. The sound is a raising or lowering of the pitch and changes as you move the joystick left and right.

Plug-in: Plug-in applications are programs that can easily be installed and used as part of your music software, running "inside" a program such as Pro Tools, or independently, such as the HALion software sampler.

Polyphonic: A musical instrument that is able to play more than one note at the same time. If you simultaneously press down two different keys on your keyboard and you can hear both notes your keyboard is polyphonic. Virtually all modern synthesizers and samplers are polyphonic.

Preset: A preprogrammed sound and control setup on a sampler or synthesizer. Presets can be made up in advance of a performance, stored in memory, then recalled instantly when desired.

Pressure Sensitivity: The ability of an instrument to respond to pressure applied to the keyboard after the initial depression of a key. Sometimes called aftertouch.

Proximity Effect: When cardioid microphones are placed very close to the sound source, a boosting of the bass frequencies occurs which is known as the proximity effect.

Punch-in: When recording, punching in over-writes a previously recorded track starting at the punch in point.

Punch-out: When recording, punching out stops the recording process started by a punch in, thus preserving the previously recorded track starting at the punch out point.

Q Dial: Rotary knob used to scroll through data or select parameters. Used on Kawai sequencers to select, among other things, a particular bar in a song. See also: Data wheel

Quantization: A timing function of a sequencer or sequencing software used to correct human-performance timing errors within a composition.

RAM: Acronym for Random Access Memory. The memory in a computer in a computer that stores data temporarily while you are working on it. Data stored in RAM is lost forever when power is interrupted to the machine if it has not been saved to another medium, such as floppy or hard disk.

RS 422: A high-speed serial communication port, which allows data to be transferred to and from an external computer at a very high rate (500K baud).

ROM: Acronym for Read Only Memory. This is computer memory, which can't be changed or erased. It is 'burned' into the computer or device. Most synthesizers have some sounds, which are in ROM memory and can't be altered. A sign of a more expensive synthesizer is having sounds in RAM memory, implying that you can alter the sounds and save variations as your own.

Realtime Controls: Occurring in actual time or live.

Resonance: A frequency at which a material object will vibrate. In a filter with resonance, a signal will be accentuated at the cutoff frequency. See Q.

Sampler: Also called a digital sampler. A type of synthesizer which derives its sounds from recording actual sounds (instruments or non musical sounds) and then storing them in computer memory, either floppy discs, hard drive, or recorded onto CD-ROM.

Sample Rate: When digitally sampling a signal, the rate at which level measurements of the signal are taken. Typical sampling rates vary from 11kHz to 48kHz.

Sampling: The process of recording a sound into digital memory.

SCSI: Acronym for Small Computer Serial Interface, which is a connection on the back of your computer or electronic instrument which allows connection to other hardware devices such as external CD-ROM drives, external hard drives, some printers, scanners, etc.

SCSI Port: The port on the back of the instrument to which SCSI devices are connected. Sequencer: A device, which steps through a series of events. A digital sequencer may record keyboard data, program changes, or real-time modulation data to be played back later much like a tape recorder or player piano. Digital sequencers use memory on the basis of events (key on, key off, etc.) while a tape recorder uses memory (tape) on the basis of time.

SDS: The MIDI sample dump standard. SDS is used to transfer digital audio samples from one instrument to another over a MIDI cable.

Serial Interface: A computer interface in which data is passed over a single line, one bit at a time. The MIDI interface is an example of a serial interface.

SFI: A file extension specifying Turtle Beach's SoundStage audio format. Typically encountered as FILENAME.SFI.

Signal Processing: The art of modifying an existing sound through the use of electronic circuitry.

Signal Processor: An electronic device which audio signals can be routed through to affect the sound of that signal. Examples: echo and reverb units, distortion devices, etc. Most electric guitarists run their instruments through 'pedals', which are small floor units, those process signals at the press of a foot pedal.

Signal to Noise ratio (S/N): The ratio between what goes in a device designed to alter or record sound, and what comes out the other end. If what you get out the other end is all distorted; the piece of equipment has a low signal to noise ratio. A very expensive DAT machine for example, will have a high S/N ratio because what you get out will sound very close to what you put in. The same goes for a very expensive digital effect processor.

SMDI: SCSI musical data interchange. A specification for sending MIDI sample dumps over the SCSI bus.

SMPTE: Acronym for Society of Motion Picture and Television Engineers who adopted a standard time code in order to synchronize video and audio. SMPTE information is in the form of Hours, Minutes, Seconds, and Frames. There are two types of SMPTE time code, Longitudinal Time Code which can be recorded on audio tape, and Vertical Interval Time Code which is recorded on video tape.

Software: The programs or sets of instructions describing the tasks to be performed by a computer.

Software Sequencer: A sequencing software package designed to be loaded into a computer. Software sequencers usually have more features and have the advantage of showing you a lot more information at once because of its computer screen.

Song Pointer: MIDI information, which allows equipment to remain in sync even if the master device has been fast-forwarded. MIDI Song Pointer (sometimes called MIDI Song Position Pointer) is an internal register (in the sequencer or autolocator) which holds the number of MIDI beats since the start of the song.

Soundcard: A circuit board that installs inside a computer (typically an IBM-compatible) adding new sound capabilities. These capabilities can include an FM or wavetable synthesizer and audio inputs and outputs.

Sound Module: See tone module.

Step Time: A sequencer mode where events are entered one at a time.

Subtractive Synthesis: The process of constructing a sound by starting with a complex sound and then removing harmonics with a filter. A low pass filter is most commonly used. The cutoff frequency of the filter is usually dynamically varied, which changes the harmonics that are removed. Using the low pass filter on the Emulator III to alter the sound is a form of subtractive synthesis. Supermode: An Emulator III MIDI function designed to enhance the Sequencer/MIDI interface. It maps data occurring on a specific MIDI channel to a specific preset within the bank. Similar to standard MIDI Omni Off/Mono mode, but more flexible. Each channel can contain polyphonic note data.

Synthesizer: A device that creates sounds electronically through the use of voltage controlled amplifiers and filters. The settings for each sound are usually saved as presets.

Taper: A digital signal processing function that fades a sound in or out between two points. Tapering permanently modifies a sound.

Terminating Resistors: Also called a terminator. A group of resistors that should be placed on the SCSI cable before the last device on a SCSI chain. Usually the terminating resistor is built inside the SCSI device. There should be no more than two terminators in a SCSI chain: one at the start, built into the EIII, and one at the end.

THD: Total harmonic distortion. An audio measurement specification used to determine the accuracy with which a device can reproduce an input signal at its output. THD describes the cumulative level of the harmonic overtones that the device being tested adds to an input sine wave.

Timbre: Tone color. The quality of a sound that distinguishes it from other sounds with the same pitch and volume.

Tone Generator: See tone module.

Tone Module: A synthesizer without a piano keyboard. Since Midi allows one keyboard to literally play another, there is little reason to acquire more piano keyboards when wanting to expand your palette of sound choices. Buying tone modules is usually a bit less expensive than the keyboard version, and saves valuable space.

Track: Sequencers borrowed this term from multi-track recording studios, referring to tape tracks. A track is one of a number of locations where a musical part can be recorded and played back. A typical software sequencer has 16-128 tracks.

Tremolo: A cyclic change in amplitude, usually in the range of 7 to 14 Hz. Usually achieved by routing a LFO (low frequency oscillator) to a VCA (voltage controlled amplifier).

Truncation: When manipulating a sample, truncation shortens a sample's length by trimming off parts of the beginning and/or end.

Undo: Cancels the results of the last operation.

USB: Abbrieviation for Universal Serial Bus; a standard bus type for all kinds of devices, including mice, scanners, digital cameras, printers, etc. USB supports a 12 Mbps transfer rate. Devices can be connected and disconnected while the computer is on.

VCA: Voltage Controlled Amplifier. A circuit whose gain is determined by a control voltage.

VCF: Voltage Controlled Filter. A filter whose cutoff frequency or resonant frequency is determined by a control voltage.

VCO: Voltage-controlled oscillator. An oscillator whose frequency can be changed by altering the amount of voltage being sent to its control input.

Velocity Sensitivity: A keyboard which can respond to the speed at which a key is depressed; this corresponds to the dynamics with which the player plays the keyboard. Velocity is an important function as it helps translate the performer's expression to the music. Velocity can be routed to many destinations on a MIDI instrument and is also translated over the MIDI line.

Vibrato: A cyclic change in pitch, usually in the range of 7 to 14 Hz.

Volatile Memory: Memory that loses its data when power is removed. The RAM memory in a synthesizer is volatile; the data on the hard disk is non-volatile.

.WAV: The Windows audio file format. Typically encountered as FILENAME.WAV

Wavetable Synthesis: A universal method for generating sound electronically on a synthesizer or PC. Output is produced using a table of sound samples, actual recorded sounds that are digitized and played back as needed. By continuously rereading samples and looping them together at different pitches, highly complex tones can be generated from a minimum of stored data without overburdening the processor.

Wind Controller: A controller instrument that is woodwind-like or brass-like in its fingering. The instrument is blown into and the air stream triggers sounds from a synthesizer or tone module. Many do not have sounds of their own and must be connected (through MIDI) to a synthesizer or tone module.

Workstation: This is generally a synthesizer or sampler in which several of the tasks usually associated with electronic music production, such as sequencing, effects processing, rhythm programming, and data storage on disk. These functions can all be performed by components found within a single instrument.

Write Protect: To protect data (either on a disk or in memory) from being written to, although data can still be read.

Zone: Typically, this is a contiguous set of keys on the keyboard; a single sound or MIDI channel is assigned to a specific zone.

Bibliography

Highly recommended books, thesis, articles and university documents on electronic music.

Uber ein Apparatur zur Steuerung und Verformung von Klängen, Herman Klein, 1959

European Electronic Music Instrument Design, a journal of the audio engineering society, ix, Harald Bode 1961

Bekannte und neue Klänge durch elektrische Musik-Instrumente, Harald Bode, 1940

The Electronic Musical Instrument Manual, A. Douglas, 1968

L'apport de l'électronique à l'expression musicale, M.C. Martin, 1950

L'initiation à la lutherie électronique, G. Jenny,1955

Heliophon, ein neues Musikinstrument, J. Marx, 1947

Elektrische Musik:ein gemeinverständliche Darstellung ihrer Grundlagen, des heutigen Standes der Technik und ihre Zukunftsmöglickkeiten, Peter Lertes, Dresden & Leipzig, 1933

Un Appareil De Musique Radio-électrique: L'Ondium Péchadre, E. Weiss, 1930

La Croix Sonore, E. Ludwig, 1972-73

21st Century Musical Instruments: Hardware and Software, Jon Appleton

La Musique des Ondes éthérées, Edgard Varèse and L. E. Gratia, 1928

Mark Twain: A Biography, Albert Bigelow Paine, New York: Harper & Brothers, 1912

Das Choralcello, H. Trabandt 1910

Das Choralcello als Konzertinstrument, H. Trabandt 1910

Magic Music from the Telharmonium, Reynold Weidenaar, Scarecrow Press

The A-Z of Analogue Synthesizers (two volumes,) Peter Forrest, 1994-98

Electric Sound: The Past and Promise of Electronic Music, Joel Chadabe, Prentice Hall, 1996

The Art of Electronic Music, Darter, Tom ed. Greg Armbuster. New York: Quill, 1984

Computer Music: Synthesis, Composition & Performance, Charles Dodge and J. A. Jerse, New York: Schimmer Books, 1985

The Computer Music Tutorial, Curtis Roads

Current Directions in Computer Music Research, Max Mathews, & J.R. Pierce, ed. Cambridge MA: MIT Press, 1989

Sound Synthesis and Sampling, Martin Russ

Electronic & Computer Music, Peter Manning, Oxford: Clarendon Press, 1985

Electronic & Experimental Music, Thomas B. Holmes, New York: Charles Scribner's Sons, 1985

FM Theory and Applications by Musicians for Musicians, J. Chowning and D. Bristow

Music by Computers, Heinz Forster, edited by James W. Beauchamp, John Weley & Sons Inc., 1969

A Bibliography of Computer Music: A Reference for Composers, Sandra L. Tjepkema

On The Sensations Of Tone. Psychological Basis for Theory of Music, Helmholtz, Hermann, New York: Dover Publications, 1954

The Evolution of Electronic Musical Instruments in the United States, Tom Rhea, 1972

Illustrated Compendium of Musical Technology, Cary, Tristram.Faber and Faber, 1992

Electronic and Computer Music, Peter Manning, Clarendon Press and Oxford University Press, 1985

Mind over Midi/for Musicians of All Levels, a Guide to the Creative Applications and Theory of the Musical Instrument Digital Interface, Dominic Milano, GPI Publications

The Sackbut Blues: Hugh Le Caine, Pioneer in Electronic Music, Young, Gayle, 1989

The Secrets of Analog and Digital Synthesis, Steve De Furia, Third Earth Publishing

Synthesis: an introduction to the history, theory, & practice of electronic music, Herbert A. Deutsch, Sherman Oaks 1985. Revised edition

Vintage Synthesizers, Mark Vail, Miller Freeman, Inc

Synthesizer Basics, Brent Hurtig, GPI Publications

Die maschinelle Musik, Aufsätze und Vorträge, Béla Bartók 1972

Theremin's Sphärenmusik, J.H. Bechhold, ed. Die Umschau #31 1927

Premieres and Experiments-1932, Marc Blitzstein, Modern Music 9 (1932).

Die elektronischen Musikinstrumente, Harolde Bode 1949

Pitch Control for an Electronic Musical Instrument, T.R. Bunting 1932

The Development and Practice of Electronic Music, Jon H. Appleton, and Ronald C Perera, 1975

Toward a New Music, Carlos Chavez 1937

Silence, John Cage, Wesleyan Univ. Press 1939

The Evolution of Electronic Music, David Ernst 1977

A Guide to Electronic Music, Paul Griffiths 1979

Joseph Schillinger. A Memoir by His Wife, Frances Schillinger 1949

A Transistorized Theremin, Robert A. Moog, Electronics World, January 1961 pp. 29-32

Bourges Electronic Music Festival. A Gathering of Giants, Robert A. Moog, Keyboard, October 1989 pp. 22—23

Build the EM Theremin, Electronic Musician Magazine, Robert A. Moog, February 1996 pp. 86—100

The Development of Electrical Music, R. Raven-Hart 1932

Clara Rockmore: The Art of the Theremin, Thomas Rhea, Computer Music Journal 13, No. 1, 61—63, October 1989

An Electronic Musical Instrument with Photoelectric Cell as a Playing Manual, W. Saraga, Electronic Engineering Vol. 17 (1945) pp. 601—603

Mein Ziel, Lev Termin, Berliner Tageblatt, 1 October 1927

Electronic Music Circuits, Barry Klein, self-distributed, contact MIT

Theremin : Ether Music and Espionage (Music in American Life,) Albert Glinsky, Robert Moog. Hardcover 2000

Manhattan Research, Inc. 2000, 2-CDs & 144-page Hardcover Book Produced by Gert-Jan Blom & Jeff Winner

Composing Music with Computers, Eduardo Miranda. Paperback 2001

MP3 for Dummies, Andy Rathbone. Paperback 2001

Virtual Music, David Cope, Douglas R. Hofstadter. Paperback 2001

Machine Musicianship, Robert Rowe. Paperback 2001

Basic VST Instruments, Paul White. Paperback 2001

Music, Cognition, and Computerized Sound: An Introduction to Psychoacoustics, Perry R. Cook. Paperback 2001

Strange Sounds: Music, Technology and Culture, Timothy Taylor. Paperback 2001

Creative Music Production: Joe Meek's Bold Techniques, Barry Cleveland Paperback 2001

Professional Sound Reinforcement Techniques, Jim Yakabuski. Paperback 2002

Studio-in-a-Box, Erik Hawkins. Paperback 2002

Remix: The Electronic Music Explosion, Bruce Gerrish. Paperback 2002

Teach Yourself Acid 3.0 in 24 Hours, Gary Rebholz, Michael Bryant, David Was. Paperback 2002

Electroacoustic Music: Analytical Perspectives, Thomas Licata. Paperback 2002

Essential Computers: Composing Music on Your PC, Rob Beattie. Paperback 2002

Music and Technology in the Twentieth Century, Hans-Joachim Braun. Paperback 2002

Liberation of Sound : An Introduction to Electronic Music, Herbert Russcol. Paperback 2002

Electronic Music on the Internet

Here is a selected list of websites that contain information on every aspect of electronic music. As the web continues to grow at break-neck speeds, more will appear every week. Please note that there is no hierarchy in this listing. It's simply a list of informative bookmarks I've compiled over the years. On the downside, email addresses and website URLs change from time to time. At the time the book went to press, all the links were active.

GENERAL SITES

The Electronic Music Foundation—**http://www.emf.org/**

120 Years of Electronic Music—**http://www.obsolete.com/120_years/**

Absolute Sound—**http://www.theabsolutesound.com/**

Adrenalin Sound Machine—**http://surf.to/adrenalin-sound-machine/**

Amazing Sounds—**http://www.amazings.com/**

American Society of Composers—**http://www.ascap.com/**

Analogue Systems—**http://www.analogsynths.com**

Anything Analog—**http://www.sonicstate.com/**

Archives of Classical MIDI Sequences—**http://www.prs.net/midi.html**

Analogue Heaven—**http://www.hyperreal.com/music/machines/ah/**

Beatseek—**http://www.beatseek.com**

Canadian Electronic Music—**http://www.canehdian.com/genre/electronica.html**

Center for New Music and Audio Technologies—**http://www.cnmat.berkeley.edu/**

Computer Control and Synthesis of Sound—**http://www.cnmat.berkeley.edu/~adrian/**

Cosmic Fantasia—**http://www.cosmicfantasia.com/**

Echoes—**http://www.echoes.org/**

Echoes Delight aka Loopers Delight—**www.loopers-delight.com/loop.html**

Emusic-lists—**http://www.ibiblio.org/mcmahon/emusic-l/**

Foundation for the Electronic and Performing Arts—**http://www.fep-arts.org/**

Harmony Central—**http://www.harmony-central.com**

Keyboard Magazine—**http://www.musicplayer.com/CDA/Player/Main/1,2228,-Keyboardist,00.html**

Macintosh MIDI User's Internet Guide—**http://www.aitech.ac.jp/~ckelly/mmuig.html**

Man Made Media—**http://www.manmade.com/**

Midwest Electronic Music—**http://www.oscillator.org**

MIDI Midi midi-Only The Best Midi Pages—**http://www.wavenet.com/~axgrindr/quimby4.html**

MIDI Composers' Exchange—**http://www.mindspring.com/~s-allen/picks.html**

Mixmag—**http://techno.de/mixmag/**

MiXViews Home Page—**http://www.ccmrc.ucsb.edu/~doug/htmls/MiXViews.html**

Mostly Early, Mostly MIDI, Mostly Women—**http://150.252.8.92/www/iawm/pages/Midi.html**

Robert A. Moog—**http://www.analogue.org/mr/moog/**

Music Machines—**http://www.hyperreal.com/music/machines**

New Empire—**http://www.newempire.com/**

Nocturnal—**http://www.nocturnalmagazine.net/**

Randy Wilson's Computer Music Homepage—**http://synapse.cs.byu.edu/~randy/music.html**

Renaissance Guitar MIDI Companion—**http://www.midi-classics.com/p1.htm**

Searching the Internet For a Certain MIDI File—**http://www.aitech.ac.jp/~ckelly/midi/help/midi-search.html**

Sonic State—**http://www.sonicstate.com/**

Synthfool—**http://www.synthfool.com**

Synthony Synthesizer Museum—**http://www.synthony.com/museum.html**

Synth Museum.com—**http://www.synthmuseum.com/**

Synth Zone—**http://www.synthzone.com/**

Tentacles/Squiduary—**http://www.yip.org/squid/**

The Sunsite Theremin Home Page—**http://sunsite.unc.edu/id/theremin/**

Bob's Theremin page—**http://www.ccsi.com/~bobs/theremin.html**

Underground Network—**http://www.undergroundnet.net/**

Urban Sounds—**http://www.urbansounds.com/**

Virtual Keyboard Museum—**http://users.aol.com/KeyMuseum/**

Virtual Synthesizer Museum—**http://synthmuseum.com/**

Vutag—**http://www.vutag.com/**

MUSICIANS & EM RELATED RECORD COMPANIES

Laurie Anderson—**http://www.cc.gatech.edu/~jimmyd/laurie-anderson/**

Laurie Anderson Official home Page—**http://www.laurieanderson.com/**

George Anthei—**http://www.antheil.org/**

Eduard Artemiev—**http://www.solaris-room.ru/**

Einar Ask—**http://www.einar.com/main.html**

Chet Atkins—**http://www.sonynashville.com/ChetAtkins/**

Ashera—**http://www.ashera.com/**

Ashley/Story—**http://www.ashleystory.com**

Louis and Bebe Barron—**http://music.dartmouth.edu/~wowem/electronmedia/barron.html**

George Beauchamp—**http://www.rickenbacker.com/us/history1.htm**

Alexander Graham Bell—**http://www.e-znet.com/kids/AlexBellLinks.html**

Graziano Bertini—**http://www.iei.pi.cnr.it/People/Bertini.html**

Ian Boddy—**http://www.ianboddy.com/**

Bojo—**http://www.bojo.net/index_e.htm**

Ron Boots—**http://www.groove.nl/**

David Borden—**http://members.aol.com/Cuneiway/borden.html**

Richard Boulanger—**http://www.nyu.edu/pages/ngc/ipg/boulanger.html**

Pierre Boulez—**http://www.concentric.net/~jadato/boulez.htm**

Glenn Branca—**http://www.tiac.net/users/blip/branca/branca.html**

Don Buchla—**http://www.buchla.com**

John Cage—**http://www.newalbion.com/artists/cagej/**

Wendy Carlos Official Home Page—**http://www.wendycarlos.com/**

Joel Chadabe—**http://www.chadabe.com/**

Harry Chamberlin—**http://www.mellotron.com/chamanu.htm**

John Chowning—**http://www.o-art.org/history/LongDur/Chowning.html**

Nicholas Collins—**http://www.lovely.com/bios/collins.html**

Mark Coniglio—**http://www.troikaranch.org/mark.html**

Ugo Conti—**http://www.emiinc.com/personnel.html**

Merce Cunningham—**http://www.merce.org/**

Roger Dannenberg—**http://www.cs.cmu.edu/afs/cs.cmu.edu/user/rbd/www/home.html**

Miles Davis—**http://www.milesdavis.com/**

Lee DeForest—**http://www.invent.org/book/book-text/30.html**

Tom DeMeyer—**http://www.ircam.fr/produits/logiciels/log-compl/bigeye.html**

Delirium—**http://www.delerium.com/**

DIFFUSION i MéDIA—**http://www.cam.org/~dim/**

Disquiet ambient/electronica—**http://www.disquiet.com/**

Tod Dockstader—**http://host4u.upws.net/dockstader/**

Homer Dudley—**http://ptolemy.eecs.berkeley.edu/~eal/audio/vocoder.html**

Jacob Duringer—**http://www.electronic-mall.com/heavenbound/show_face.htm**

Mark Dwane—**http://www.markdwane.com/**

Keith Emerson—**http://www.keithemerson.com**

Emerson, Lake, & Palmer—**http://www.emersonlakepalmer.com/**

Brian Eno—**http://music.hyperreal.org/artists/brian_eno/**

Electronica Primer—**http://www.plato.nl/e-primer/**

Christopher Franke-Home Page—**http://www.sonicimages.com/**

Grandmaster Flash—**http://www.grandmasterflash.com/**

Peter Frampton—**http://www.frampton.com/**

Robert Fripp—**http://www.elephant-talk.com/**

Fred Frith—**http://www.fredfrith.com**

Philip Glass—**http://www.philipglass.com/**

Jeff Greinke-Official Site—**http://www.hypnos.com/greinke/**

Laurens Hammond—**http://www.mitatechs.com/links2.html**

Paul Haslinger—**http://www.sra.at/persons/217/6873.htm**

Jimi Hendrix—**http://www.jimi-hendrix.com/**

Alan Holdsworth—**http:// www.calweb.com/~geprman/he.html**

Dick Hyman—**http://www.home.earthlink.net/~spaceagepop/hyman.htm**

Iasos—**http://iasos.com/**

Jarre, Jean-Michel—**http://www.jeanmicheljarre.com/**

Henry Kaiser—**http://www.henrykaiser.net/**

Kalvos and Demian New Music Baazar—**http://www.goddard.edu/wgdr/kalvos/index.html**

John Kerr—**http://www.xs4all.nl/~johnkerr**

Kraftwerk—**http://www.kraftwerk.com/**

Krause & Beaver—**http://www.wildsanctuary.com/bk.html**

Mars Lasar—**http://www.marslasar.com**

Don Leslie—**http://www.theatreorgans.com/hammond/faq/mystery/mystery.html**

Linden Music (Kit Watkins)—**http://kitwatkins.com/**

Roger Linn—**http://www.drummachine.com/newpages/rlinninterview.html**

Loop-Monthly Dark Music Ezine Digest—**http://www.welcome.to/Loop**

Lovely Music, Ltd.—**http://www.lovely.com/**

Tod Machover—**http://www.media.mit.edu/~tod/**

George Martin—**http://www.beatlesagain.com/bgeorgem.html**

Miya Masaoka—**http://thecity.sfsu.edu/~miya/**

Max Mathews—**http://www.csounds.com/mathews/**

Lyle Mays—**http://www.lylemays.com/**

Bob Moog Big Briar.com (Bob Moog)—**http://www.bigbriar.com**

Materiali Sonori—**http://www.matson.it/**

Joe Meek—**http://www.concentric.net/~meekweb/telstar.htm**

Pat Metheny Group—**http://www.patmethenygroup.com/**

Patrick Moraz—**http://www.monmouth.com/~storyofi/biograph.htm**

Giorgio Moroder—**http://www.algonet.se/~jonwar/moroder.html**

Multimood Records—**http://www.algonet.se/~harakiri/**

Multiphase Records—**http://www.mphase.com/**

Gordon Mumma—**http://www.lovely.com/bios/mumma.html**

Tom Oberheim—**http://www.siliconbreakdown.com/oberheim.html**

New Albion Records—**http://www.newalbion.com/**

Ben Neill—**http://www.benneill.com/**

Pauline Oliveros Foundation, Inc.—**http://www.artswire.org/pof**

The Orb—**http://www.theorb.com/**

Joe Paradiso—**http://www.media.mit.edu/~joep/**

Zeena Parkins—**http://www.sigov.si/uzp/city/site/music/cvparkin.html**

Les Paul—**http://www.beacham.com/paul/paul_radio.html**

Jeff Pearce-Official Site—**http://www.hypnos.com/pearce/**

Roger Powell—**http://www.algonet.se/~bassman/photos/rp.html**

The Artist Formerly Known As Prince—**http://www.nuvo.net/hammer/prince.html**

Projekt Web—**http://www.projekt.com/**

Miller Puckette—**http://www.crca.ucsd.edu/~msp/**

Steve Reich—**http://www.stevereich.com/**

Robert Rich—**http://www.amoeba.com/rrframeset.html**

Terry Riley—**http://terryriley.com/**

Clara Rockmore—**http://www.geocities.com/Vienna/1859/**

Steve Roach—**http://www.steveroach.com/**

David Rosenboom—**http://www.shoko.calarts.edu/~david/**

Ryuichi Sakamoto—**http://www.sitesakamoto.com/**

Mario Schönwälder (Manikin Records)—**http://www.manikin.de/**

Klaus Schulze Official home Page—**http://www.klaus-schulze.com/**

Raymond Scott—**http://raymondScott.com**

Jonn Serrie—**http://vipinfo.com/jonn/**

Mark Shreeve—**http://www.synthmusicdirect.com/collide.cfm**

Flavia Sparacino—**http://www-white.media.mit.edu/~flavia/**

Laurie Spiegel—**http://www.dorsai.org/~spiegel/**

Morton Subotnick—**http://www.newalbion.com/artists/subotnickm/**

Michael Stearns—**http://www.michaelstearns.com/**

Karlheinz Stockhausen—**http://www.stockhausen.org/**

Saul Stokes—**http://www.hypnos.com/ss.htm**

Tim Story—**http://www.timstory.com**

David Sylvian—**http://www.imusic.interserv.com/showcase/modern/davidsylvian.html**

System 7/777—**http://www.easynet.co.uk/pages/system7/sys7.htm**

Tangerine Dream Official Homepage—**http://www.tangerinedream.de/**

Serge Tcherepnin—**http://www.wwa.com/~johnp/history.htm**

James Tenney—**http://www.music.mcgill.ca/~gems/tenney/**

Robert Scott Thompson—**http://www.aucourantrecords.com**

David Tudor—**http://www.emf.org/tudor/**

Vangelis—**http://bau2.uibk.ac.at/perki/Vangelis.html**

Barry Vercoe—**http://sound.media.mit.edu/~bv/**

vidna Obmana—**http://www.vidnaobmana.org/**

Andreas Vollenweider—**http://www.vollenweider.net/**

Scott Wedge—**http://www.synthmuseum.com/emu/emuemul01.html**

Chris Wren—**http://www.drwren.com/chris/**

Frank Zappa—**http://www.zappa.com/**

Peter Zinovieff—**http://www.ems-synthi.demon.co.uk/emsstory.html**

John Zorn—**http://www.browbeat.com/zornlist.html**

Companies & Organizations

Aardvark—**http://www.aardvark-pro.com**

ACO Pacific, Inc.—**http://www.acopacific.com**

A.D.A.M. Audio GmbH—**http://www.adam-audio.de**

Akai—**http://www.akai.com/**

Alesis—**http://www.alesis.com**

American Composers Forum—**http://www.composersforum.org**

Analogue Modular Systems, Inc—**http://www.analogsynths.com/**

Analogue Org—**http://www.analogue.org/**

Arboretum—**http://www.arboretum.com**

Audio Engineering Associates—http://www.wesdooley.com

Berklee College of Music—**http://www.berklee.edu**

BIAS (Berkley Integrated Audio Software)—**http://www.bias.com**

Cakewalk—**http://www.cakewalk.com**

Canadian Electroacoustic Community—**http://www-fofa.concordia.ca/cec/home.html**

CEMI-University of North Texas—**http://www.scs.unt.edu/cemi/cemi.htm**

Center for Studies in Music Technology—**http://www.music.yale.edu:/**

CCRMA Stanford University—**http://ccrma-www.stanford.edu/**

CCMRC Santa Barbara—**http://ccmrc.ucsb.edu/**

Center for Research in Computing and the Arts (CRCA)—**http://crca-www.ucsd.edu/**

CERL Sound Group—**http://datura.cerl.uiuc.edu/**

Deep Listening—**http://www.deeplistening.org/dlc**

DigiTech—**http://www.digitech.com**

Digital Guitar Archive—**http://waynesworld.ucsd.edu/DigitalGuitar/digitar_archive.html**

Dolby Laboratories, Inc—**http://www.dolby.com**

Electro-Harmonix—**http://www.ehx.com**

EMS-Electronic Music Studios—**http://www.hinton.demon.co.uk/ems/ems.html**

E-mu Systems, Inc—**http://www.emu.com/**

Ensoniq—**http://www.ensoniq.com/**

Eventide, Inc—**http://www.eventide.com**

Expression Center for New Media—**http://www.xnewmedia.com**

Fairlight—**http://www.fairlightyesp.com.au**

Guitar Player Magazine—**http://www.guitarplayer.com**

Faculty of Music, McGill University—**http://lecaine.music.mcgill.ca/**

Harvard Computer Music Center—**http://www-mario.harvard.edu/**

Harvestworks—**http://www.harvestworks.org**

Hearts of Space—**http://www.hos.com/**

House of Techno and electronic music—**http://www.house-of-techno.com/Eindex.html**

In-Site Magazine—**http://www.in-sitemagazine.com**

International Alliance of Women in Music—**http://150.252.8.92/www/iawm/**

International Alliance for Women in Music—**http://music.acu.edu/www/iawm/home.html**

International Computer Music Association—**http://music.dartmouth.edu/~icma/**

IUMA, Welcome to IUMA FutureNet—**http://www.iuma.com/**

Journal of New Music Research—**http://www.swets.nl/jnmr/jnmr.html**

Keyboard Central—**http://www.keyboardmag.com/**

Keyboard Magazine—**http://www.keyboardonline.com**

Korg USA, Inc—**http://www.korg.com**

Kurzweil Music Systems—**http://www.youngchang.com**

Leeds University Department of Music—**http://www.leeds.ac.uk/music.html**

Lexicon—**http://www.lexicon.com**

Lightworks—**http://www.lightworks.com/**

Liquid Audio—**http://www.liquidaudio.com**

Logitek Electronic Systems—**http://www.logitekaudio.com**

Lucid Technology—**http://www.lucidtechnology.com**

MAZ Soft Synths—**http://www.maz-sound.com/synths_text_only.html**

Mellotron—**http://www.mellotron.com/**

MIDI Guitar Unofficial Home Page—**http://www.epix.net/~joelc/midi_git.html**

MIDI Space—**http://www.webproducers.com/midispace**

MIDI title search—**http://www.aitech.ac.jp/~ckelly/midi/help/midi-search.html**

MIDIWorld—**http://midiworld.com/**

MIT Media Laboratory—**http://www.media.mit.edu**

Music Machines—**http://machines.hyperreal.org/**

Musical Instrument Technicians Assoc.—**http://www.mitatechs.com/index.html**

NAMM—**http://www.namm.com**

Norwegian Network for Technology and Music—**http://www.notam.uio.no/index-e.html**

Novation Synthesizers—**http://www.nova-uk.com**

Oberheim—**http://www.gibson.com/products/oberheim.html**

Opcode Systems—**http://www.opcode.com/**

PAIA Electronics—**http://www.paia.com/paia**

Pauline Oliveros Foundation—**http://www.artswire.org/pof**

Phonetik—**http://www2.phonetik.uni-muenchen.de/AP/APKap2.html**

Propellerheads Software—**http://www.propellerheads.se/**

Roland International—**http://www.rolandcorp.com/**

Sinkhole experimental music magazine—**http://www.sinkhole.net/magazine/**

Spotted Peccary Music—**http://www.spottedpeccary.com/**

Sonic Foundry—**http://www.sonicfoundry.com/**

Sonic State—**http://www.sonicstate.com/**

Sound on Sound Magazine—**http://www.sospubs.co.uk/**

Serveur WWW de l'IRCAM—**http://www.ircam.fr**

UCSC EMS Home Page—**http://arts.ucsc.edu/EMS/Music/**

Virginia Tech Center for Digital Music—**http://server.music.vt.edu/technology/vtcdm.html**

Vocoders-PAiA Vocoder—**http://www.paia.com/~paia/vocoder.htm**

Wavestation—**http://www.danphillips.com/wavestation/**

Winham Laboratory CMIX—**http://www.music.princeton.edu/winham/**

Wired—**http://www.geocities.com/SunsetStrip/Plaza/4626/news.htm**

XLR8R—**http://xlr8r.com**

Zeta—**http://www.zeta.net/**

Yamaha—**http://www.yamaha.com/**